# HOW TO MAKE ANYONE LIKE YOU!

*Proven ways to be a people magnet*

## LEIL LOWNDES

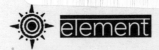

**Dedicated to my dearest friends Giorgio and Phil
who taught me the meaning of
love and friendship**

Element
An imprint of HarperCollins*Publishers*
77–85 Fulham Palace Road,
Hammersmith, London W6 8JB

The website address is:
www.thorsonselement.com

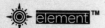 ™

and *Element* are trademarks of
HarperCollins*Publishers* Limited

First published by Thorsons, an Imprint of HarperCollins*Publishers* 2000
This edition published by Element 2002

9

© Leil Lowndes 2000

Leil Lowndes asserts the moral right to be
identified as the author of this work

A catalogue record of this book is
available from the British Library

ISBN-13   978-0-7225-4024-4
ISBN-10   0-7225-4024-8

Printed and bound in Great Britain by
Clays Ltd, St Ives plc

# Contents

# Introduction

# How to be a people magnet

I bet you know some folks who are human magnets. It's not that they're overly good-looking, rich or bright. But they walk into a room of strangers, and people smile. They walk into a singles bar, and people stare. They walk into a negotiation, and the suits on the other side of the table instinctively smell that they are 'big time'.

If they're single, everyone wants to be their date. If married, passionate partners are grateful to be their mate. If they're in need, faithful friends would charge over the hill, run through fire, or walk on broken glass for them.

But wait a minute! They don't have anything you haven't got – maybe less. So what's the secret?

That's what *How to Make Anyone Like You!* is all about.

##  How we're going to find the answer

From the time we are little tykes rattling the cot rails for attention until the time we catch a cloud to carry us to the great beyond, we want people to like us. Kids call it 'popularity', whereas adults prefer 'charisma' or 'leadership' ability. But even if the generations can't agree on a word for 'it', they know what it is. And everybody wants IT.

Usually people classify this coveted talent in three parts. When talking about business, they say 'communications skills'. When referring to being comfortable with strangers and making friends, it's 'social skills'. And when love is in the air, the ability to win hearts is all-important. Then they say someone has 'sex appeal'.

Having researched exhaustively, lectured extensively, and written books on all three subjects, I want to let you in on a little secret. *It's all the same thing!* Quite simply, it's that quintessential quality that makes people like you and want to be part of your world today, tomorrow or forever. And that's what we're going to learn in *How to Make Anyone Like You!* Each section gives you another way to enrich your life through finding loyal friends and true love:

Part I, 'Making strangers like you, instantly!', gives you confidence booster shots and party tactics. Then it teaches you some lovely little tricks to spread sunshine and make strangers smile, wherever you go.

Part II, 'Friends and lovers', is about finding (then binding) friendships and romantic love. It shows you how to find a wide variety of people to enhance your life, and then walk the talk that most people only talk. If, as Shakespeare said, 'All the world's a stage, and all the men and women merely players', this section helps you choose the players you want in your life, then gives you ways to win them – and qualities to *keep* them.

Part III, 'Cupid's secrets', reveals some surprising truths that the cunning little cherub tried to hide from us, but recent research has excavated. We've turned these nuggets into sexy ploys you can use to entice lovers – and hold on to them!

Part IV, 'Recruiting Knights for my personal Round Table', helps you build a solid support system of people with a vast span of skills. Like King Arthur and his Knights of the Round Table, you will emerge with an army that may someday save your life, as it did mine.

Part V, 'Marketing me', reintroduces you to someone you've lived with all your life. You get to know *yourself*, in a deeper and different way than ever before. Then you learn methods to market this unique person to potential friends and lovers, just like Hollywood celebrity-makers promote a star.

## ✸ The fatal FUD factor (Fear, Uncertainty and Doubt)

Throughout the book we work on eliminating the number-one people repellent: Fear, Uncertainty and Doubt – otherwise known as the FUD factor.

Norman Vincent Peale, one of the founders of the 'I can do' way of thinking, spent 25 years trying to stamp out the FUD factor. He knew the world was already too full of worry worts and wet blankets who believe the only thing the world will ever give them on a silver platter is tarnish. Hundreds of motivational speakers and feel-good gurus since Norman have tried to inject our brains and veins with positive thinking juice to get rid of it. But it's easier said than done. You don't make it go away by standing on a chair, beating your chest and shouting 'I'm the best! Everybody loves me!'

Even Dale Carnegie tried to teach us how to win friends and influence people. He did a really good job, but he neglected a couple of crucial factors. When it comes to finding friends and lovers, one size does NOT fit all. Those folks who can pick and choose their friends and lovers found *that* fallacy years ago.

Another fumble that success coaches make is that they give us *their* opinion of what works – or what's worked for *them* – not what's been proven in controlled studies conducted by responsible researchers around the world. *How to Make Anyone Like You!* is different from any other book on relationships in that specific sociological, anthropological or psychological studies support everything I say.

Most motivators make a third big mistake. They tell us what to do – and then they don't even wait to see if we agree. They preach from the podium, then step down amongst great applause but with little commitment from the audience to comply. Or they write a book and, when their readers finish the last page, they close the book and (again), most likely, their commitment.

*How to Make Anyone Like You!* isn't going to let you get away with that! You are going to be asked to read this book with a pen in your hand and a promise in your heart!

# Friends, lovers and Knights

*'I get by with a little help from my friends.'*
John Lennon

It's *not* just a song. We all need a little help from our friends. If not now, tomorrow. Or the day after. Or the year after...

Some people never realize it until it's too late. They invest in stocks, bonds or property thinking that money is going to give them the security and happiness they seek. Sadly, they neglect the most important investment of their lives – time spent finding, making and nurturing true friendships, and *true* lasting love relationships

Sometimes we are a nation of blockheads so blinded by sex that we don't see the true love for the birds and the bees. (Not that there's anything wrong with the birds and the bees – we're going to talk about those captivating little critters. But with no myths, no false magic.) We're going to get real about love and sex. Because all too often the lovebird sings sweet lies, and the bee stings too hard. We're also going to talk about friendship because, as we mature, same sex and other-sex non-sexual friends take on an increasingly important role in our lives.[1]

So what is a true friend? Someone you trust? Someone you can call at four in the morning? One friend told me, 'It's someone who knows all about you and loves you anyway.' Another said, 'It's someone close enough to tell you you've got spinach between your teeth, and then laugh *with* you, not at you.'

Some people, especially men, have trouble understanding the value of same-sex friends. Or they'll make jokes about it. When I read the paragraph above to one male friend of mine, Charlie, he said. 'Yeah, Leil, but you missed something. If he's really a *true* friend, he'll lend you his toothbrush!'

While Charlie was chuckling at his own tasteless joke, I asked myself, 'Why is it that guys seem to have a hard time admitting they need or want other male friends?' In the 19th century, men formed deep bonds with each other, confided the most intimate details of their lives, wrote letters of love to each other, and even slept in the same bed. But gay? No way! These friendships were not only accepted, they were respected by both men and women. Today, men run like dogs with cans tied to their tails when the subject of deep feelings for each other comes up.[2]

Here are some of the types of relationships we're going to explore in *How to Make Anyone Like You!*

## ✿ Platonic male/female friendships: 'There's no such thing!' (Or is there?)

Many people, especially men, say there's no such thing as a platonic (no sex) friendship between a man and a woman – unless the two just plain don't find each other sexually attractive.

The issue is further complicated by differing definitions of a platonic relationship. I asked one of my girl friends to define a platonic relationship and she said, 'It is a friendship with an esteemed and appreciated individual of the male gender with whom sexual intercourse is neither advantageous nor desired.'

I then asked a male friend to define it. His answer was, 'A platonic relationship is a transparent and sadistic ruse by which attractive and otherwise eligible females destroy the ego and spirit of a male acquaintance who shows romantic interest by announcing to said acquaintance, "I just want to be friends", thereby ripping out the poor bloke's heart and shredding it to pieces.' (He later admitted he had once been emotionally clobbered by a woman with that cruel club called 'I just want to be friends'.)

Excuse me – if I may interject my opinion here (after all, I *am* the author of this book) – I definitely feel men and women can have a platonic relationship. I should know, I have a great one. In fact he's more than a friend; he's my roommate! (New York City apartment prices make strange *non*-bed fellows.) Phil and his candour about his various triumphs and tribulations with the weaker (ha!) sex will flesh out and corroborate many of the studies upon which this book is based.

## ✹ And, of course, love: The magic that makes the world go round

Ah, yes, love. Love between a man and a woman is so mysterious, so miraculous, so marvellous, it defies simple definition. It is the most deranged, delusive – and yet strangely most desired – state of all. This is the one we say we have no control over. We don't speak of falling in friendship or falling into a network against our will. Yet we talk of falling in love, as if we tumbled into the boat against our will.

Once we've fallen into the love boat, most of us forget to inspect the hull to see if it's full of holes. We don't even look at the charts to see where the relationship is going to take us! It's a beautiful sunny day, so we just smile, hoist the sails and let the winds take us out to sea.

He called? He sent flowers? He told you he loves you? It's like a huge wave lifting you to the crest and you feel like you're on top of the world ... You laugh, you talk, you sing, you dance, you make love and your universe is spinning.

She said she's 'not ready for a relationship'? She wants to be 'just friends'? You suspect she's seeing someone else? The wave crashes, you're sucked under, and you think you're drowning.

Now the early sunshine turns to a black sky, an ominous foreshadowing of a tempestuous storm. Blinded by the wind and the waves, you're unable to steer the relationship and keep your balance in the rocky love boat. It becomes a nightmare from which you can't awake!

We're going to talk a lot about love – how to get it, how to give it, how to keep it. You'll also get some navigation lessons on how to circumvent the storms.

## ❁ Men's friendships: 'I love you, man!'

The emotions between men run deep, but they're suppressed. In fact, some men even have trouble coughing up the words, 'my friend'. Manny, an old college chum, is like that. Over the years I've heard him talk about John, his closest friend. He'll say, 'John, yeah, he's my main man', or 'my pardner'. Or maybe, 'my amigo', 'my compadre'.

If he does say the 'F' ('friend'), he toughens it up with a string of virile adjectives. When I started writing this book, I asked him, 'Manny, how many men friends do you have?' Like it was a new word in his vocabulary, he scratched his head and responded, 'Friends? You mean buddies, honest-to-goodness, ignore-their-buck-naked-wife *friends*?'

'Well, yeah, Manny, I guess you could say that. Isn't there some guy you like whose relationship isn't based 100 per cent on chasing babes, booze or baseball? Some guy who really knows you and understands you?'

He shrugged and said, 'Understands me? Most men don't need to be completely understood.' I could sense from his smug smile he felt good about expressing that titbit of ideology.

But it quickly disappeared when I asked, 'OK, who can you share your feelings with?'

Manny rubbed his neck and said, 'Oh come on Leil. You're not going to give me any of that old Robert Bly mens sensitivity stuff, are you? I think I know what you're getting at. But I'm not one of those creme puffs who starts beating drums and dancing naked back into the woods to get in touch with my infantile self.'

'Women wanting us to express our *feelings* [his nose scrunched at the word] presumes we have feelings. And, sure, we've got one or two. But they remain submerged and, if we air them, it violates their validity.' Then, pointing one finger in the air as though making a profound philosophical statement, Manny pronounced, 'The strength of the genie comes from being in a bottle.'

And, he added, 'You can put that in your pipe and smoke it!'

I decided not to pursue it further – for the moment.

## ✺ Women's friendships: 'Oh, why can't a man be more like a woman?'

At least that's how most women feel about friendship. We're the self-proclaimed experts on friendship. But are we really?

How do you define being an expert on friendship? If you define it as having more friends, it's women.[3] If you define it as being more sensitive to each other's unspoken needs, it's women.[4] If you define it as genuinely liking their female friends better than anyone in the world, it's women. (One study showed many women like their best friends better than their husbands![5]) If you define it as talking about their friendships and admitting them more openly than the less gentle sex, it's women.[6] If you ask who is able to receive more comfort from their same-sex friends in later life, it's women.[7] If you define it as knowing the intimate details of their friends' lives, it's women. (Seat any two women together on a long train trip and, by the time they reach their destination, they could write a novel about each other. Seat typical males together at adjoining desks, and two years later most don't know each other's wives' names – or if they even have wives!)

If you define it as knowing that having friends helps you live longer, improves your immune system, slows the ageing process and reduces the chance of colds, flu, high blood pressure and heart disease, it's women.[8] All pretty strong evidence that women are better at friendship. But, experts? We'll see.

##  Networking friends: So who are these Knights?

Most people, if they decide to go on holiday, say, 'It was lucky we had our friend, Tom, the Travel Agent.' If they get sued, 'It's lucky we had our friend, Laura, the Lawyer.' If your dog Goofy gets sick, 'It's lucky we had our friend, Vinnie, the Vet.' And so on through every situation that sooner or later hits us in the face. And even though, if you were a betting man or woman, you would place bets that a particular something would never happen, that particular something *always* happens – and *always* catches you by surprise.

Was it just luck that Tom, Laura and Vinnie were friends when you decided to go globetrotting, when you got sued for leaving a banana peel on your pavement, and when Goofy got green around the gills?

Not if you're smart. Everyone needs Toms, Lauras and Vinnies in their life, and a lot of other friends with a vast selection of skills upon whom they can call in times of need. I call these folks, both men and women, Knights.

For the analogy, I went back – way back – to when I was all curled up in my flannel pyjamas, hugging my teddy bear, about to drift off to sleep. Mum is reading my favourite story to me...

There was a sword stuck in a stone, and whoever could pull it out would become king. Nobody succeeded until a freckle-faced kid named Arthur came along and slid it out like a knife out of butter. He then became king, King Arthur, and married a fair maiden named Guinevere. The part I liked best was when, right after the wedding, Merlin the magician rose, toasted King Arthur and his new Queen Guinevere, cleared his throat and spoke in solemn tones.

'Today is the first day of the Knights of the Round Table; you all have your allotted chairs. No seat is more important than any other. But, when one knight dies, another will take the place, with the name on the seat changing by itself.' With that, he said, 'I leave you now to the wise counsel of your King. Goodbye and God bless you all.'

When Merlin had taken his leave, King Arthur rose and called for silence. Often the last words I'd hear before entering dreamland, was King Arthur asking each knight, 'Are you loyal to your king, and to each other?' Sometimes I tried to stay awake to hear each of the 150 knights swearing their sacred oath in sequence, one for all, and all for one. But I usually fell asleep by the time I got to the fourth or fifth knight.

I didn't mind, though, because my knights came back for an encore in my dreams. They would slay fire-breathing dragons snorting gusts of purple smoke and orange flame, and rescue damsels in distress. These visions made me feel safe all day long. I truly believed that King Arthur and the Knights of the Round Table were real, and would magically appear to rescue me if ever I should need them. But, just as King Arthur had to do without Merlin one day, I grew up and had to do without believing that King Arthur and his knights were real. But now I've replaced the valiant mythological Knights of the Round Table with real ones. I have Knights, both female and male, who will slay any dragon of a problem for me and rescue me when I am in distress. And, of course, I will slay any of their dragons within my realm of possibility. One for all. All for one. In modern-day parlance, it's called a 'Network', and we all need a good one.

How do I know that? Because something really, really bad happened to me one summer – something I'll tell you about later – and if I'd had my 'druthers never would have happened. But it changed my life for ever and made me realize that love and friendship – giving it and getting it – is the most important thing in life.

So, if you are ready to start filling your life with friendship, love and a terrific support system, let's go! Have your pen filled with ink so you can sign off on some of the clauses in this personal contract between you and yourself – and marking the ones you'll have to come back to. You're making a plan that will enrich the rest of your life. Maybe, some day, like it did mine, it will even save it.

By the way, while carefully constructing this plan, don't forget to enjoy the journey. As John Lennon also wrote, before he was gunned down in the driveway of the Dakota,

> *'Life is what happens while you're busy*
> *making other plans'*
> John Lennon

# Why this book is guaranteed to work!

## It is not a book – it's a contract!

A very personal contract between you and the person you are most responsible to in life – yourself.

The definition of a contract, according to dearly departed (but oft-quoted posthumously) dictionary man Noah Webster, is 'a binding agreement usually between two or more persons or parties'. Since we all have 'two or more persons' residing within ourselves, we'll take liberties with 'two'.

As women, looking in the mirror, we're continually having conversations like this, asking our reflection:

YOU 1:   Shall I wear these old jeans today?
YOU 2:   Nah, they make you look like a busted sofa!
YOU 1:   They're not *that* bad, and tight jeans are sexy.
YOU 2:   What, are you kidding? You look like you were poured into them and forgot to say when.

Or, you're a single man, asking yourself:

YOU 1:   Should I ask her out?

YOU 2:   Of course, not, stupid. She'll say no.

YOU 1:   Yeah, but if I don't ask her, I'll never know. What if she says yes?

YOU 2:   You? Lamebrain! Why would a gorgeous woman like her want to go out with an ugly-ass blot on the landscape like you?

And so the two factions within you slug it out. But not to worry – soon you'll know how to write a contract between the internal warring parties so your best side always wins.

*How to Make Anyone Like You!* is one long contract and it has many clauses. Don't worry if you can't promise to comply with every single one. Neither can I – yet. (But I'm working at it.) All I ask is that you consider each clause carefully. Then, if – and only if – you agree to make the suggestion a part of your life, put your signature on the dotted line under it.

## ❀ Everything in the contract is backed by sociological studies

If you read one of the clauses in the book and the information I provide you with is not sufficient to convince you to sign it (the clause), then I would beseech you to check the Notes. This is where you will find the proof in the original studies.

But do be warned – most of the studies are written in a strange dialect, which I call Academese. This curious scholarly style gets a '10' in its precision, but only a '2' in clarity for the layman. Here's an example. What do you think the following sentence means? You've got thirty seconds: 'When the level of analysis of a construct is open to debate, Klein et al. suggest that fairness and research rigour will be enhanced by measurement strategies that allow for empirical testing of appropriate levels of analysis.'

Huh? You're a much better reader than I if you understood that they were just saying: 'When you're not sure of the results, it's better to test it a way that's easier to measure.'

In any case, I ploughed sluggishly but smilingly through studies that tell us some crucial can't-live-without information (like why watching old television shows such as *Beverly Hills 90210* or *Melrose Place* can be dangerous to your health, whereas watching *Roseanne* isn't! Or why men love helping women with some problems but not others – and where they draw the line.

I took the often surprising results of these studies and put them into plain English. Sometimes, I fear, it's in too plain English. I hope you and the serious researchers will forgive the linguistic liberties I've taken with their very significant works.

## ❀ It contains confidential testimony from thousands in my seminars

For eight years, I have been conducting communications skills and relationship seminars all over the English-speaking world, and have perhaps learned as much from my students as they have from me – especially when it comes to the confusion men and women have about each other. The two sexes continue to baffle each other in the boardroom, the bedroom and beyond. Yet they are hesitant to ask, 'Why do you...?' and 'How do you really feel about...?'

In both my corporate and public seminars, they can ask questions, anonymously and without embarrassment, by writing them on a card signed only by 'M' for male or 'F' for female. I then put the questions to the group and the women answer the men's questions, then vice versa. Revealing only the asker's gender has a unifying effect on the opposite sex, and they sally forth with often surprising (but always sincere) answers for you.

With these three guarantees in your pocket, get your pen poised so you can start signing off on the clauses that will make you into a people magnet.

# Part I

# Making strangers like you instantly!

# Chapter One

# Hi! How do you like me so far?

Think back to your college or sixth-form days. Remember the Big Man On Campus, the Prom Queen, the Cheerleaders – the real 'cool' kids. In most schools, these were the kids everyone envied. These were the kids everybody dressed like, tried to walk and talk like, and the ones they wanted to be seen strolling into class with. If you were like most teenagers, you probably wanted to date them or be their best friend. You wanted them to like you, and you hoped some of their stardust would rub off on you.

But, deep down, did you really like them? I mean really like them? Here's a test. Let's say you are paddling a canoe on a big lake and suddenly you spot two men who can't swim on a quickly sinking raft. They're both howling, 'Help me, Help me!' As you row frantically towards the raft, you see that one of them is Luke, the Big Man on Campus. The other is... Oh no. It can't be! It's Frank! He's your dorky, doggedly-devoted, forever-faithful follower from the old neighbourhood where you both grew up. Your canoe is tiny and you only have room to row one of them to safety.

Now, one hand on your heart, the other on the Bible, who would you choose? Frank? Of course you would. How do I know? Because, surprising new studies show that being liked and popularity in the sense we knew it in school are NOT the same thing. And, when the chips are down, we help people we really like first.

## But is being popular *really* being liked?

It's a strange phenomenon, yet it happens all over the world. As soon as two or more kids get together, they form a pecking order, just like chickens on a farm. Ask any kid, from reception class up, 'Who are the popular kids? And who are the unpopular kids?' He or she can tell you immediately.[9]

Up until recently, everyone thought being popular in school was, by definition, being liked by lots of people. But when researchers started asking schoolkids confidentially, 'Who is popular?' and 'Who do you like?', they got a big shock. Not only did many students not like the popular kids, they resented them. They wanted to be in their clique only to increase their own status. And 11 per cent of the students admitted to downright despising the kids everyone else considered so cool.[10]

Upon further questioning, researchers discovered that many of these cool kids were indeed mean.[11] They created a false sense of exclusivity by not ever hanging out with their less popular schoolmates. Often it was to cover their own insecurities. That's not the kind of popularity we're talking about here.

This covert cliquish of popularity that caused two boys to kill is not what were talking about here. We are exploring the qualities that empower you for kindness and compassion, and make people want to be part of your world today, tomorrow and forever.

## What's your OQ? (Optimism Quotient)

To find out precisely what qualities make people like us, the American Sociological Association conducted a vast study.[12] The results? At the top of the list was having a positive optimistic personality and confidence in yourself.

I'm sure you've seen the TV interviews with the athletes just before the tennis match, the football game, the wrestling match. The reporter asks the tennis player, 'Do you think you're going to win?' She replies, 'Definitely.' In another interview, the reporter asks the opponent the same question, and her answer is the same – 'Absolutely.'

Or a reporter asks a boxer, 'Are you going to win?' He replies 'I'm-a gonna kill da mudder fudder.' Then he asks the contender the same question. He answers, 'Ha! I ain't gonna swap leather for more den 15 seconds wit dat powder puff before he kisses da canvas.'

Whenever I heard these interviews, I thought 'What vulgar crude arrogance. *One* of them must know he's kidding himself. *Both* sides can't be cocksure of success.'

I'm older and wiser now and I realize that, to be successful, you *must* be genuinely confident. You can't just put on the face of confidence for the competition – or for the meeting or the party or the date. You have to feel confidence pulsing through your veins. Your heart has to be the drum that beats out the rhythm of confidence. Every word that comes out of your mouth has to be the lyrics of confidence.

Olympic athletes don't just 'get it up for the game'. They practise getting into what some of them call The Zone so that it's all there for the competition. Leading up to that is years of training their bodies to move instinctively, without losing precious seconds stopping to figure out what to do next.

Likewise, you must train your body to react instinctively for success, without thinking about it. Your game isn't throwing a javelin or hurling a discus. It's waking up each day like the little choo-choo train who said 'I can do it.'

Perhaps you remember the children's story of the little red choo-choo that had to climb a big mountain. It was huffing and puffing and having horrendous difficulty. But with each huff and puff, the little train expressed, 'I think I can. I think I can. I think I can.' And the little red choo did.

In fact, because of the little red choo, I met a friend in college who remains a good mate to this day. I was at a fraternity house party and, due to a severe case of shyness, was trying to meld into the wallpaper. Since nobody was talking to me, I ambled over to the fireplace and feigned interest in a toy wooden train engine on the mantelpiece.

A few moments later, above my head behind me, I heard a Texas drawl, 'Excuse me ma'am, but I just couldn't help but admire you while you're admiring my choo-choo train there.' I whirled around to find myself facing a huge chest. I slowly followed it up with my eyes until I reached the face of a tall grinning Texan. Sensing my shyness, he proceeded to tell me a story, the story of how his father had given the train to him when he was a kid, as a symbol of the 'I can do anything' thinking.

He made conversing easy and we spent the rest of the party talking ('makin' chin music', he called it.) Soon we got around to the subject of what we wanted to do after college. He told me that when his dad passed away without having taken out any insurance, the family was left with nothing but the house they lived in. That inspired him to enter the field of selling life insurance.

Two things stuck in my mind about that conversation. First, Dale told me a *true* story – the story of what *inspired* him to enter the field. He didn't just wind up selling life insurance because that was the best way to make a buck. He created a *true and inspiring story*. (Keep that in mind, because we'll get back to it in Part V, when we talk about marketing yourself the way celebrity makers market stars.)

The second characteristic I remember was the calm assurance he exuded from the top of his ten-gallon hat to the tip of his pointy kill-a-cockroach-in-the-corner boots. He didn't say, 'I *want* to sell life insurance.' He didn't say, 'I'll *try* to be the best life insurance man in Texas.' Dale said, 'I *will* be the best life insurance salesman in Texas.' And today he is.

It's no wonder. People enjoy buying from him because he never lets his own problems get others down. He had a beautiful office building just on the outskirts of Dallas. During a big storm there several years ago, his roof blew off, the trees came crashing down, the office floors were badly flooded, and most of the furniture and paper records were destroyed. His phones were obviously out of order, so that night I called him at home and asked if his office survived the storm.

He said, 'Honey, I bet you been walkin' a hole in the carpet over this. It was blowin' so hard you could spit in your own eye. But don't you worry, everybody's fine. Though the office got plucked cleaner than a Thanksgiving turkey, we'll be back in business better 'n ever within the week.'

And so he was. Even when he was talking about a torrential rainstorm, Dale was able to spread a bit of sunshine on his listeners.

## Chapter Two

# How to spread sunshine wherever you go

Dale carried a pocketful of sunshine with him, which made people glow wherever he went. Not only did he always look on the bright side of things, but he looked at *everything* from the other person's perspective, thus winning their hearts. I think that was one of his most winning ways.

One rainy morning several years ago, when I was giving a speech in Dallas, Dale and I met at a coffee shop for a very early breakfast and then a tour of his new offices. We were the only customers in the coffee shop. He placed his order by saying to the waitress, 'Ma'am, I bet *you* hate the smell of ham and eggs this early, but...'

'No problem!' the waitress said, grinning from ear to ear. Dale was looking at his order from her standpoint.

Paying the tab, he said to the cashier, 'How do you like that? I'm your first customer of the day and *you're* stuck trying to make change from a 50-dollar bill. I sure hope it doesn't clean *you* out.'

'No problem,' said the cashier, smiling broadly and forking over the $35 change.

On the way to his new building, we stopped at a petrol station. 'Buddy, it's a durn shame *you* have to come out in this rain just to fill up some dude's gas tank.'

'No problem, sir.' Smiles.

As we entered Dale's lobby, the doorman held the door for us. Dale's greeting? 'I sure am sorry. They're gonna be some sloppy galoshes messin' up *your* floor today.'

Under his big rainhat, I could see the doorman's enormous, no-problem smile.

The phone was ringing as Dale unlocked his offices. The secretary wasn't in yet, so he grabbed it. All I heard was, 'I'm so sorry ma'am, *you* just wasted your quarter. You're going to have to look up that number again 'cos no one named Betty Ann works here.' Even a wrong number got Dale's looking-at-it-from-his-listener's-perspective treatment. As he hung up, I imagined the caller smiling, even though she'd just wasted her time and money on a wrong number.

I've dubbed Dale's knack of putting everything in his listener's perspective 'In Your Shoes' communicating. Recently, I've started using it with everyone I can. The results are phenomenal! Smiles break out all over. Try it. You can use it in practically all conversations. You'll find it works especially well with strangers.

For example, suppose you are on holiday and you are hopelessly lost. You have no idea where your hotel is. Thank heavens, you spot a policeman and you can ask directions.

Instead of saying, 'Hey, where is the Midtown Hotel?', or even 'Excuse me, could you tell me where the Midtown Hotel is?', venture an 'In Your Shoes' way of asking.

*'I know it's not your job*, but could you direct me to the Midtown Hotel?'

*'I bet you're really tired of people asking*, but could you direct me to...?'

*'I bet you're thinking, "Oh oh, here comes another lost tourist."* And you're right. But could you...?'

*'I know you're here on a much more important assignment to protect life and limb,* but could you tell me where...?'

Not only will you get a smile, but you'll get extra good directions.

> Whenever you say anything to anybody, pretend you are not the speaker, but the listener. What is the listener thinking and feeling when you speak to him or her? Then, whenever appropriate, speak from your *listener's* perspective. Try it! You'll see scowls turn to smiles, dullness turn to delight and NO turns to YES!

Here is the first clause in *How to Make Anyone Like You.* Since it is for both men and women, I've marked it with both ♂ and ♀. If you are going to make a sincere effort to speak from your listener's perspective, then go ahead and sign on the line. That is your commitment to yourself.

**CLAUSE 1 ♂ ♀**

## In Your Shoes

From now on, I will hear everything I say through my listener's ears and, whenever appropriate, phrase it from his or her perspective.

# Chapter Three

# Making everyone feel special

One time I complimented Dale on how he made sincere contact, no matter how brief, with everyone. His answer? 'Well, why not? Why not make every moment and every person in your life count? It gives them joy and it gives you joy. It's a win–win situation.'

Throughout the day, we exchange no more than a few words with dozens of people – bank clerks, cab drivers, shop assistants, bus drivers, waiters, ticket collectors, cashiers, flight attendants. We're usually so absorbed in our own thoughts that they become 'non-people' to us. They are robots who open doors, take our tickets, swipe bar codes on our groceries, take our money and give us change. Likewise, we are non-people to them. We are just one more customer to open a door for, take a ticket from, or swipe the bar codes for.

Whichever side of the counter you are on, here is a way to bring even more sunshine into both the stranger's day and yours. After you've conducted your business, give the stranger an extra second or two of eye contact before looking away. He or she, feeling your eyes, will look up. You both will feel the pulse of electricity between you. It's like a flashing neon sign which reads, 'We are really communicating' and 'I think you are special.'

When I was a flight attendant, I passed meal trays to thousands of passengers, only to hear back a mumbled thank you, which had the sincerity of TV canned laughter. Instantly inspecting the size of the bread roll or counting the number of peas, they seemed oblivious to the fact that there was a human hand holding their tray. What a treat it was for me when the rare passenger looked me right in my eyes, smiled and, unrushed, unmumbled, articulated 'Thank you' or 'Thank you, you're doing a great job.' (How much do you want to bet I didn't give *that* passenger priority service for the rest of the flight?)

I'm sure you've had that same empty feeling when, making a purchase at the chemist's, the sales assistant places the change in your hand and her eyes never meet yours. Here you could be the abominable snowman and, if the repository for the change (your hand) looked human, she would never have noticed.

Be sure to discharge a little blast of joy into everyone's life. Keeping your eyes on theirs for that transitory, fleeting second says so much. Translation:

I find you interesting.
I think you are attractive.
I like you.
We are on the same wavelength.
Our auras are touching.
It is a brief moment in both our lives, but we are both here, now.
I respect you.
You are a person to me.
You are special.

When you say 'Thank you' to the cashier at lunch, give her an extra moment of lingering eye contact. When you say 'Thank you' to the bus driver, give him an extra shot of eye contact. When you say 'Thank you' to the porter who has carried your bag, give him an extra beat of eye contact. When you say 'Thank you' to the lady who does your service wash at the laundrette, give her an extra flash of eye contact.

As you go throughout the day, miraculously transform non-people into VIPs with an extra moment of eye contact. Give the painter an extra pulse of the peepers. Give the seamstress an extra shot of the shutters. Give the porter an extra beat of the blinkers. In a eye-blink, you alter the encounter from ordinary 'business as usual' into a special one. At the end of the day, the twinkles in your smiling eyes will probably have added up to less than one minute – 60 seconds. But it makes a world of difference to how people respond to you.

**CLAUSE 2** ♂ ♀

## Extra Beat of My Blinkers

To turn mundane minutes into magic moments, I will let my eyes stay in contact for an extra second with everyone I speak with.

# Chapter Four

# Win their hearts, in 10 words or less

One of my duties, when I was a flight attendant, was to stand by the door as passengers were disembarking and wish each of them farewell. Now, this presented a problem, because saying goodbye more than 100 times in a row gave the impression of a Barbie doll on one triple-A battery.

In order to avoid this, I determined that my voice, when speaking at a low-to-normal tone in a crowd, carried about four metres. I then calculated that five passengers in a row with all their carry-on luggage covered that four metres. Ergo, the sixth impatient passenger couldn't hear me. Quick arithmetic on the fingers of one hand told me I should prepare five different 'Goodbyes' so no passenger felt that he or she was getting a canned one. My riff simply became, 'Goodbye', 'So long', 'Good bye, I hope you enjoyed your flight' and, depending on our destination, a 'Cheerio', 'Adios', 'Ciao', 'Sayonara' or 'Auf Wiedersehen'.

To my surprise, only one of the farewells above brought sincere smiles, not the fake smiles given by people who have been squashed in narrow seats and forced to turn the other cheek for eight hours. Can you guess which it was?

The *sincere* smiles came from the folks to whom I said, 'Goodbye, I hope you enjoyed your flight', which I call 'The Expanded Thankyou'. When I felt the warm response, I started expanding or specifying all my thank yous to people, on the plane and off.

The Expanded Thankyou also helps wriggle you out of those unpleasant little predicaments we find ourselves in every day. Just last week, when I was buying a lipstick, a lady in the cosmetics department waited patiently as I vacillated between the cardinal red, the crimson red, the coral red, the ruby red, the scarlet red or the vermilion red. Finally, much to her relief, I made a decision. Upon parting, I said, 'Thanks for your patience with my indecision.' She gave a big smile and lied, 'Oh no, it's no problem. I know how important it is to get just the right colour.'

I've even turned the tables now, and when I disembark from a plane as a passenger, I thank the flight attendant with 'Thanks for doing such a super job feeding us all.' If the pilot is there, I'll say, 'Thanks for such a great landing in all that wind' or, simply, 'Hey, thanks for getting us here.'

> The best way to say 'Thank you' (and give the pleasure the word intends) is to tell *why* you are thankful. Specify the reason for your 'Thank you' with a little extra padding. Big smiles and 'No problem!' will be your reward for detailing your gratitude.

**CLAUSE 3** ♂ ♀

## The Expanded Thankyou

Before saying 'Thank you', I will think to see if it fits to tell why I am thankful. Then I'll say, 'Thanks for...'

Now, obviously if there are three or four reasons you are thankful, you don't need to list them all. Just the top one will do. Women, you're not going to say to the sexy waiter, 'Thank you for your excellent service, your suggesting that great wine, and for being such a *hunk*!' 'Thank you for your excellent service' will suffice.

Once you get comfortable padding your 'Thank you's', you can start padding other pro-forma words as well. Instead of 'Good morning', you can say, 'Hi, I hope you're having a good morning.' Instead of 'Have a nice day', you can say, 'I really hope you have a lovely day.' It's less than ten words, but it's astounding what a little originality and personalizing your greeting will do.

# Chapter Five

# The magic wand – your body

The potency of human physical contact is powerful. When two bodies touch, you can actually feel the energy oozing out of one and flowing into the other.

A handshake, a hug, even an embrace between people, especially strangers, must follow convention. You can shake hands with a stranger when introduced. You can hug a stranger at a ball game when your team has won. You can even embrace a stranger if you have both suffered a grievous loss. Grief counsellors at airports after a crash use the embrace to console as often as they use words.

One kind of touch between strangers, however, is not regulated. In fact, it is so fast, so fleeting, you're not even sure it happened. In fact, it *must* be so brisk that no one could mistake its intent, especially if coming from a man. This is the accidental or trifling touch.

It can be hands touching when exchanging money, or shoulders brushing on the bus. The imperceptible flash of electricity between you is fleeting, yet forceful enough to create warmth.[13] It is saying, 'I accept you. You are not, like the ancient lowest caste in India, untouchable.'

It can also be a longer, light touch on the shoulder instead of a tap when you want to get someone's attention.

Several months ago, I was taking the last train home from Boston and was in a deep sleep. As the train pulled into Penn Station in New York, I slowly and happily came out of dreamland. When I was fully conscious, I looked up into the beautiful, dark, kind face of the conductor. He had his hand on my shoulder, was shaking me ever so gently, as he said, 'Here we are, ma'am. New York City. End of the line. Did you sleep well?'

I suppose some might think his lengthy touch was inappropriate, but I knew it came from a good heart and nothing else. I'm sure he would have awakened a male passenger with the same tender touch.

How much better it was than many pokings, jabbings, nudgings, prodings, thrustings or loud-mouthed touchless 'Ma'am,' wake up's I'd received on various trains, planes and buses over the years.

One cautionary note. Women can use this trifling touch more securely than men. *Due to our extreme sensitivity to sexual harassment issues, men must be more prudent.* However, if done in good taste with no questionable motives, men may also spread sunshine with the trifling touch.

---

It is transitory, yet it contains the potency of an embrace. It is ephemeral, yet it invokes strong subconscious emotions. The trifling touch, when tastefully employed, creates a subconscious excitement between people.

**CLAUSE 4** ♂ ♀

## The Trifling Touch

I will try to find appropriate occasions to allow my hand or shoulder to fleetingly touch another's. It is like a quick-as-a-wink caress. Rather than tapping someone on the shoulder to get attention, if *appropriate*, I will apply a longer, tender touch.

## Chapter Six

# Like Hallmark Cards, a smile for every occasion

Iwas once patiently awaiting my appointment in the doctor's waiting room with four or five other patients. One of them was a cantankerous old curmudgeon of a man, who grumbled to the nurse each time she came in for the next patient. I would have placed my bets that he hadn't smiled in a year.

While he was sitting there grumbling to himself, a woman with an adorable six-month-old baby came in and sat across from him. Everyone looked at the woman and smiled, but not crusty old crab.

After a few minutes, when everyone had gone back to their reading, I saw the baby giving the grouchy old guy a big toothless grin that seemed to be for him and him alone. How long do you think the old lemonpuss held out not smiling? Not two seconds. He cracked a smile that threatened to fracture his face from ear to ear. When the nurse came to get me for my appointment, he didn't growl at her. He was still smiling like the first spring flower after a long cold winter, and cooing, 'Well, hello, there little fella.'

So what warranted this exceptional reaction? Was it that the baby was so cute. Perhaps that's part of it. But mainly it was because the baby's smile was not quick and plastic. It was slow, flooding and *genuine*. It was not the stretched professional smile of the travel agent or ticket collector. It was not the quick-flash ingratiating smile of the beggar or the porter. It was not the bluffing frozen smile of the negotiator, or the conniving smile of the used-car dealer. *It was a slow and flooding sincere just-for-you-because-I-like-looking-at-your-face* smile.

Nobody told the little mite, 'Now be sure to smile at strangers, especially ugly old crabs like the one who is sitting in the doctor's office.' The baby obviously didn't see a cranky disagreeable old man. He saw something he liked in the old crab's face. And that's what we can do, too. See the beauty in everyone's face (it really is there if you look hard enough!). Smile at that.

> The most obvious difference between a real smile and a sincere smile is timing. A real smile is slow – really slow. It floods over our faces. It seems to well up from some-where inside our heart and, when our heart is just too full from enjoying what our eyes behold, it spills out into a smile. That smile says, 'Wow, I really like what I see.'

**CLAUSE 5** ♂ ♀

### Slow, Spillover Smile

From now on, no more automatic one-size-fits-all smiles. I will look at each person, see the beauty in him or her, and let the smile s-l-o-w-l-y erupt from my heart and spill over on to my face.

## Chapter Seven

# Why do we prefer one person over another?

Several years ago I was helping my friend Deborah pack up her linen and crockery because she, her husband Toby and their two daughters, aged 4 and 5, were moving from New York City to San Francisco. She was telling me she was worried Julie and Lucy might not fit in with the kids there.

'Deborah,' I said, 'you've got to be kidding. You think the girls are going to go up to another kid and, in a real New Yawk accent say, "Shaddup schnook?".'

'No,' she protested. 'I mean, they're used to being *well liked*. All the kids in their nursery school enjoy playing with them, and now they have to start all over.'

'Start all over?' I asked with a touch of friendly mockery. 'I see – like politicians winning over a new constituency?'

'Well, sort of,' she replied. 'I've worked very hard to give them the skills that make other kids want to play with them. In San Francisco, they'll be starting from square one again.'

'You mean, you gave them a course in Popularity 101?'

'Well, I guess you could call it that,' Deborah replied.

I chuckled, shook my head, and took a few more dishes off the shelf to wrap. How could tots Julie's and Lucy's age care if they played with one kid or another? What qualities could a well-liked tot have that a not-so-well-liked one didn't? At that tender age, I thought, they certainly couldn't have clearly defined personalities. Or could they?

I figured this was just another of Deborah's fads. She'd been through them all – Rolfing, Tantra, the Alexander technique, the Feldenkrais method and, when she got pregnant, she had Toby going to some New Age fathering classes.

'Impossible,' I muttered to myself. Deborah obviously heard me, because she said, 'Leil, I'm not kidding. I have given the girls the most important skill they need to make friends.'

'You mean they can tell jokes better than the other kids?' I asked. 'I can just hear their comedy routine now. Lucy will go up to another kid and say, "Hey, didja know my big sister Julie is so dumb she has to take off her shoes to count to 20?" Then Julie will pipe up, "Yeah, when she grows up they're going to use my sister as a mould for making dumbbells."' Tastelessly, I chuckled at my own depraved humour.

'Stop it, Leil!' Deborah said, 'I'm serious. Can you guess what one learned skill makes them more popular?'

'Listening.'

'Sort of,' Deborah said, 'but it has nothing to do with hearing.'

'I give up.'

That was all the invitation she needed. Deborah went diving into a box of books she had already packed and pulled out a copy of the *Journal of Genetic Psychology*. Opening it to a dog-eared page, she handed me the journal and commanded me: 'Read!'

I looked at the unwieldy title: 'The Association of Children's Nonverbal Decoding Abilities with Their Popularity, Locus of Control, and Academic Achievement'.

'What does *that* mean?' I asked.

'That means, in plain English for you, Leil,' she said, 'that the better my girls are at reading other people's emotions by their non-verbal signals and tones of voice, the more well liked they'll be. I've taught the girls to watch whoever is speaking very carefully and respond first to their *body language*. That's the most important. Then comes responding to the *sound of their voice*, and only finally their words. Most people get it backwards.'

The study fascinated me because I knew that we receive information in just that order: 50 per cent is visual, what we see; 30 per cent is auditory, what we hear; and only 20 per cent derives from someone's actual words.

Deborah then told me how she had trained the girls to be little experts at this. Every evening she played a game called 'Guess How I Feel'. Deborah would make a movement like rubbing her neck or wringing her hands and the girls would identify it. Each time they played 'Guess How I Feel', the signals got more subtle.

They also played a game called 'Truth or Lies?', where, for example, Deborah would put her hand to her mouth or fidget while telling them a story. She would then ask the girls whether they thought she was telling the truth or not. (Hand over the mouth is a common signal of lying.)

Still sceptical, I said, 'Oh, come on Deborah, I was expecting something a bit more mundane from you. You know, some psychology – Jungian, Adlerian or Freudian, at least.'

'You don't think it will work?' she asked.

'I'll eat my hat if it does,' I responded.

##  Deborah gets the last laugh (and Leil eats her hat)

The next year, in what has now become my annual visit to Deborah and Tony's in San Francisco, was Deborah's year for Pilates, an exercise regime where you work out on a machine that looks like an ancient torture rack.

One afternoon her class ran late, so she asked me to pick the girls up at nursery school. When I arrived at the school, the principal invited me to come to the playroom and get them. As we walked down the hall, she was gushing about the girls. 'Everyone loves Julie and Lucy. They're such nice girls, and so smart!'

We entered a large classroom where about 35 children were running in circles, jumping, laughing and tossing toys all over. Lucy was sitting in a large circle with about a dozen other kids, who were playing a game similar to an old TV game show called 'To Tell the Truth', except the kids formed two teams, the telling team and the guessing team.

One kid on the telling team named Sally started by saying, 'My parents promised to take me to Disneyland for my birthday this year.' The next kid, Willie, said, 'My parents promised to take me to Disneyland for my birthday this year.' And so on down the line, each said, 'My parents promised to take me to Disneyland for my birthday this year.' I couldn't help but notice Lucy. The other kids were listening to the speaker, but Lucy's eyes were glued to the speaker.

Just as the final kid, Jason, finished saying, 'My parents promised to take me to Disneyland for my birthday this year', Lucy piped up with 'Willie is the *real* one.'

Willie nodded in confirmation. 'Hooray! Hooray!' Everyone started clapping. The wide-eyed principal leaned over to me and said, 'I just don't know how she does it. It's truly phenomenal. She guesses right almost every time. Just hearing one sentence, she knows who's telling the truth. It's almost eerie.'

I agreed that it was indeed phenomenal. However, I knew little Lucy had no mystical or supernatural powers. Deborah had told me the secret.

As I was helping Julie on with her coat, I overheard Lucy talking with Willie.

'When are you going to go to Disneyland?'

Little Willie with downcast eyes said, 'Next month.'

Lucy obviously knew something was wrong. 'You don't wanna go?' she asked.

'I wanna go, but...' Willie, still looking down, started digging his toe into the floor.

Like the most exquisitely trained psychiatrist, Lucy didn't say anything. She just kept looking peacefully and sympathetically at Willie. 'It's just that', Willie continued hesitantly, 'I'm going alone with just my dad because, he and Mom, well my dad moved out last month and...'

Lucy put her hand on little Willie's arm, looked right into his eyes, and neither kid needed to say another word. No wonder all the kids loved Lucy. She knew how to listen with her heart more than her ears.

> Listening with your heart is watching people carefully to see how they *feel* about what they are saying. It is 'listening' to their gestures, 'listening' to their fidgeting, 'listening' to their skin flushing, 'listening' to their eye contact, and 'listening' to everything else you can *see* about the person who is talking.

**CLAUSE 6 ♂ ♀**

## Listen to Their Heart

Whenever people are speaking, I will be sensitive to their body language and try to determine how they feel about what they are saying. I will then respond to that as much as their words.

# Chapter Eight

# Fine-tuning your tongue

The second language lesson I learned from Dale came as a bombshell, especially coming from a guy who cut his teeth on a gun barrel. On his last business trip to New York, we decided to meet for lunch. I arrived at the restaurant a bit early and waited five minutes, ten. Just as it was coming up on 15, I spotted his big ten-gallon hat hovering above the crowd like a flying saucer. He handed it to a beaming hat-check attendant who pretended he needed help from another to carry it.

When he reached the table, he said, 'Oh, I bet you were about to send the bloodhounds out for me. But don't you worry little lady, ol' Dale knows how to take care of himself, even in Noo Yawk City.'

Dale said, 'I'm as hungry as a goat on a concrete pasture. How about you?' A minute later, while looking at our menus, he peeked sheepishly over his and said, 'I hope you weren't offended by what I just said.'

'The goat?' I asked sincerely.

'No, that "little lady" bit. I durn near got my mouth washed out with soap last week at the office. And all I said was the "switchboard gal" was sick that day. Well, my right-hand gal, er person, Stephanie, set me straight.'

This piqued my curiosity and I asked him to tell me more. He said, 'Well, I knew my tongue was as wild as unbroken bronco and it needed some ropin'. So I took her to lunch and she told me a slew of things.'

'Like what?'

'Like I wouldn't say "my lawyer guy" or "accountant guy" so why say "switchboard gal"? I should've said "switchboard operator". Then she said that if I were going to refer to a female, I should say "woman", not "gal" or "girl" or "lady".' He thought for a second and then said, 'So I guess that means "little lady" is out too?'

'Well, yes, Dale, it does,' I said. 'But if you can prove with a birth certificate and residency papers that you were born and bred in Texas, people will forgive you.'

'Whoa, Miss Leil, I say a mighty big thankyou to that. But I don't deserve any excuses. My body may be in the second millennium, but my mouth is still in the first. No, this ol' Lone Star fella has to change his ways when it comes to the, uh, "other but equal" sex.

'Stephanie suggested a couple of good books for me to read. I told her, "I sure would like to read 'em, but I know I'm not going to find the time." I asked her if she would write me a little crib sheet to make me poh-litically correct.' Here Dale reached into his pocket and pulled out an obviously well-studied dog-eared piece of paper. 'Here's the inventory of tricks I'm trying to train my tongue to do,' he said.

It just so happened I also had a written list of linguistic do's and don'ts in my purse that day because my tongue, too, was lagging behind my awareness. For example, when giving a speech, out of habit sometimes I'd slip and call my female audience members 'ladies'. I could see by their expressions that some of them took offence.

Dale and I swapped our lists and simultaneously cracked up. Practically all of his 'DON'T SAY' list for men was on my 'DO SAY' list for women, and vice versa.

I asked Dale if I could borrow his list and present it here.

'Why, sure, little lady – er I mean Leil – that would be an honour.'

> The differences in the way men and women should speak in order to win hearts, not wound them – to make careers, not break them – gets men discombobulated and women in a tizzy. To cut the confusion, simply follow the six reduced rules in Clauses 7 and 8.

Gentlemen, follow these rules and 90 per cent of the ammunition in the workplace war between the sexes will be demolished. Innocent female employees will no longer feel ravaged and pillaged. You will no longer be accused of dictatorial tactics. And the office battle of the sexes may soon take its place in ancient history alongside of the Battle of Hastings or the Seven-Year War.

**CLAUSE 7 ♂**

## Dis-Guys My Dialogue

When speaking to women, I will avoid gender-specific terms, all sexual references at work and speak less didactically. I will always:

- state an observation (or ask a question) as a preface to stating what I want.
- soften any requests or commands with phrases like 'Could you...?', 'Would you be able to...?', 'Could I ask you to...?'
- be a bit more tentative when, for example, interrupting her with a question: 'I'm sorry to bother you, but...'
- minimize facts and use more feeling words such as 'I'm pleased/moved/irritated/enthusiastic...'

- add lots of tag lines, such as 'What about you?' and 'What do you think?' to solicit her opinion
- even (horrors!) throw an occasional 'I'm sorry' into the mix.
  For men only

Women, here is your part of the peace treaty. When you follow these simple rules, your male colleagues, friends and sweethearts will *actually* understand you, and you'll go up a notch in their estimation.

**CLAUSE 8 ♀**

## De-Gurrl My Dialogue

When speaking to men, I will...

- lower my voice, speak more directly, less hesitantly and say what I want.
- say what I mean in complete sentences; no beating around the bush.
- be straight on, with no humble introductions; stamp out phrases like 'I'm sorry to bother you, but...' or 'I know this is a silly question, but...' (and 'while I'm at it', 'I'll never say', 'I'm terrible at maths!')
- minimize feeling words and substitute facts
- drop all tag lines
- never apologize unless I mean it.
  For women only

These clauses are not just for the office. Husbands who 'Dis-Guys' and wives who 'De-Gurrl' their talk will have more harmony at home. And dating 'Dis-Guysed' guys and 'De-Gurrled' girls will have a lot more respect for each other. In other words, these two clauses will make the other sex like you a whole lot better. (See Appendix A for examples.)

I knew Dale saw the folly of his ways and genuinely planned to change. I told him, however, that I hope he didn't change his Texas charm.

'Yep,' he said. 'I've been told I could charm the knickers off the Queen Mother.'

Old habits are hard to break...

## Chapter Nine

# Never hear 'You're not listening!' again

Have you ever talked to a nail sticking out of wood? It doesn't nod. It doesn't say 'Uh huh'. It seldom smiles. It just stands there until you have finished speaking. Gentlemen, with all due respect, you listen like a nail – which, when listening to other men, is great. That's how you've been taught to listen. That's how to signal to other men that you *are* listening. However, if you listen that way to a woman, she'll want to take a hammer, give the nail (you) a thwack on the head, and scream, 'Why aren't you listening?'

Last year I spoke at a terrific Women's Leadership Conference in Mexico, which was attended by several hundred women and half a dozen brave husbands or significant others who had come along for the sun and the beaches.[14] About 10 concurrent sessions for women and one for men, on themes ranging from entrepreneurial to spiritual, ran at any one time. I attended a variety of seminars but, on the last day, the one which caught my eye was a men's one, called 'Living with a Successful Woman'.

Totally inappropriate, of course, for me to attend, so I asked the facilitator if I would be able to purchase the recording. Alas, no arrangements had been made – guess the men didn't want their wives or significant others to hear all that male bonding in female-bashing. (Amazingly, there was none of the latter – just the opposite. This remarkable muster of males was very proud of their successful wives. As one man said, 'especially when I look at the monthly bank statement of our joint account'...)

The facilitator generously invited me to attend and I accepted, only if the participants had no objections and I could be a fly on the wall. So that my presence wouldn't inhibit the men, I sat behind a big screen, where I could hear but not be seen.

At the beginning of the session, the facilitator suggested each man introduce himself and speak about his successful partner and their relationship. The first man started speaking... And speaking... And speaking... He must have gone on for about 10 minutes and I began to wonder if the other men had left because I heard nothing. No 'uh huhs', no comments, no questions, no nothing. *Had they walked out?*

No. It soon became evident that each man was speaking in turn and those constant little noises that we women make to show our support of the speaker were conspicuously absent in their dialogue. Or, I should say, during their monologues.

Holy mackerel! I thought. This is unusual. I was so surprised by the phenomenon that, after the conference, when I returned to my office, I combed through a batch of studies on male/female listening. Some pretty eye-opening results.

We think women are better listeners? No way! We just listen *differently*. We constantly nod to let the speaker know we are listening. We make supportive noises to confirm that we understand what is being said. Until that moment, I didn't consider my innocent way of overlapping, sportive statements to be interruptions. But many men would! Be careful, sisters. We have to adapt a different listening demeanour around men. (As men should when they speak with us.)

Conversely, men only nod when they agree with the speaker. They might argue that the male way of listening is superior because he isn't thinking about his momentary responses.

We think women talk more than men? Again, no way! Men talk much more than women at work. For them, talking is a form of competing and getting their ideas across. When they're at home, their silence simply means they're taking a rest from having to compete.

Women interrupt each other more, but in a non-competitive way. It is mainly to jump in with their own encouraging statements.[15] Like those little plastic ducks you can balance on the side of a glass, we are constantly nodding our head. All that says is, 'I understand what you're saying.'

A picture of a male listening is definitely a still life. A picture of a woman listening is high animation. Want the other sex to stop saying, 'You never listen to me'? Listen the way they listen.

CLAUSE 9 ♀

## Listen Like a Nail

When speaking with a man, I will cut the constant nodding and little supporters like 'Uh huh', 'Yes', 'Oh', and other cooing noises. He'll think I'm interrupting! (Imagine that...) I will get it into my head that if I just stand looking at him while he speaks, he'll think I'm a great listener.

For women only

**CLAUSE 10** ♂

## Listen Like a Dunking Duck

To let a woman know I am listening, I will sprinkle my conversation with supportive statements like 'Uh huh' and 'Yes, I see.' I'll also nod to confirm that I understand what she is saying. I'll get it into my head that nodding does not mean that I agree with her.

For men only

Incidentally, when it comes to language, what's good for the Western goose may not be good for the Eastern gander. For instance, if you're travelling to the Far East, toss linguistic advice over the Japanese screen or, at least, take it with a splash of teriyaki sauce. Say you're an English mother and you come upon your kid in the kitchen gleefully taking raw eggs from the refrigerator and dropping them one by one on the floor. 'Whee!', PLOP; 'Whee!' PLOP. Naturally, you'd go berserk and, at the very least, say, 'No, stop!' A little physical intrusion in the form of a warning finger might even be in order.

The Japanese mother, on the other hand, feels that saying no means losing status. Discussion means gaining status and harmony.[16] So the Japanese mum says to her little mite, 'Oh, isn't that interesting? Who drops eggs on the floor, Kieko? Do you know anyone who drops eggs on the floor? Have you ever seen anyone dropping eggs on the floor? Mr Egg is saying "Ouch." '

In fact a Japanese gentleman named Ueda wrote a paper called 'Sixteen Ways to Avoid Saying "No" in Japan' – and this guy was serious![17]

## Chapter Ten

# Fragging the fatal FUD factor

There may be some differences in thinking between the Orient and the Occident, but one is universal. We must have confidence if we hope to win at any game, be it athletic, business, social or romantic.

Olympic athletes, performance artists and even business-people, who want always to be at their best, are turning increasingly to sports psychologists. I have the good fortune to know one named Stan who, with one simple technique, made a great difference in my life.

We were having a quick lunch in a coffee shop one day when he told me he was working with a Japanese Olympic skater whose name he asked me not to use – we'll call her Tesuko. He said she had all the talent and skill she needed to get a gold medal. Nevertheless, she lacked confidence in her-self – a fatal flaw in athletes, as in all of us. (When reporters asked her, 'Will you win?', her answer was, 'I'm going to try.' Not good enough, Tesuko!) Stan told me that unless you truly know in the depth of your heart that you are a winner, you never will be. You have to believe it constantly – not just while competing, but while sleeping, eating, showering, talking and partying. Stan calls that constant assurance being in The Zone.

##  But what about me? I'm no Olympic athlete

I asked him whether finding The Zone, as he called it, would work for the rest of us who were *not* going for a gold medal.

'What do you mean?' he asked. 'We're all going for gold. Maybe not a gold medal for ice skating, skiing or track. Still, we're going for gold in our jobs, in dealing with our families We're going for gold in making friends and finding love, or making it last. Everyone's definition of gold is different, but the method of getting it is the same. You get in The Zone or you wind up like a pancake on ice.'

I asked him, 'So where is this Zone place?'

He said, 'For some people it's right in their own back yard. For others, it's very far away and takes a very long time to get to.'

My next question was, of course, 'Well, how far is it for me?'

'I don't know,' he answered, 'But if you like, we can find out. Let me ask you to do the same thing I asked Tesuko.' Stan drew the following sketch on a napkin.

| | | | | | |
|---|---|---|---|---|---|
| _____ | CN | CS | CB | CL | CA |
| _____ | CN | CS | CB | CL | CA |
| _____ | CN | CS | CB | CL | CA |
| _____ | CN | CS | CB | CL | CA |
| _____ | CN | CS | CB | CL | CA |

'Now,' he said, 'on the five lines, write the five people you talk with the most in your life. If you have more than five whom you deal with every day, you can add more lines and put the same letters beside the lines.'

Before continuing to read, please could you do the same. List five people you know and who know you pretty well. They can be same-sex friends, other-sex friends, lovers, brothers, sisters, spouse or significant other – someone who you feel has an influence on you. For now, ignore the letters beside the lines and just write their names. We'll return to the exercise in a moment.

Lack of confidence had eliminated Tesuko the year before, and now Stan had only three months to work with her and make her honestly feel 'I am the best.' This was his number-one tough challenge because Tesuko had grown up in Japan, where the joyful arrogance and good-natured bantering and boasting so widespread in our sportsmanship was nonexistent. A Japanese motto, translated, says, 'The nail that stands out must be hammered down.'

To make matters worse, Tesuko was romantically involved with a man who, out of his own insecurity, belittled Tesuko. The number-two challenge Stan faced was showing her how her boyfriend, Akiro, was sabotaging her self-image. Only if he could accomplish this could he go for the goal – qualifying Tesuko to go for gold.

The five people Tesuko wrote on her list were her mother and father in Kyoto, with whom she spoke every day on the phone, and her sister, who lived in the States. Then there was her best friend, an English girl named Jenny, and, of course, Akiro.

Stan asked Tesuko to think about her conversations with each person on her list, then circle the set of initials that most accurately described how much (if at all) they criticized her.

Before continuing to read, please do the same. Circle CN if the person whose name is on that line Never Criticizes you. Circle CS if they Seldom Criticize you. CB is an interesting one: it stands for 'Criticizes Beneficially'. Circle that if, at times, that person does criticize you, but it has a positive effect. You feel they give their criticism without rancour and it helps you grow. Mark CL if the person on that line Criticizes you a Lot, and CA if they are Always Criticizing you.

Tesuko's list looked like this: her mother and sister – CN; her father – CS; her girlfriend, Jenny – CB, and her boyfriend, Akiro – CA.

Stan's first step to helping Tesuko get in The Zone was to get her talking about herself, her life in Japan, her new life as an Olympic athlete, her training, and about her relationships. Throughout her narrative, he interjected questions about her feelings: 'How do you feel when your sister is watching and you've skated really well?' 'How do you feel when Jenny is watching and you've skated really well?'

Stan noticed that whenever she talked about her family, who were so proud of her, her back straightened, her deep-brown eyes sparkled and a soft, confident smile framed her lips. This was the feeling Stan needed Tesuko to have – always. Conversely, whenever Tesuko started talking about her boyfriend, her shoulders tensed up and her eyes fell.

##  When you love the one who hurts you

Then he asked Tesuko the million-dollar question – the one that, when Tesuko tried to answer, she broke into tears. That question was, 'How do you *feel* when your boyfriend is watching and you've skated really well?'

Tesuko realized, at that moment, that she had *never* skated well when Akiro was watching.

##  How you can go for gold

Now go back to your list. If all of your relationships are CS (Criticize Seldom) or CN (Criticize Never), you are very fortunate indeed. Supportive people surround you. If you have any CBs on your list, make sure they are indeed Criticizing only Beneficially, and that you are genuinely growing and improving by their guidance. The problem comes if you find any CAs (Criticizes Always) or CLs (Criticizes a Lot). If you do, and can eliminate them from your life (or at least diminish your exposure to them), please do.

However, if you want or need to keep a relationship with someone who criticizes you a lot – well, this person a 'Trasher' – you must get him or her to stop reproaching you, if you are going to be successful in stamping out Fear, Uncertainty and Doubt. You can't feel good about yourself if someone important to you is constantly gnawing away at your self-esteem.

You must take the Trasher aside and tell them how it makes you *feel* when they criticize you. Be very specific. Describe your symptoms. Describe the result. For example, you might say, 'George, I know you think you are telling me this for my own good. Nevertheless, every time you criticize me, I get short of breath. My heart beats faster. I begin to feel worthless, and then later I find myself getting angry. I don't want this to happen. You are too important to me.'

You must also decide on an ultimatum if they continue to criticize. Depending on your relationship, this can be as light as walking out of the room or out of the house – or as strong as walking out of their life.

Obviously you can't walk out on your parents or a marriage which is otherwise good, or if you have children. Choose your ultimatum carefully, because when they start to criticize non-beneficially you must stick with it.

---

The reason why juries are sequestered in trials is so they won't be influenced by the media or what their friends or family say. It's the same here. You can't have contact with people who are constantly criticizing you and still feel good about yourself. If these folks (we'll call them 'Bitchers') are not crucial in your life for other reasons, well, they've just gotta go! As my Mother would say, 'Give them their walking papers. Now!'

**CLAUSE 11** ♂ ♀

## Ditch the Bitchers, Talk to the Trashers

I will tell the Trashers in my life how I feel when they criticize me and give them an ultimatum. As far as the Bitchers are concerned, it's either 'Stop criticizing me' or it's 'Bye-bye, Bitcher'.

The tale of Tesuko has a happy ending. In the weeks ahead, she and Stan spoke more about her relationship with Akiro. It was Tesuko herself who came to the conclusion that she should sever the relationship.

I guess she wasn't the first woman to be attracted to a 'bad boy'. And she won't be the last. Some women are addicted to the bad boys, so much so that science has given it a name. It is called the 'Stockholm Syndrome'.[18] Researchers have come up with some pretty interesting theories on why these men hold such attraction for some women, and we'll explore these later in Part IV.

Right after breaking up with John, I sent Stan an email. He wrote back saying, 'Leil, I know you did the right thing. Even though he obviously excited you, I could tell it was a destructive relationship. You were very smart for cutting it off swiftly and surely.' He then said, 'I'd like to share this definition of a "smart woman" that I found posted on the Web.'

##  Confidence alone isn't enough

Of course, Tesuko and all Olympic athletes need not only confidence to win; they need extraordinary skill. Likewise, to make people like us, we need extraordinary social skill. I begin most of my seminars asking participants why they decided to take the programme. The two most prevalent reasons given are 'fear of walking into a room full of strangers' and 'making small talk'.

The next two clauses will help you over those two everyday experiences, which many people find are excruciatingly painful. (If you're one of them, there's no need to be embarrassed.) *The New York Times*, one of the few publications with the ability to officialize a phenomenon, has put Social Anxiety Disorder on the map. More than half the population suffers from it at one time or another.

## Chapter Eleven

# How to work a room like royalty

Entering a room full of strangers is like jumping into a cold swimming pool. The worst part is standing on the edge, fearful of how it's going to feel when you smack against the icy water. But once you're in, it's not so cold after all, and you can start enjoying the swim.

You stand at the doorway of the party. Everyone is laughing, schmoozing, drinking, munching and having such a good time. They all seem to know each other. Your knees are knocking together so loudly that you're sure in a minute they're all going to turn and look at you.

Here is how to avoid such upsetting episodes in your life. You're well armed with your good eye contact, a sincere smile and just the right handshake. You look good – except for that frozen look of sheer animal fear on your face. Naturally you want to replace it with a confident smile, but you would feel like a grinning idiot smiling at no one.

Here's the tactic. I call it The 'Emperor's New Clothes'. Perhaps you remember the story of the emperor who was given a beautiful new suit of clothes that supposedly only the right-eous could see. To all those who were *not* righteous, the suit would be invisible. Well, the emperor made a proud procession through the streets and all of his subjects oohed and aahed in admiration of the new suit. (Naturally, they all wanted everybody else to think they were righteous and could see it.) Then, one honest little kid shouted, 'But the king has on nothing at all!'

You will need your imagination, but don't worry, you don't need to get naked!

## Step One

As you stand at the door of the party, let your eyes settle on an empty space between several people on the far side of the room. Give the empty spot a big warm smile and a wave. You mustn't be concerned that you're beaming at a barren spot of wallpaper. The person to the right and left of it probably won't even notice and, if they do, they won't look to see who you're smiling at.

If you do know someone on the other side of the room, all the better. But, even if they are facing the other direction, grace their posteriors with the same warm greeting you'd give their beconing faces.

## Step Two

Now you start your regal procession of one through the gathering. Think Queen Elizabeth. Think presidential candidates and 'I want your vote.' As you make your way through the throng of your subjects, give a smile, a nod and small acknowledgement to every third or fourth person as you pass.

Will they know you're faking it? Absolutely not. Everyone else's insecurity will be in high gear and they'll think you know everybody. Those strangers you've smiled and nodded to will assume all the others were *real* acquaintances and you must have just mistaken them for someone else. Either that, or you're a really famous person and, after all, *noblesse oblige* (the noble are obligated to acknowledge their court).

If you come upon someone you really do know, you're in luck. Now you can stop and chat a while. They'll feel lucky that, out of all the people you know at the party, you chose them to exchange a few words with.

Now you're in the pool. You can either tread water with a found acquaintance, or keep the breaststroke up until...

## Step Three

You catch up with your imaginary friends at the far end. 'Hmm, where did they go?' Oh, well, by now you have made a favourable impression on everyone you have acknowledged and on everyone who was merely watching you. So you take the last and final step of the procession.

## Step Four

You look for someone to introduce yourself to. Another party-goer standing alone is an excellent candidate. This loner has probably noticed you gliding confidently through the crowd greeting all your fans, so he or she will be honoured that you chose to stop and talk.

No solo souls standing around? Then head for the bar or the table of hors d'oeuvres, where you'll find plenty of humans lurking. The food is not only fodder for feeding the folks, it's fodder for conversation with anyone else grazing at the trough.

'Hi, those carrot sticks look healthy, don't they? But I'm not in a healthy mood. Have you tried any of the other goodies yet?'

'Hello, think they'd laugh if I asked for a rum and coke?'

Incidentally, if you can refrain from holding something in your hands, do. Open arms make you more approachable, and your hands are free for shaking other people's hands.

## CLAUSE 12 ♂ ♀

## The Emperor's New Clothes

Whenever entering a room where I don't know anyone, I will spot imaginary friends on the other side of the room, and begin a regal glide toward them, acknowledging every third or fourth 'old acquaintance' as I pass. Upon reaching my mark, I will strike up a conversation with another 'stand-alone' (who will feel honuoured that someone obviously so well connected as I am should grace them with my attention!).

You may feel a tad silly the first time you use this technique, but I have used it for years and have suggested it to many friends, who now swear by it. Happily, not one of us has ever encountered a kid like the one who told the hypocritical spectators, 'But the king has on nothing at all!' Nobody's going to shout, 'Ha ha, she's really bluffing and doesn't know anybody here.'

# Chapter Twelve

# Nice shake!

Now we get into the realm of the first highly choreographed human contact, the handshake. In some societies, a handshake is more valid than a 20-page contract. For example, in the diamond district of New York, countless millions of dollars of precious gems are bought, sold and traded – not on a contract, but a handshake. You break a contract and they can sue you. But you break the trust of a handshake and they break your kneecaps. And that's just for starters!

But let's talk about the tiny contract between any two people who shake hands. It reads, 'Hello, I am open to a minute or two of conversation with you to see if we interest each other.'

You extend your hand in friendship and, for those first moments your epidermis touches that of a new person, you are emitting (and receiving) thousands of subliminal signals. A handful of limp linguine whispers falteringly to your new acquaintance, 'I am a passive loser with no people skills, and furthermore I am not the least bit interested in meeting you.' The opposite isn't much better. The power crunch shouts in your new acquaintance's ear, 'I'm really a wimp inside and I'm going to try to prove I'm not by squeezing the hell out of your hand!'

Then there's 'The Topper', who floats in from above expecting you to kiss his/her ring; 'The Puller', who yanks you in so suddenly that you totter on your toes; 'The Rifler', who extends his arm so straight out that you want to raise your arms and beg, 'Don't shoot!'; and, of course, the 'Two-Handed Shaker', who, no matter what he says next, you know he's after your vote, your money or your body.

The handshake that it gives me the most pain to talk about is the 'Cold Wet Paw' because, though decades have passed, I will never forget my anxious high-school years as a mushy mitt-shaker. At the first sign of nervousness, I didn't break out in controllable zits like many of my more fortunate friends. They could cover their embarrassment with a dab of calamine lotion. There was nothing I could do about my cold, wet flippers. I tried everything – from little white lies about my sore hand, to pretending I didn't see theirs suspended in the space between us in expectation of mine joining it for a second or two of good fellowship. I resorted to carrying a handkerchief and doing quick swipe before each shake. But this was to no avail. The swipe was too obvious and the hand too moist. My palms were a permanent perspiration factory.

Every June our school had what was called 'The Best of...' award ceremony. An award was presented in the auditorium to the student who had the best painting in art class, the best science project, the best athlete, and the best essay in creative-writing class. I was to be the proud recipient of this last.

The joy of my magnificent moment was marred by fantasies of extending my wet paw in front of the whole school. I prayed the presenter's suffering (and my own) would be brief.

The big day arrived and I had made preparations to reduce the disgrace. I was waiting with the other recipients in the wings of the auditorium stage. Just as my name was called, I managed to give my hand an unobtrusive shake (like a dog emerging from the river) and a final swipe on a hanky, before stashing it in a backstage plant (which, I am sure, welcomed the moisture).

I strode proudly on stage and extended my right hand to Miss Leigh, the presenter. Still clasping my right hand, she handed the award to me with her left. We both turned to the photographer, who clicked. No flash. He clicked again. Nothing. Mumbling something about having to change his repeater bulb, he dived into his photo bag. Miss Leigh let go of my hand, which by now was starting to overflow with perspiration. During the two minutes it took the photographer to change bulbs, Miss Leigh, sensing my shyness, gave the group a supportive little dialogue about the joys of creative writing. Little did she know that I was dying inside and that I felt beads of perspiration dripping from my hands, in a fairly even flow now and forming a little puddle on the floor.

Ah, the photographer was ready. Miss Leigh straightened up, repeated 'Congratulations, Leilie', and picked up the plaque. There was no circumventing the dreaded moment now. I couldn't tell her I'd just sprained my wrist in the past two minutes. Or that I suddenly decided I was going to become a surgeon or maybe a concert pianist, and therefore couldn't let mere mortals touch my hands.

With a big smile, she offered her right. I stared at it, frozen in fear. I didn't dare let nice Miss Leigh clasp the cold wet fish I was hiding behind my back. A few seconds, which felt like hours, must have passed, because I heard the audience tittering. I had no choice but put my icy wet paw into Miss Leigh's warm arid hand. It was like watching an arctic wind freeze her smile into ice.

As she called out the next student's name, she was compelled to take a handkerchief from her purse on the podium and wipe her hands. Good intentions aside, it was as unobtrusive as a cow walking across the stage. The audience roared with laughter.

This happened way back in the 1970s – a lifetime ago. Yet, to this day, envisioning that mortifying moment, the pain comes back with a rush as fresh as this morning's tabloid headline: 'Timid teen attempts to drown teacher (nationwide hunt under way)'.

Over the years, I have realized that I am not alone. Some people today are (nearly) as pathetic as I was. Fortunately, for them there is a cure to the mushy-mitt syndrome. Modern science gives us – drum roll, please – *antiperspirant*. If it works under your arms, it works on your hands. My hands still tend to perspire on important occasions but, dressing for an event, no roll-on or spray for me. I use old-fashioned jar antiperspirant and I make sure I massage it into my armpits with my bare palms.

But enough of the 'Don'ts'. Here are the 'Do's' for your handshake. Just as during your annual physical your doctor listens to your heartbeat and peers into your eyes with that blinding little torch, here are the five points the handshake doctor would check you out on.

In fact, I open many of my communications seminars by having people shake hands with someone they don't know. Then, in the middle of the shake, I tell them to freeze.

Try it with a friend. Shake hands and, in the middle of the shake, become motionless. Have someone check you on the following five points.

## Are you looking into each other's eyes?

This is pretty basic. Yet, out of temerity or disinterest, many people catch themselves, at the critical moment of contact, looking away. Here is a trick you can play to make sure your ocular nerve is focused in the right place – while your hands are pumping, make a mental note of your shakee's eye colour.

## Are the webs of your thumbs touching?

What are the webs? Think of your hand as a big duck's foot. The web is the part between his toes; in this case, your thumb and forefinger. Whenever shaking hands, you want to slide in with your hand until your webs press together in good fellowship. As you confidently glide your hand in, you'll be surprised at how many people grip and stop you before you get to their web. It sends out subliminal signals that they are afraid of intimacy.

## Are you putting light pressure on their metacarpus?

Their what? The metacarpus are the bones on the back of your hand. I said *light pressure*. That's why the bone-crusher is called the bone-*crusher* – these tiny bones are delicate, crushable fossils. (And, the older you are, the more fossilized they become.)

## Are your palms close enough together that you could hold a marble between your palm and your partner's?

If your palms are pulling away from your partner's, you give the feeling that perhaps you have something to hide – like those buzzers kids hide in their palms!

## Are your palms 100 per cent perpendicular to the floor?

If you extend your hand knuckles up, palm down, you are saying, 'I'm the boss! Anything I say goes. If I say "Jump", you ask me, "How high?"' If you extend your hand palm up, you give the impression of a beggar, and the shaker feels that he or she has to cross your palm with a tip.

With these five checkpoints, you will be a perfect shaker in no time.

CLAUSE 13 ♂ ♀

### My Five-Star Handshake

Whenever I shake hands, I will make sure that: I maintain eye contact, our webs are touching, I exert light pressure, and that our palms are marble-close and perpendicular to the floor.

Now you know the basics of The Five-Star Handshake, let's give it a little fine-tuning. How many pumps? Two should suffice, lest your shakee thinks you're trying to draw water. Check your arm. Is it slightly bent? If it's too straight, it signals that you are fearful and are saying 'Stay away!' If it's too close, it could be anxiety-provoking. Your shakee might fear that you've pulled his or her hand in so tight they'll never get it back.

Are you leaning forward, inadvertently signalling, 'You, I like you and would like to get closer to you.' Or are you leaning back, which in the language understood around the world says, 'I'm trying to get as far away from you as is socially possible'?

And, of course, shake with one hand – unless you are giving your condolences: 'I'm so deeply sorry your parakeet passed away.' Let there be a momentary linger at the end of your handshake. If you are holding good, strong eye contact, and a bit of your dental work is showing in a sincere smile, it anchors the good fellowship that only a handshake has the power to make.

I've been trying to break the habit, but in the past few months I've been judging everyone's handshake. More than once have I had to bite my tongue, to stop myself saying to a new acquaintance, 'Nice shake!'

# Chapter Thirteen

# The Hugganary

'What about hugs?' you might logically ask. It seems like people are hugging more these days, and it's meaning less. True, but I'm not here to try to change uncomfortable customs; just to try to make them more meaningful.

Several years ago, at a convention, I learned the meaning of the more commonplace hugs.[19]

First is the *A-Frame Hug*. On the opening day of any convention, you spot everybody giving this one to folks they haven't seen since the last convention. Since they can't remember each other's name (and obviously haven't given them a thought since they went through the identical charade the year before), they cover it with a hug. Like pairs of cards with their tips balanced tent-style (like an 'A'), they are cheek-to-cheek but their bodies and feet are as far apart as humanly possible. The accompanying dialogue is always, verbatim, an effervescent 'Hello, how *are* you? It's so good to see you.'

One step up is the *A-Frame Patter's Hug*. This is similar to the above, with the addition of each patting the other's back. The added unspoken dialogue is, 'It's been a long time. I really don't want to touch you though.' The A-Frame Patter's

Hug is also employed by friends of the opposite sex when they are genuinely happy to see each other but their respective spouses have accompanied them on the trip, so they don't dare upgrade to the more desirable Heart-to-Heart Hug.

Which, of course, brings us to the *Heart-to-Heart Hug*, which is (in my estimation) the first true hug. This is the uninhibited hug between two friends who really do like each other and are not uptight about it. Their full upper bodies are touching and their lower bodies are still separated, but by a smaller space. The underlying message is, 'We're good friends. I really like you, but we're not having sex.'

Women, unless one of them is too well endowed, often give each other the Heart-to-Heart Hug. Men do too, but theirs lasts a fraction of the time that the female version does. One study on men's hugging showed that, even during these fleeting hug-ettes, men often suffer marked psychological distress lest one get the wrong idea.[20] I've often seen men, in a natural overflow of genuine sentiment, instinctively give each other a quick hug – and then look around furtively to see if anyone noticed.

Now we come to the famous *Big Bear Hug*, my favourite. It is known round the world and named after the celebrated grizzly bear.

Perhaps the Bear Hug is intensely poignant to me because I once had a boyfriend who was a *real* big bear-hugger. In fact, not only did he hug a bear, but he trained it to dance! Alfred (my boyfriend – not his real name, but he looked like one) kept Barney (the bear – his real name, and he *definitely* looked like one) in a big geodesic dome made of fencing material in his garden in Iowa. However, he often travelled to New York with Barney to shoot movie scenes or commercials

When Barney wasn't working, Alfred would charge admis-sion for tourists to come and watch him dance with Barney. They made a striking couple. Alfred was a slender, Aryan type with longish blond hair. Alfred was tall, but Barney was taller (3 m), heavier (weighing in at more than 450 kilos – before breakfast) and much, much hairier. That's a lot of bear to dance with. Just one of Barney's paws is larger than Alfred's head. It was an upsetting thought to think of my relationship at the mercy of a bear. If Barney ever got upset with Alfred, he could smash his beautiful head with one swipe.

Alfred invited me out to Iowa to visit him for a few days and I learned the meaning of 'bear hug' the first time I saw them perform together. The show started and Alfred gave Barney one of the dozens of commands he knew, such as 'Turn around.' Barney stared at Alfred blankly for a minute. Barney repeated, 'Turn around, Barney.' Then, to the delight of the crowd, Barney lifted one of his massive paws and started his turn in a clockwise direction. When he had completed his pirouette and several other graceful (for a bear) moves, Alfred went berserk with praise. He reached into his pockets, which were stuffed with chicken gizzards, necks and legs, and held them out. 'Good Barney!' 'Good Barney!' he boomed.

When Barney had greedily and happily devoured the prize, he clasped Alfred in a BIG hug. From that moment on, no one in the crowd would ever have the same image when they heard the words 'bear hug' again. For the rest of their lives, 80 kilos of Alfred being surrounded almost 360 degrees by 530 kilos of Barney will flash before their eyes. And whenever they give someone a bear hug, it will be bigger, and warmer, and longer, than ever.

But let me tell you about the last time I saw Alfred and Barney do their thing. Everything had gone as planned. Barney had performed a dozen or so of his amazing feats. But this time, during the great hug, it must have dawned on Barney for the first time that Alfred couldn't move! And as long as Alfred couldn't move, he wouldn't make him do any more silly things like ballerina turns. And maybe being top bear was better than getting chicken and wolfing it down for a crowd of tourists.

'Let go,' I heard my dear Alfred say in a firm voice muffled by bear fur. I could hardly see my man inside of big Barney's grasp.

'Let go,' he repeated, more muffled, but louder. Barney looked down at the tousled yellow head buried in his chest, then looked at the frightened spectators.

'Let go, Barney,' Alfred said one more time. Barney respond-ed by dropping some bear slobber on top of Alfred's head. Finally, after what seemed like an eternity to me, he loosened his grip. Alfred, grinning from ear to ear, emerged from Barney's grasp, drenched but exhilarated. Alfred then blew up into Barney's mouth (a sign of esteem and affection among bears) and more great globules of bear slobber slithered down on Alfred's head and down his back. Alfred seemed to love it.

I found myself becoming ill.

As a finale, Barney lay down on his back and put his paws in the air. Just kidding, Alfie.

Somehow, I just couldn't bring myself to kiss Alfred after that. The end of a beautiful relationship. I guess it ended, as so many relationships do, by seeing my man in the arms of another.

But, to this day, the feeling between man and bear hugging each other was more sincere than I've ever seen with two human beings hugging each other.

Since that day, I have tried to avoid superficially hugging someone unless I *really* feel it. But, when I do, I'll hold them tight, if only for a second, like Barney held Alfie (and I'll try not to slobber on their head).

You can't go anywhere these days without seeing people everywhere in A-frame position throwing pretentious French kisses in the air. If someone lifts her arms, bends over at the waist, and comes at you with that 'I'm soo cool because I'm going to give you zee French hug' look in her eyes, there's not much you can do to avoid it. But try to make the moment mean something by making it (at least) an honest hug.

**CLAUSE 14** ♂ ♀

# The Honest Hug

Whenever I hug someone I *want* to hug, I'll hold on tight, for just a second or two longer, to make it a REAL hug.

# Chapter Fourteen

# The secret of confident conversing

The secret of conversing comfortably and confidently can be reduced to three easy pieces. Dozens of studies have unveiled what makes a successful socializer, and they all came up with the same answer.

My all-time favourite study in this area is titled 'The Behavioral Assessment of Social Competence in Males'.[21] That's a fancy way of asking, 'What makes a guy cool?' Even though this particular study involved men, the same rules apply for women.

## What separates social 'winners' from social 'losers'?

Researchers chose two groups of men to participate in their study. The first group was already successfully socializing. They were invited to many parties, were popular with women, and well liked by all. These fellows dated a lot and were 'winners' in the social scene.

The second group, alas, were not 'winners'. In fact, they were 'losers' in the social scene. They wanted desperately to date but, but they were either hesitant to ask a woman out or were continually getting turned down. Since the two groups of men were equally good-looking, researchers set about isolating what made one group of guys 'winners' and the second group 'losers'. They put the men through a series of tests.

## Would you like to dance?

The first test took place at a social dance. The men were just told to ask someone to dance. The women (who were 'in' on the study) were to respond by saying, 'I'm not really much of a dancer.'

*Results* Upon hearing this, the men who were successful with women simply laughed and responded with variations of 'I'm not either. Shall we sit?', not as a rejection of them, but simply as a statement of fact.

The less successful guys responded with a wide variety of 'Oh', 'Er', 'Um, well' and the like, and then they gave up. In short, the 'losers' interpreted the female's answer as a rebuff.

## Hi, how are you?

In the second test, researchers taped conversations between attractive women and the 'winners', and between the same women and the 'losers'. This time the women did not know it was a study. It was the gentlemen's assignment to chat with a woman for a while and eventually ask her for a date.

*Results* The difference between the 'losers' (most of whom were turned down for the date) and the 'winners' (who often got an affirmative answer) was this. The 'winners' chatted, asked questions and, immediately upon the woman's answer, offered their own experiences or views. Many of them then asked her another question, to include her and keep the exchange going. In other words, they allowed very few pauses in the conversation. There was a continuous flow of energy. The conversations had a nice melody to them.

Now – the 'losers' had equally interesting and intelligent things to say. But, unfortunately, there were more awkward gaps in the conversation. They paused too long or hummed and hahed before answering. The musicality of the exchange was off, which made the women uncomfortable.

Researchers also timed the length of the men's answers to questions asked by the women. For instance, when a woman asked, 'Why did you move to Sacramento?', the 'winner' would give a longer answer, and then throw the ball back in her court. A 'winner's' answer might sound something like this:

'Well, there were several reasons actually. One, I'd read a lot about Sacramento. I'd heard that it had a rich cultural life, especially theatre. The weather is great, and the people very friendly. Also, I'm toying with the idea of studying Veterinary Medicine and California State University has the reputation of being very strong in that department. My sister moved here a few years ago and she's been telling me nothing but good things about the city. How about you: were you born here or did you move here?'

The 'loser's' answers might be, 'Uh, well, because my sister was here and I wanted to go to California State University.'

There was a third plus. The 'winners' had high energy in their voices. They sounded truly interested in what they were saying, and the energy was catching.

The 'losers' had many more pauses and shorter answers. When they did talk for 30 seconds or more, their voices were monotonous – not someone you'd want to listen to all evening.

To summarize: there were two main differences between the 'winners' and the 'losers'.

First, the 'winners' did not expect rejection. When they got turned down for the dance, they just let it roll off their backs and they carried on the conversation. Expecting rejection is always a self-fulfilling prophesy.

Second, the melody of the conversation was smoother. When you hear a song for the first time, you listen to the melody before you decipher the lyrics. It is just the same with conversation. The melody of the 'winners' was good because they reacted quickly to the women's questions and therefore eliminated awkward silences. When they did answer, rather than giving one-sentence answers they talked longer. Their voices were energetic. They showed that they were enjoying speaking with the woman. They also showed that they were interested in her by ending many of their responses with a question.

**CLAUSE 15 ♂ ♀**

## React Faster, Answer Vaster

I'll practise the 'winner's' conversational style: keeping the energy level up by not allowing long pauses, talking longer or giving longer answers to questions, and throwing the conversational ball back to the other person by asking a question.

## Chapter Fifteen

# Shyness stinks! (Not only that, it can trash your life)

O K, let's get real serious about shyness, because shyness is serious – real serious. Think back to when you were...

Age 4: Your mother called you 'cute' when she ran into one of her friends in the grocery market and you hid behind Mum's skirt. 'She's shy,' your mother would smilingly tell her friend.

Age 10: Your dad was proud that, instead of going out and playing with the other kids, you preferred to stay home and play with your chemistry set. 'Looks like he'll grow up to be scientist,' he bragged to his mates. (Little did he know that the other kids terrified you so much that you had fantasies of making a bomb with said chemistry set and blowing up the whole neighbourhood.)

Age 15: At the dinner table, you tearfully tell Mum and Dad how shy you feel around the other kids, and you get the shakes whenever you have to talk to someone of the opposite sex. They look at each other and smile understandingly. 'Oh, don't worry,' they say. 'It's just a passing phase. Everybody feels shy. You'll get over it.'

Your parents had no idea that they could be ruining your life by the way they treated your shyness.

First let's dispel that 'You'll get over it' inaccuracy. Between 30 and 48 per cent of adults suffer from shyness, and consider it a lifelong hindrance.[22] Of these folks, 13 per cent are in anguish due to an acute case of the ailment. Shy people, at first meeting, are considered to be less intelligent and they consider themselves to be much less attractive than they really are. Because of their shyness, they never feel complete. They never attain a satisfactory 'sense of self'.[23]

##  Wait, there are more bummers!

They have difficulty making friends, they date less and, if they do, they're for ever botching up the friendship or love affair.[24] Shy people are less likely than those who suffer with other types of anxiety problems to find a partner and get married.[25] Shy women who do marry are less apt to blend raising a family with fulfilling outside interests or career. Then they are more apt to suffer loneliness and Empty Nest syndrome when their kids grow up.

Furthermore, shy people are slower to get into a satisfactory career. And, when they do, their careers are more unstable, right into midlife. They seldom find a job that uses their talents adequately.[26]

Had enough? Well just one more round. Shy people suffer more from self-deprecatory thoughts,[27] inhibited behavior,[28] loneliness,[29] anxiety attacks[30] and depression.[31]

Can I put it any stronger? Shyness sucks. Insecurity is the pits. It can trash your life. And the time to chuck it is NOW.

I'm no stranger to shyness. Right on through college, I suffered a severe case of schmooze-aphobia. I was much too timid to go to any social events alone. Early on, I had tried one event, where I stood in the same spot all evening rivalling the wallpaper for attention – and the wallpaper won.

In those days, I didn't even have the benefit of role models. There were no movies where the socially challenged star miraculously overcame his or her geekiness and become popular. Kids are luckier now. There's a spate of teen movies with the evergreen Cinderella theme of mousie-geek turning into hottest babe in class and being courted by the in-crowd, or the dorky dude winning the cream-cracker eating contest (or some other unexpected awe-inspiring feat) and thereby getting the girl and being loved by all.

## ❁ So, if schmooze-aphobia is a disease, what's the cure?

Only in the 'misery likes company' department is it consolation to know that ten million American adults regularly suffer Social Anxiety Disorder.[32] If you're not one of those ill-fated ten million, then you've probably still suffered an occasional attack of SAD – like when you have to give a speech, or walked into a party of strangers where you're expected to make sociable chit-chat. The symptoms are familiar: racing heartbeat, blushing, trembling, wishing you could say, 'Beam me up, Scottie' and be teleported to *anywhere* except where you are.

Without getting too deeply into a depressing discussion of dopamine, noradrenaline and serotonin, suffice it to say that a chemical imbalance is often at the root of shyness or schmooze-aphobia. For severe chronic cases that inhibit one from functioning, psychiatrists can prescribe an antidepressant to increase the level of the neurotransmitter serotonin in the brain. But medication is not a satisfactory solution, and it takes a lot more than a little yellow pill to make fear disappear, a big orange one to make us more sociable, or a whopping red one to suppress the 'fear till you tear' syndrome. Personality by prescription is a long way off, if ever. There is no quick fix, but there are a excellent few home remedies for alleviating shyness. (They are the ones I used and, happily, they worked.)

The first one is force yourself to talk to strangers. Do I hear, 'But my parents told me when I was a kid to never talk to strangers?'

You're a kid no longer. Avoid accosting strangers in dark alleys at night but talk to neighbours and other harmless-looking street strollers in your neighbourhood. But smile, open your mouth, and talk to people queuing up at the bank or waiting to get into a busy restaurant. A shyness clinic in California actually suggests getting on elevators you don't need to jump on – just for the ride and to snare unsuspecting strangers to talk to.[33]

Another helpful hint is to get a dog – and the funnier-looking, the better! I once invested in a Siamese cat who walked on a lead. This putting one foot after another, after another, after another, after another, while on a leash, was such a rare feat for cat that passers-by made constant comments. I learned to laugh the 100th time someone asked if my cat's name was Lassie.

People *always* have something to say about animals. I once was introduced to a short, rotund chap who works in the world-renowned Fulton Fish Market. I had always wanted to see the market and I talked Marco into giving me a tour one morning. As he passed each booth, everyone gave him a big wave and a smile and said, 'Hi Monkey Man', as though he were a celebrity. I asked Marco what they were talking about. He said that he had a pet monkey, which he usually carried on his shoulder but, alas, the monkey had a hangover that morning. However, obviously everyone was used to talking to Marco and his imbibing monkey.

Whether we walk with monkeys on our shoulders, cats on leashes or ride on elevators that go nowhere, the trick is to start talking with people everywhere. The more you do, the easier it gets.

Learning how to be a natural-looking winner and to glide smoothly through any social occasion like a hot knife through butter is not easy. You know all the right things to do, but putting them together, well that's another matter. The best way to proceed is to practise one or two clauses at a time. Perhaps just use

Clause 1 (saying everything as though I were 'In Your Shoes') and give everyone Clause 2 an 'Extra Beat of My Blinkers' for a few days. When those become second nature, add Clauses 3 and 4 ('The Expanded Thankyou' and 'The Trifling Touch'), and so on.

Getting these skills perfected is like learning to ski – one of the most humiliating experiences of my adult life, incidentally. (If you have kids, teach them to ski NOW, so they don't ever have to endure what I did.)

There I was, a fully grown and, if I must say, pretty coordinated adult. I had bought new skis and a pretty snazzy skiing outfit and showed up for my first lesson. What could be so hard? The instructor gave me the simple directions – 'Bend your knees, keep your back straight, lean forward. Fine. Now look down the hill, lean into it, and keep your weight on the downhill ski.' YEEOOOOOOOOOOOW!

It was a long, long time before I was able – without concentrating on all those separate activities – to enjoy the pleasure of the fluid grace of my body speeding down the mountain, savour the feel of the cold wind on my cheeks, or even conjure up a smile for the other skiers.

Like learning to ski, think of the movements individually. Practise the 15 clauses we've covered so far on all those people you ambush in the elevator, or pin down on the street corner, and you'll soon be sliding through social occasions with the grace of a champion. Don't worry so much about the words at first – it's the melody that counts. Make your voice enthusiastic and keep your body language open and friendly. Make everyone you speak with feel special.

**CLAUSE 16** ♂ ♀

## Always Talk to Strangers

If shy, I will talk to at least 10 strangers a day. I'll put enthusiasm in my voice, a twinkle in my eye, and practise these first 15 clauses until I get them perfect.

# Chapter Sixteen

# Does this confidence make money?

Having the attitude that people will like you isn't only good for getting dates or socializing at parties. Confidence makes a lot of pennies – which leads to pounds, which, for one company, led to millions of pounds (or, rather, dollars).

A University of Pennsylvania Psychology professor gave a personality survey to reps at a major life-insurance agency. He asked (among many other questions) if, when they met someone, they believed the person would like them. The ones who answered, 'Sure, they're going to like me. Why not?' were called the 'optimists' for the sake of the study. The rest were neutral or pessimistic about people liking them.

The optimists among them had no more training and no more experience. But, in the months that followed, the optimists sold 37 per cent more than the not-so-confident ones!

'Whew!' thought top management at the insurance company. 'This Professor Martin Seligman's study is very impressive.' Because of it, they decided to go out on a limb: they took a chance and hired 100 wannabe reps who had actually *flunked* the standard industry exam, but were real optimists on how much they could sell.

The company was being pretty optimistic by taking such a courageous move, but it paid off. These happy flunkers sold 10 per cent more than the average guys and gals who had passed the exam.

So what happens when an optimist fails? Seligman said that when Gloomy Guses or Calamity Janes say or do the wrong thing, they tell themselves, 'No wonder I botched that; I'm terrible at social/business situations' or 'I'm terrible when it comes to meeting women/men', whereas Mr Sunshine or Ms Positive says, 'Whoops, I'll figure out precisely what I did wrong and resolve not to do that next time.'

Seligman explained that a similar dynamic shows up when things go well. The black crepe hanger says 'It was just dumb luck – couldn't happen again,' whereas Dr Pangloss pats himself on the back and says, 'I knew my hard work would pay off!'

> The secret lies in the questions we ask ourselves. Your brain is a colossal computer. You ask it a question, and it will find an answer. If it doesn't find an obvious one, it keeps searching, and searching, and searching – even if it has to go back to when you were two years old. Still no answer? Well, the brain is so determined, it will give you an answer, even if it's the *wrong* one. To have total control over your mind, learn how to ask the right questions.

Suppose you make a mistake, you hit your head and say, 'Why am I such a turkey?' Whizz, whizz, the disk starts spinning and voilà! Your brain has found an answer. You're a turkey because you've always been a turkey, and you always will be a turkey. Now you feel miserable and the next move you make is a turkey move.

But, suppose you ask yourself a different question upon making a mistake. Your brain asks, 'Hmm, what can I learn from this?' or, even better, 'What can I do differently next time?'

You'll be sure to find an answer and therefore probably not make the same mistake twice. The biggest 'winners' in life and in love are just people who have made each mistake once – and only once. They also develop long arms so they can give themselves a daily pat on the back for the things they did well.

**CLAUSE 17 ♂ ♀**

## What Can I Learn From This?

Whenever I put my foot in it, and before I take another step, I'm going to sit down and ask myself these magic questions:

- What can I learn from this?
- What else can I learn from this? and
- What else can I learn from this?...

I'll keep asking until I run out of answers. Then, I'll ask, 'What can I do differently next time?' (Finally, I'll give myself a pat on the back for the things I did well that day.)

# Chapter Seventeen

# Ah, mystery of life (and how optimism saved one!)

One of the most pleasurable aspects of networking (and you'll get a great game plan for that later) is that sometimes a relationship that started as a professional one turns into a true friendship. And where there is true friendship there is trust. This trust allows you to cross the line and say things off the record to your friend that you would never say publicly.

I'm proud to say that one of those friends is a highly esteemed cardiologist in New York who is on the staff of two important hospitals, and a professor at one of the best medical schools. She lectures frequently and has been the Cardiology Consultant for several major publications. In other words, Carolyn (her name is changed) has credibility – big time. But Carolyn told me something across a dinner table that she could never say to a reporter, or even a fellow cardiologist. Yet she is as convinced of it as she is of her own heartbeat.

She has no way of proving it, but, she said, 'If a patient truly believes he will survive – I mean, truly, *truly* believes it, and isn't just trying to convince himself, he will get better – the chances are astronomically increased that he will.' Here her voice faded off and her eyes began to water as she leaned forward to tell me about one of her patients, who had had three heart attacks and was being treated for serious coronary artery disease. When George was rolled down the corridor of the hospital for open-heart surgery, his family thought they'd never see him again. '*I* didn't think they would, either,' Carolyn said.

'I visited him, clasped his hand, and he gave me a weak smile. He could hardly speak as he said, "I'm not going to make it, am I, Doc?" This man had complete trust in me. I had been treating him for six years and he knew I always gave it to him straight. I'd yelled at him when he kept smoking and told him every cigarette was another nail in his coffin. Once I grabbed a cigarette out of his mouth in my waiting room, right in front of other patients, and told him that if he was hell-bent on continuing to smoke I was going to drop him as a patient. Furthermore, if he wanted to kill himself, I told him, do it somewhere else!

'Anyway,' Carolyn said, 'he'd believe *anything* I said.' She said she just stood over his bed looking into his eyes, not knowing what to say. She had never lied to him before. But this time it was different. She knew that if she told him what she really thought, his family would never see him again.

He asked her again, 'This is it, huh?' Carolyn is a deeply religious woman and would never tamper with the truth. Unless...

'Oh, come off it,' she lied. 'Unless you've got some cigarettes hidden under that blanket, of course you're going to make it. You're going to be fine.'

He believed it, and he was.

George died several years later, Carolyn told me. But she knows that big whopper she told him gave him the strength to pull through, and it gave him and his family a few more years to share. Carolyn's religion doesn't permit her to say 'God'. But she laughed as she looked heavenward and said she knows she'll be forgiven for the big whopper she told George.

There are even times when being an optimist can be a matter of life and death.

# Chapter Eighteen

# Pass the Pollyanna please

If you already have kids, or someday plan to, one of the greatest gifts you can give your children is the gift of optimism – the faith that they can do whatever they want.

Carolyn was brought up in the days when the most accepted women's aspiration was to go to college and bag a good husband. But her family didn't hesitate for a moment when she told them she wanted to grow up and be a heart doctor instead. My Texan friend Dale could trace his optimism back to his father's 'I think I can, I think I can' choo-choo train optimism (*see page 24*).

I have another super-achiever friend. When Benissa – with her almond eyes, smooth milk-chocolate complexion and glistening black hair – comes to work in the morning, she could easily be mistaken for one of the top models in the agency her firm represents. Instead, she followed a career in law and is senior partner at a prestigious Los Angeles firm specializing in the entertainment industry. No small accomplishment, since entertainment law is extremely competitive and you've got to be a whole lot better than really good to make senior partner. Add this to the fact that she's a woman (an African-American woman at that), and you've got one big winner here.

I was expressing my admiration to Benissa one day and she said, 'Thanks, but I always expected to wind up doing this kind of work.'

'But,' I started to falter here, 'being born in the 1950s, before civil rights and all that, uh, you never thought you'd get this far, did you?'

'Sure,' Benissa replied. 'Dad always made me feel I could be anything I wanted to be. Remember when Neil Armstrong first stepped on the moon, 1969? I was ten years old then.'

'Yes,' I replied.

'Well, we lived in a really poor neighbourhood in Brooklyn then. But Dad took the whole family on the subway into New York City to watch it on a big screen in Central Park. I was shorter than everyone else, so Dad had me hoisted up sitting on his shoulders. I'll never forget that feeling. I was taller than anyone in the whole park. And when Buzz Aldrin put his foot on the moon, that was *me* taking one great step for mankind.

'That night, when we got home, I told Dad I wanted to be the first woman on the moon. Instead of saying, "Yeah, you and two million other kids – off to bed now," he smiled at me and we sat down to construct a serious game plan. "First, you'll have to study astronomy and physics. Then you'll need some engineering background..."

'I went to bed happy that night, knowing that if I wanted to be a female astronaut I could be. And that was always Dad's attitude,' she told me. 'Anything I wanted to be, I could be.

'As I got older, I decided against my extraterrestrial aspirations and decided I wanted to be a lawyer in the entertainment industry right here on terra firma. And, well, that's what I am – still dealing with stars, I guess. But a much less predictable kind,' she added.

Benissa's father knew how important it was that his daughter believe she could do whatever she wanted. He had given her one of the most valuable gifts in the world – the gift of 'You Can Do'.

**CLAUSE 18** ♂ ♀

## Give the Gift of 'You Can Do'

I will never tell any young people in my life – my brothers, sisters, cousins, my own children – that something is too difficult or they cannot accomplish a certain goal. In fact, I'll help them take the first step, even if it's in what I consider to be an impossible direction.

# Part II

# Friends and lovers

*How to find them, how to keep them*

## Chapter Nineteen

# Why have friends?

*Or Pollyanna plummets into*
*Pandora's Box*

When I was a grinning little kid with too many teeth for my face, people passing me on the street would call out, 'Well, hello there little Pollyanna.' (She was the mythological muse who was always happy, always smiling.) Well, I got bigger – and finally, my face began to fit my teeth. But people kept calling me 'Pollyanna' ... because I kept smiling.

And *meaning* it! Each day, I had ever more things to be happy about. By my own reckoning, I had a charmed life. Just ask me why and I would have started blathering on about how I somehow managed to flirt with all the 'glamour' jobs. I became a model (after a nose job, that is), a cruise director (cracking jokes for passengers who would laugh at *anything* because that's what you do on a cruise), a Broadway actress (well, I had *one* Broadway role) and a Pan Am flight attendant ...

Was it really glamorous? Once, while kneeling in the latrine, straining stinking water for a passenger's lost contact lens, someone asked me what I was searching for. I replied, 'I'm looking for the glamour in my job.'

Whether the jobs were glamorous or not is definitely debatable. But I certainly made them sound that way at parties!

Then, by the age Barbie dolls are expected to grow up, I'd somehow managed to convert my fun jobs into more serious endeavours. I tacked a few more university credits on to my degree, became a communications skills consultant, a corporate trainer, professional speaker and author. Soon my business life was brimming with blessings. Four books, a couple of cassette series, representation by the best speakers' bureaus ... I had a lot to smile about. I was doing the work I loved, and loving the work I was doing. I was *still* Pollyanna.

I won't say my friends called me that any more, because now I didn't have a whole lot of friends. But, then, I didn't really take the time to invest in finding and nurturing friendships. After all, that would have gobbled up hours that I'd rather have spent writing or planning a speech. I was a certified workaholic. Besides, I had one really good friend in my PMR (Platonic Male Roommate) Phil. And I had a boyfriend, too. His name was Giorgio. (You can tell by his name that he's from out of town.)

Not only was my life happy, it was also secure. All my ducks were in order, as they say. I had insurance on my house, my car and my body, which covered everything that could possibly go awry (save a broken fingernail).

Yet, the best insurance of all, I arrogantly told myself, was my own mind. I had confidence, thanks to my training in communications skills that, no matter what happened, I could talk my way into – or out of – anything I wanted.

## ✸ Suddenly last summer

Then, suddenly, one summer, as I was walking to a meeting – one that I had been looking forward to for some time – I felt a curious leaden weight on my heart, an alien joylessness. Why? I had just been chosen by the National Association of Female Executives as their Speaker of the Year to do a cross-country tour of breakfast talks. This was the luncheon to meet the Executive Director and Tour Coordinator.

*Why* wasn't I my usual exhilarated self about it? *Why*, when I arrived at the restaurant, did I discover I'd misread the clock and was an hour late? *Why*, as I stared at the menu, was the thought of food repulsive? *Why*, as they chatted animatedly about the exciting itinerary, was I unable to concentrate? *Why*, when it came time to respond, was I uncharacteristically and catatonically mute?

A puddle of perspiration trickled from my palms on to the napkin in my lap. Babbling fraudulent excuses, I bolted to the bathroom, leaving the two women looking at each other and wondering, I am sure, why the committee had ever chosen me. I grasped the sides of the sink to steady myself. Slowly I looked up into the mirror. Staring back at me, I saw the ghoulish face of a frightened stranger with smeared make-up. *What was happening to me?*

##  Pollyanna plummets into Pandora's box

The next few weeks were a blur. I felt a poisonous black fog pressing down on me and squeezing out all my energy. With each breath I sucked in fear and exhaled any residual happiness. I lost nearly two stone (11.5 kg) and all my joy of life. By late August, I was a sorrowful eight-stone (50 kg) scarecrow dangling from a five-foot nine (175 cm) frame.

By September I realized I was not just having a series of bad-hair days. I found myself, the author of *How to Make Anyone Like You!* afraid to talk to people; the author of *How to Make Anyone Fall in Love with You* unable to put lipstick on my lips or powder on my nose. I let my machine answer the phone and only returned calls when absolutely necessary. The producers of my audio cassette series, ironically called *Conversation Confidence*, had just rolled out a national advertising campaign. And I, like a child in the protection of my mother's skirts, wanted to hide behind the curtains, frightened of talking to the neighbours. My book, *Talking the Winner's Way,* had just come out and I had to cancel the author's tour because my interviews would have sounded like 'Talking the Loser's Way'.

The smallest task became an insurmountable challenge. I would stand frozen in the supermarket aisle facing a shelf of soups. Tomato? Vegetable? Chicken noodle? Beef barley? Making a choice was an impossible task. Sometimes, I would see a poverty-stricken old woman squeezing each orange before deciding which to spend her few food coupons on. I would have traded my life for hers in a heartbeat. She was able to make a choice.

My friend Phil was confused and worried. To keep him from questioning further, I told him I was suffering a 'hormonal imbalance – you know, one of those woman things'. (Men never question 'female conditions'.) But I knew my mind, day by day, was melting away.

Enter Giorgio, a ship's captain by profession and, as I grate-fully discovered, a care-giver by nature. Giorgio took me to my little weekend cabin and stayed with me around the clock. He cooked for me, cared for me and tried the impossible – to comfort me during my ever-worsening nightmare.

Sometimes I truly believed it really was a nightmare, and if I screamed loudly enough I would wake up. But, woefully, there was no awakening from the mysterious malady.

September was just the beginning of the indescribable and inexplicable horror that lasted three months, fifteen days and seven hours. By October, checking email or balancing my cheque book and paying bills became mind-boggling tasks. Numbers danced on the page to mock me. When I wrote cheques; I added wrong, transposed numbers, and made puz-zling mistakes. (The bin men must have smiled as they returned my cheque written for $4465.00 [£3000] instead of $44.65 [£30]!) The terrifying words 'Tear on perforation and fold' or 'Write account number on your cheque' were printed on bills just to taunt me. Did they have no mercy for the helpless?

**The bottom of the pit**

In November the anguish became too intense to bear. I frightened Giorgio when I told him I wanted relief at any cost. When he walked me to a nearby park, he held my hand securely because I told him every passing car looked to me like a machine which, if I timed my lunge just right, could end my suffering. In the park, I looked up at the cliffs and mentally measured each, calculating if it were high enough (and the landing hard enough) to assure instant relief.

December came and temperatures plummeted below zero. Now I was reduced to writhing and curling like a caterpillar with a pin through its belly on the couch. Because I had been unable to open the bills, the gas company disconnected me. And, for once, Giorgio couldn't help. Because English was not his mother tongue, it was difficult for him to call and explain that it was just an oversight, and that the cheque was forthcoming.

Years before, when I was a flight attendant, I once asked the instructor of a crash training course, 'How long should we stay with a downed plane to help passengers?' The reply was, 'Until the fire gets too hot, or the water gets too high.'

Well, now the fire *was* too hot, and the water *was* too high, to keep fooling Phil. In as unfaltering a voice as I could muster, I called him and told him the truth – that I was suffering what the doctors called a 'severe depression'. Could Phil assist me by opening my mail, paying the bills on my account, and just sending the cheques to my country home so Giorgio could steady my hand as I signed?

As though I'd told Phil I had a toothache and asked for an aspirin, my friend readily replied, 'Of course, Leil.' Then, he tried to comfort me by putting me in elite company. He said, 'Many great writers have experienced a severe depression – Albert Camus, William Styron, Virginia Woolf, Jack London, Ernest Hemingway...'

I appreciated his effort, but had no ego left to massage. And, besides, he neglected to mention that the last three of these fallen artists put an end to their anguish by their own hand.

In mid-December, I was able to calm the howling tempest in my brain just long enough to have the first thought in months that was not completely tormented and self-obsessed. For a glimmering moment, I was filled with gratitude to Phil and to Giorgio, and overcome by the incredible *power of friendship*.

In the following weeks, I started having ephemeral flashes of rational thought. I devoted those moments to thinking of my two dear friends, and how each was giving 100 per cent of his capability. Each had a very different contribution. Giorgio, a loving and patient care-giver, couldn't tell a piece of junk mail from a tax return, or speak English to the gas board. And Phil, a brilliant writer and a virtuoso of organization, couldn't take care of a cat, unless he'd programmed it into his computer.

My mother used to say, 'God takes care of fools and children.' Well, I was no child during this insidious meltdown of my mind, so I suppose I am a fool. Nevertheless, I'm a fortunate fool for having at least two good friends.

I now truly believe that 'Friends are God's way of taking care of us.' Without one, the life I'd carefully constructed would have shattered. Without the other, I might not even *have* a life.

## ☀ So what's this got to do with making people like you?

Everything. Until this bout of depression, my doctrine was 'We are our own best friend.' Like so many motivational speakers, I preached this from my podium. I proclaimed that, no matter what adversity should come our way, we would always have our own mind and spirit to sustain us.

Now, I know that there is no dungeon darker than the mind, and even your own spirit can betray you. You can become your own worst enemy. When that happens, you need friends and loved ones to intervene and shield you from the vicious and well-armed adversary who knows every back alley of your brain.

I had purchased many kinds of insurance policies. However, I never paid premiums on the most important one. This is one you can't buy, but you still must pay for. The currency is not money. You pay in your time, your personality and your love. It's the insurance of having loyal friends and true love. It's the only one that will save you when you really need it.

## ✿ Pandora's box suddenly snaps shut

30 December: Curled on the couch in foetal position which had now become my permanent pose, I struggled to lift my leaden head to look at the clock. As I watched, as I had so often before, the second hand creep with excruciating sluggishness from 4.04 p.m. to 4.05 p.m., something was happening. I felt a refreshing breeze on my back for the first time in months. Was the poisonous fog starting to swirl upward and outward, ready to suck the torment out of my brain. *Could it be?* Was I really seeing a brilliant streak of the day's waning sunlight through the window for the first time since September?

At 4.05 p.m., the writhing caterpillar uncurled and shed its skin. I felt like a butterfly escaping its cocoon. I stood up tall, threw my shoulders back and my arms floated up in the air. Dare I think I was free?

Dazed, I turned momentarily to look behind me down at the couch, which had been my hideous home for so long. I saw a depression in the shape of my knees and head – like the contour of Mother's corpse in the mattress at the Bates Motel in *Psycho*.

That's what my experience is to me now – a scary movie that's over. Why my brain decided to take a three-and-half-month holiday, I'll never know. One doctor suggested that a workaholic's life that is not balanced with friends and loved ones leaves an emptiness that leads to a crash. Another explained a life of being manic can induce a depressive period.

He said it's what they used to call a 'nervous breakdown', and now they have a fancier word, 'unipolar', which simply means a once-in-a-lifetime humongous depression. They both humbly agreed that modern medicine does not have the answers. All I know is that my brain, if it was going to go on holiday, could have chosen a better place to spend it than in hell!

May I pause for a 'public-service announcement', which, I pray, never becomes relevant for you? But if it does (it has been estimated that one in ten people will suffer from depression) and your mind should ever plunge into that abyss, please don't let pride shield you, as it did me, from immediately seeking the help you need. Tell your doctor when you detect the first dark shadow. And keep the faith. You will come back. And, I promise, when you do, you will see life with more serenity and joy than you ever imagined possible. And your spirit, having been contorted and twisted into unfathomable shapes, will possess even more capacity and desire to love.

31 December: I spent a glorious New Year's Eve with Giorgio, Phil and his girlfriend, Colleen. 'Pollyanna' had the happiest New Year ever. And her New Year's resolution? Make more friends, and help others to do the same.

Hence this book – *How to Make Anyone Like You! Proven Ways to be a People Magnet*.

# Chapter Twenty

# Friendship's first commandment

 **Thou must have something to give in order to receive**

You've heard the phrases, 'Nothing is free in life' or 'There is no free lunch.' Is it sad, but true? I don't think so. It's just true, but true. No, I'm not a cynic. And yes, I believe deeply in the power of love. Let me explain.

My friends Phil and Giorgio gave everything of themselves, 100 per cent selflessly during the days when I thought there would be no tomorrows. Did they care for me night and day for what they thought they were going to receive in return? No, they did it because they were my true friends.

But let's carry this back to its logical inception.

Question: Why were they my true friends?

Simple answer: Because they liked me.

Now let's go another step back.

Question: Why did they like me?

Here the answer is not so simple. Perhaps they liked my way of thinking, or the knowledge I had shared with them, or the laughs we'd had together, or the things I had done for them, also selflessly. Whatever it is, true friends are people who have a history together. They are people who have received something from each other. That something can be anything.

*Perhaps the something is new knowledge.* Anaïs Nin wrote: 'Each friend represents a world in us, a world possibly not born until they arrive, and it is only by this meeting that a new world is born.'

*Or maybe it is self-knowledge.* Thus the expression, 'The best mirror is an old friend' (George Herbert).

*Or helping you grow.* Henry Ford maintained: 'My best friend is the one who brings out the best in me.'

*Or just making your days more pleasant.* John Lubbock said: 'A friend is like a sunny day spreading brightness all around.' (And John should know all about things like sun'n'stuff because he was an English astronomer.)

*Or helping you make sense of your own thoughts.* A friend is one to whom one may pour out all the contents of one's heart, chaff and grain together, knowing that the gentlest of hands will take and sift it, keep what is worth keeping and with a breath of kindness blow the rest away, says an Arabian proverb.

*Or someone who won't judge you.* Mother Teresa believed: 'If you judge people, you have no time to love them.'

*Or maybe the gift they give you is comfortable silence,* the contentment to be with them when you didn't feel like talking. 'When the silences are no longer awkward, you know you are around friends' is a proverb.

*Maybe the gift your friend gives involves some self-sacrifice.* 'A friend is someone who is there for you when he'd rather be anywhere else.'

*Or keeps you on track with your dreams when you falter,* or believes in you when you've ceased to believe in yourself. 'A friend is someone who knows the song in your heart, and can sing it back to you when you have forgotten the words.'

Whatever the reason for your being friends, you have given them something of value, and they have done the same. To have a good friend, you have to be one. Khalil Gibran

(Lebanese/US novelist and artist) wrote: 'Friendship is always a sweet responsibility, never an opportunity.'

##  You don't make friends, you *earn* them

If we were chiselling friendship truths on a tablet, the first commandment would be: 'Thou must have something to give in order to receive.'

Does that sound dangerously like barter, 'tit for tat'? It is, in a way. If I had not given selflessly of myself to my two friends, they might not have done the same for me. Had I been humourless, stupid and selfish – in other words, if I had no 'gifts' to give them, they would not have been inspired to give theirs to me. Had they been the same, I would not have been inspired to give mine to them.

In fact, many a true and lifelong friendship or love relationship develops just because of someone's specific gift. I met Phil at a writing seminar 'back in DOS days', as he says. At the time I was trying to make sense of (then) new words like COBOL, PASCAL, FORTRAN and other 'insider' words that many computer techies tried to trick us with. They said we had to understand all that just to boot up our machines. Anyway, Phil and I had a brief conversation – or I should say he listened patiently and knowledgeably to my whining monologue of computer woes.

'Hmm, I might be able to help you with that,' Philo announced.

HALLELUJAH! It was like the skies opening and the computer God saying, 'You have been saved.' Phil came over the next afternoon and got my computer up and humming happily away in just a few hours. Naturally, out of gratitude, I asked him to stay for dinner and a friendship developed.

What did I have in return? No talent as valuable as his to share, but I did have some empty space in my loft, which I was thrilled to rent out to a fellow writer and computer genius. Thus he became my PMR.

##  And yes, you earn lovers too

Would a great hue and cry go up if I were to say that, although a true love relationship is selfless, caring and altruistic, you have to bring something to the table before you can earn that love. You can earn it with your God-given gifts, or ones that you develop.

A vast body of research called the Equity Theory (which is covered much more thoroughly in my book, *How to Make Anyone Fall in Love With You*), has shown beyond reasonable doubt that people make decisions about a potential love partner with all the reckoning that they would in buying a house or a horse.[34]

What is the legal tender that counts in love? Equity Theorists reduced it to six elements: looks, money, prestige, intelligence, personality and character.[35] They call it the currency with which one buys a good partner.

In my relationship seminars, I often ask participants to write down secretly on a card how critical each of the qualities is in a potential love partner. They sign the cards with only 'M' for male, and 'F' for female. Before you read the following consensus of their comments, you might want to consider how important the big six qualities are for you in a potential love. Then compare your answers.

## How important is physical appearance?

### Men

'Very important.'
'Unless she had good qualities too, I'd get immune to her good looks.'
'I always feel proud taking out a good-looking woman.'
'Damn important. I'd be a liar to say otherwise.'

**Women**

'Not that important.'

'Not important that he be "typically" good-looking, but I like character in a man's face.'

'Not that important but I do like him to have a good body.'

## How important are possessions or money?

**Men**

'Not at all.'

'Hey, it's cool if she has money, but it doesn't make any big difference.'

'Well, I'd be a little put off if she started asking me for money early in the relationship, but how much money she earns isn't crucial.'

**Women**

'I certainly wouldn't marry a man just for his money, but I like him to earn more than me.'

'It's becoming less important now that I'm earning more, but I guess I'm still a little old-fashioned.'

'Sure it's important.'

## How important are status and prestige?

**Men**

'It's not important.'

'Never really thought about it that much.'

'I wouldn't want her to have a bad reputation, but she doesn't have to have a lot of status.'

## Women

'Depends on how you define status. I like people to respect him.'
'If he's a good man, he'll automatically have that, no?'
'I am attracted to power.'

# How important are information and knowledge?

### Men

'I like a woman to be bright.'
'I hate stupid women.'
'I want my woman to be smart, but maybe not quite as smart as me.'
'I like her to be intelligent but not go around showing it off.'

### Women

'Very important.'
'Intelligence is a big factor for me.'
'Education is not all that important but I like him to have "street smarts".'
'I want to know he's smart enough to take care of his family.'
'I have my Master's degree so I suppose I'd like him to at least have that.'

# How important are social graces and personality?

### Men

'Yes, I like a girl with a great personality. That and looks are the two most important things to me.'
'I want her to be fun to be with.'
'Sure, I don't want her to embarrass us at social functions.'

'I'm a businessman and I'd like my wife to be able to entertain smoothly.'

**Women**

'He doesn't need to be a laugh a minute, but I like a guy with a good personality.'
'Social graces are important to me. I'm sick of guys who don't know what fork to use.'
'Personality is extremely important.'

## How important are character or inner nature?

**Men**

'Very important.'

**Women**

'Very, very important.'
'It's probably the most important thing.'

So there it is, straight from the sources' mouth. Breaking the qualities and 'assets' down into these six categories, of course, has its fallacies. People define words differently. Additionally, this doesn't take into consideration other factors like religion, age, how many children they want, how their family feels about the partner and what their 'definition' of a relationship is.

That aside (and that's a pretty *hefty* 'aside'), what I did find fascinating, was the accuracy with which Equity Research was able to predict whether two people would be happy together, based on what they bring to the table. If you want to determine what chances Equity Theorists would predict you and a chosen partner have for riding happily off into the sunset together, then you can do the quiz in Appendix A. (But keep your tongue firmly implanted in your cheek throughout.)

I present this only as an example of how some researchers are *so* convinced of the 'tit for tat' in relationships that they have broken it down into calculable numbers. This, of course, supports my thesis that the way to draw more friends and lovers to you is to have more gifts to share. Or, as Equity Theorists would say, more 'currency'.

Some couples who would otherwise part, stay together for a variety of reasons – for religious motivations or 'for the sake of the children'. But friends don't have those ties. They are free to move on. So, if you want dynamic friends to be drawn to you, you *must* keep growing. When people become too predictable, boredom sets in and the relationship suffers. It's not crass. It's simply true in any friendship or love relationship: you trade benefits, be they as simple as making each other's days more pleasant or opening new worlds for him or her.

**CLAUSE 19 ♂ ♀**

## Growing My Gifts

To draw more friends and lovers to me (and/or be a better friend and lover to those I have), I will consciously grow my gifts in all areas – appearance, knowledge, finances, personality, prestige and, most importantly, character.

## Chapter Twenty One

# Ways to say 'I love you' to a friend

Many women today value their friendships with other women as much as they do their relationships with men – maybe more. Just ask Emma, Mel B, Victoria and Mel C. (Who? do I hear fellow baby-boomers ask?) They were the Spice Girls then, who reflected the modern feeling about women's friendships in their song 'Wannabe'. You've heard it even if you couldn't understand the lyrics: 'If you wanna be my lover, you gotta get with my friends. Make it last for ever, friendship never ends.'

Well, sister baby-boomers, we should take pride that we were the first to acknowledge that a woman could have deep feelings for a woman, or that a man could have deep feelings for a man, with nothing sexual between them. This was an awareness we passed on to our own Emmas (or Mel Bs, Victorias or Mel Cs). In their parents' day, it wasn't that way. A woman wouldn't think twice about changing plans made with a female friend, even at the last minute, if a date with a male came along.

##  Plan private pleasures for precious people

One Saturday evening, when I was 17, my best friend Stella and I had planned to go to the movies. She'd even borrowed her brother's car so we could make an evening of it and drive to Chinatown for dinner afterwards.

On that Saturday afternoon, the phone rang. I assumed it was Stella, calling to set the time she would come by in her brother Spencer's snazzy little Nash Rambler. (Incidentally, Spencer was a pretty snazzy rambler himself. I'd had a secret crush on him ever since I saw him at Stella's house two years earlier. But it was an unrequited infatuation, for Spencer already had a steady main squeeze.)

When I picked up the phone, instead of Stella I heard the nasal voice of Freddie, a freckle-faced fellow with skunk breath I had met at a party a few weeks earlier. Unfortunately, Freddie was, as we used to say in those days, strictly from Dullsville, USA.

My mother happened to be walking by my room as I said to him, 'Oh, gosh, Freddie, you know how I would love that. Going to the party with you would be super.' (In those days, we were carefully taught to lie to save men's egos.) My mother was beaming at me from the doorway. 'But', I continued, 'I have plans to go to the movies with my girlfriend tonight.' I could imagine his flabbergasted freckles paling in incredulity that I was turning him, a *bona fide* male, down for an engagement with a *girlfriend*. After I hung up, I looked at my mother and sensed something was terribly wrong. She reminded me of a duck whose feathers are unruffled on the surface, but underneath the feet are paddling frantically.

Mama cleared her throat and asked, 'Leilie, dear, did I just hear you turn down a date to go to a party with a *boy* just because you told Stella you'd go to the movies with her tonight?'

'Yes, Mama, that was Freddie, and going out with him would be duller than watching paint dry. I like Stella a hundred times more than I like him.'

'Nevertheless, dear,' she chided, trying to suppress her exasperation, 'you can see Stella any time and Freddie is a *date*.'

'Mama, his breath is so bad I could smell it over the phone.'

My mother gave me a strange look, probably questioning for a fleeting moment her daughter's sexual orientation. Her retort was, 'Well, you'll never meet any boys in a movie. You know I've always said, "Go out with the creep, look over the crop."' With that piece of misguided wisdom, Mama strode out of my room (not her finest moment).

The next call was from Stella. I told her what happened and we both got a big laugh out of it. I could tell that underneath her laughter was a tone of gratitude. Our feelings for each other were seldom verbalized, but always understood. She planned to pick me up at seven.

I mentioned Stella's brother – tall, handsome, considerate, strong, gentle, intelligent, witty AND, I discovered recently, broken up with his previous girlfriend. Just guess who rang my doorbell at seven? You're right. (God is good.)

Spencer took my arm to help me down my front steps to his car, where Stella was waiting like the Cheshire cat.

I had never told Stella about my crush on her brother. But, looking back at it, of course she knew. Part of being a good friend is knowing things about your friends that they don't want to say, and respecting that boundary.

The three of us had a great time. But the highlight for me was after the movie, when we went to a Chinese restaurant to 'eat Chinx' as we used to say. Spencer looked at me and said, 'It really was great of you to turn down the date with that Adonis Stella told me about.'

'That *what*?' I asked choking on my chow mein.

'Yes, Stella told me about the football player who wanted to take you to the big Phi Sigma Kappa bash tonight.'

'But ...' I started to protest.

'Oooooh,' squealed Stella, 'just try one of these dumplings,' she said as she squished a whole fried pork dumpling dipped into hot pepper sauce into my mouth, temporarily incapacitating my tongue. 'They are dee-lish!'

'No, really, I admire your loyalty to my sister,' he said as I tried to extinguish the fire in my mouth.

I looked at him and tried to smile with my mouth full of ice cubes. When he smiled back, suddenly in my heart I heard a twelve-piece orchestra striking up the chords to 'Falling in Love Again'.

If Stella had told me she was going to bring her brother, I would have been thrilled. But not anywhere near the degree I was when it turned out to be a carefully conceived surprise just for me.

Had I listened more carefully to the orchestra playing in my heart, I would have heard the strains of another song – one dedicated to Stella called 'That's What Friends Are For'.

**CLAUSE 20** ♂ ♀

## Plan a Sweet Surprise

Sometimes it is more difficult to say 'You are very special' to a good friend than it is to say 'I love you' to a lover. I will plan a surprise for a good friend to let him or her know of my feelings.

 **'I love ya, man', and all that jazz**

Fellas, I'm just talking to you now. Suppose you have a good buddy, a real pal. You'd stick together thick or thin, lose or win. You'd rush to the ramparts with a broken beer bottle to help him. You love the guy. And, in all these years, you've never said a word about how you feel. Do you have a friend like that? And did you ever tell that amigo, that compadre of yours how much you value your friendship?

If you answered 'Yes', congratulations. You are a rare and fine specimen of manhood indeed. If you answered 'No', no problem. You've answered the way 95 per cent of guys do. In addition, you probably thought, 'Don't need to say it. He knows.'

And, yes, you're right, he probably does. And you can leave it at that. The spill-your-guts-at-the-drop-of-a-beer-bottle so-called men's movement of the 1980s has pretty much blown over and, confused as they are, most men are still pretty happy just being a guy and acting in all the guy ways.

So why should I bring up the subject of letting a friend know how much he means to you? Well, because you bought this book called *How to Make Anyone Like You! Proven Ways to Be a People Magnet*. And I assume you knew it meant not just love between a man and a woman. So, even though your buddy knows how you feel about him, maybe you should give him a shot before he's floating around, all flipped over and glassy-eyed, in the goldfish bowl.

This following Clause enriches your friendship with your buddy. He probably won't tell you, but when you let him know how much he means to you he will appreciate it big time. However, you want to do it at the proper time and in the proper way. You know the old saying, 'There is a time and a place for everything'? Well, they've even done studies on where and when one real man can tell another real man of his affection and still retain full butch status.

How about you? Put a tick mark by the place or places where you think the old boy would enjoy hearing how important he is to you.

In a public place                     _____

In private, where no one can hear   _____

At a sporting event                  _____

While watching TV together        _____

At a wedding or funeral           _____

Just walking along the street      _____

In the showers at the gym         _____

Pass the envelope please. Well, 'In the showers at the gym' is definitely out if you want to keep your reputation as a skirt-chaser. The place men felt most comfortable giving or receiving a hug or hearing, 'I love ya, man' was in public.[36] Researchers determine the reason for this is that public displays of affection between romantic partners is less appropriate in public than in private. So, counterintuitively, two males hugging in public seems the antithesis of romance.

The best place, as decreed by a study called 'The Male-to-Male Embrace: Breaking the Touch Taboo in a Men's Therapy Group', is a wedding, funeral, graduation or some other emotionally charged event.[37] That's when sometimes the sentiment wells up in real macho types who would never dream of saying anything warm and fussy to their good ol' buddyroo. It just sort of spills over at one of those events, where it's appropriate to cry. (Well, a suppressed tear or two as the women are wringing out their handkerchiefs.)

> Gentlemen, if you wish to inform another gentleman of your esteem and affection, and not lose one ounce of testosterone, here's how: Choose a public place, preferably an emotionally charged one such as a wedding, funeral or graduation. You're safe letting it all hang out – for about three seconds. Then pull back. You've strengthened the bond and still remain stud-duck in the pond.

**CLAUSE 21** ♂ ♀

## I Love Ya, Man

I'll choose the time and the place and how to say it, but sometime in the next two weeks I'm going to let that ol' buddy of mine know how much he means to me.

For men only

## ✿ Actions speak louder than words (just ask any guy)

The next time you are at a sporting event, let your eyes scan the crowd. Lots of men. Everywhere men. Busloads of men.

Two males at a baseball game – without taking eyes off the field for hours, or saying a word other than 'Kill the ump' or 'Gimme me a coke and a hot dog. What? Six fifty?' – are having as deep a communication as any two women sharing their most intimate secrets.

They're on the same wavelength, just like two guys riding the crest of the same breaker on their surf boards, or two men's hands on the same bent rod trying to tug a massive fish out of the ocean. That's intimate communication, guy style. I once saw a film of six skydivers, holding hands, something that men would never do except 3000 metres up in a free fall. It was like their souls were as one and they were all entering the pearly gates together. (Could have happened!) Yeah, guys bond through stuff like that.

Men, here's a clause that will help you strengthen your friendships with other men, macho style. Women, don't feel left out. You too you can use it to augment your cross-sex friendship, or even a potential love relationship. Whatever your motives, it helps the user to bond, big time, with the boys.

First write the name of a dude you'd like to schmooze. Then, under his name list some activities you know he enjoys. Fly fishing? Karate? Racketball? Backpacking? Scuba diving? Whitewater rafting?

Name of a male friend _____

Some of his favourite activities _____

_____

_____

_____

_____

_____

Now go over the list of activities and see which you have done, or could bluff your way through well enough to keep your friend's co-enthusiasts moaning, 'Who brought that nerd into our big-deal interest?'

Say your mate Bob is a white-water rafting fanatic, and you reckon you could hang on to the white-water raft as well as any thrill seeker. Get some tickets, say your prayers, and then suggest the two of you do it. Say your friend Sam loves live shows, Bill likes basketball and Dick likes folk dancing. Then there's Arthur. He's the opera buff. Are you lukewarm on live shows, football, folk dancing or opera? Doesn't matter. You're not lukewarm on friendship or love with Sam, Bill, Dick or Arthur. Call the lucky chap and tell him that you've got some tickets for ... whatever. Ask him to join you. Whatever your mate's or potential mate's offbeat bag is, do it! Who knows – you may even enjoy 'it'. (What, me bungee-jump?)

Now, where this gets hot – no, explosive – is when a woman puts together this little package for a male friend. If there's any romance potential there, this bonding match can light a stick of dynamite between them. (Women, when was the last time you called a man up and told him you had tickets to a football match?)

Once this technique worked, quite by accident. I have a friend Tara who is an editor in a publishing house. She is now married to the president of the company, a distinguished gentleman named Marvin. When she met him, he was as eligible and sought after as Bill Gates was at Microsoft in his single days. The female editors didn't go so far as to wear 'Marry Me Marv' T-shirts like the 'Marry Me Bill' T-shirts wannabe Mrs Gateses did at Microsoft. However, other female employees shamelessly let the first button on their blouses come unbuttoned, or a shoe dangle while speaking with him. Nevertheless, publishing mogul Marvin was strictly business all the way.

One Thanksgiving, Tara's brother (who was a zealous hockey fan) came to visit her. He coaxed, cajoled and finally convinced poor Tara – who didn't give a flying puck about hockey – to accompany him to a big National Hockey League game.

Unfortunately, for Tara's brother, a business emergency cut his stay short. So there sat Tara with two expensive tickets for the best seats in the house. Tara had only one other slight connection with hockey in her life. She remotely remembered having seen photos of hockey players in Marvin's office. She wouldn't have noticed, but she remembers wondering what they were doing with those funny-looking sticks.

Quite correctly, she sent an email to Marvin telling how her brother couldn't use the tickets and if Marvin or any of his friends would like to go, please accept the tickets.

In less than sixty seconds after she clicked the 'send' button on her computer, Marvin was on the threshold of her cubicle to say thank you. Now, gentlemen, a 175-centimetre gorgeous red-head gives you two tickets to a sold-out game you've been dying to go to ... Who are you going to take?

'Tara, do you enjoy hockey?' he asked.

Now, women, suppose you despise the sport, but fancy the man. Don't you think you could justify just one eensy teensy little lie?

Tara said, 'I do!'

Men bond not only to other men by doing things they enjoy together, but they bond to women by doing things *he* enjoys together. Less than a year later Tara was answering 'I do' to another of Marvin's questions.

It came out (after their marriage) that Marvin had always admired Tara's excellent work, not to mention (because he was too reserved) her beauty. Tara had always respected Marvin's wisdom and administrative abilities, not to mention (because she was too reserved) the fact that he was a hunk. Sometimes all it takes is a little puck to bring people together.

CLAUSE 22 ♂ ♀

## Do My Mate's Bag

If there is any male with whom I want to reinforce my relationship, I will get tickets or make arrangements for us to go.

Women, let me issue a word of warning if you simply wanted to strengthen a friendship with a man and do not want him to get the wrong idea. When I told this story to a female friend of mine, she said he'd probably assume the woman was making a pass at him. I argued that I thought he'd just take it at face value because, when it comes to men, they miss so many things.

But, rather than argue with nothing to substantiate my claim, I did a little research. She was right. If an action could be taken either sexually or non-sexually, men will probably go for the former.

In a study called 'Can Men and Women Differentiate Between Friendly and Sexually Interested Behavior', approximately eighty men and eighty women were shown films of a male and a female acting in either a friendly or sexually interested fashion.[38] Men read a lot more sexiness into all the vignettes than did the women. It was probably wishful thinking, so be careful.

## The power of gifts (or a great way to get rid of junk you don't want!)

Are you a squirrel or a caterpillar? Some people are like squirrels, which hoard and amass everything. They seem constitutionally incapable of throwing anything away. (Unfortunately, that's me.) Others are like caterpillars, who are constantly shedding their skins and moving around in a new one. Like the date stamped on the top of a milk carton, everything in the caterpillar's life has a 30-day expiry date. (That's Phil, my PMR.)

It's almost a ritual now. Every Tuesday and Thursday evening, together, we lug the garbage down from our three-flight walk-up to the street for pickup. Inevitably, a few hours later, I'll have trouble sleeping, thinking about how I'll miss one whatsitsname or another that we've just junked. I then tiptoe to the door of his room to make sure I hear the rhythmical regular breathing of deep sleep. That's my cue to sneak down in the dead of night – to rescue that thingumabob.

Once, we had struggled together for almost an hour to carry a huge armchair down to the street. Long after he had gone to bed in exhaustion, I was still rearranging the furniture in my room. As I adjusted and readjusted the bed, couch and a few tables, I had one empty corner – the corner that was *perfect* for the just discarded armchair!

I raced to the window. Whew, it was still there. 'Hmm, now a dilemma. Should I awaken Phil and, with great embarrassment, ask him to help me lug it up again?' No, the humiliation would have been too great and, besides, he'd never let me forget it. Instead, I went down to the corner and found the panhandler who frequented our corner. 'The Bum' (by his own designation) and I were old friends by now. We had a deal: he wouldn't hold his hat out as I passed, especially if I were walking with friends. In return, I would cross his palm weekly with a little tip.

This time, I had bigger rewards for 'The Bum'. I asked him if he would like to earn ten dollars by helping me carry something? He smiled from ear to ear – until I pointed out the big armchair. His dismayed expression made me reconsider my weekly donation. Nevertheless, we got the chair upstairs and, the next day, Phil, spotting the chair as he passed my room, respectfully didn't say a word.

For some time now, Phil had been suggesting a 'let go of clutter' system he'd been using for years. It was, quite simply, throwing out three things a day. I tried it. The first day it was an old lamp, a tape recorder that I'd been planning to have fixed for three years and an earring that I'd lost the mate to two years before. The second day it was a ripped sheet I knew I'd never sew, an old WordStar computer book and three left gloves whose mates had been lost.

I held to this schedule for a week and it was working well. I began to appreciate this shedding of flouvia. So, can you imagine my dismay when Phil's (then) girlfriend, Felicia, a flight attendant, started bringing me little presents from places she travelled to – Tchotchkes, she called them. (Yes, even Irish girls use Yiddish words in New York.) Tchotchkes (pronounced 'chatz-keys') are little anythings. She brought me an ivory-carved cigarette holder from Alaska (I don't smoke), Droste chocolate from Holland (I don't need the calories) and a coffee mug from Brazil (I prefer cups). Thanks to Felicia, I now have a box overflowing with ashtrays from around the world, little bottles of spirits from the plane, exotic shampoos and hand lotions from hotels' amenities trays, three miniature Eiffel towers and one leaning tower of Pisa – junk, all junk. All things that I will gratefully shed, three by three.

But here's the rub. I adored Felicia for her thoughtfulness. Her little nothing gifts were a lovely tribute; much nicer than a postcard on which the sender has written in invisible ink between the lines, 'Ha ha, look where I am now and you are not.'

I was genuinely sorry when she and Phil broke up. Felicia and her tchotchkes had made me think about the concept of gift-giving which is, by comparison, conspicuously absent in our culture.

Gift-giving is *expected* between any two parties doing business in practically every other European or Asian culture. Each has unspoken rules on *when* and *how* you give the gift. Before doing business abroad, bone up on the particulars. Do you present your gift when you first meet, or at the end of the meeting? In private or when others are around? Wrapped or unwrapped? Open it when you receive it or open it later? The list goes on. The important thing is not the value of the gift, but the fact that it is a gift.

Pick up little gifts not only while you're traveling, but also while at home. It shows that you revere the receiver.

Incidentally, be aware of some gift-giving dos and taboos around the world. You are probably not sending the message you want if you give alcohol to Arabs or chrysanthemums to Germans. And giving a clock to the Chinese or knives to Americans sort of says, 'Drop dead!'

**CLAUSE 23 ♂ ♀**

## Casks for Chums

I will constantly be on the lookout for casks, little gifts for my colleagues, my friends – and folks I'd like to make my friend.

# Chapter Twenty Two

# Standing up for your friends

A girl named Priscilla – my eyes narrow even now as I write her name – was THE most popular girl in my school. All the girls wanted to bask in the shadow of this self-appointed princess. They tried to walk like her, talk like her and dress like her. Monday, if Priscilla wore a sequined sweater to school, on Tuesday, you'd be blinded by the swarm of sequined sweaters in the classrooms. In fact, one Friday morning she came to school with a dime rather than a penny in her loafers. By 10 a.m. on Friday morning, not a pair of 'penny' loafers was walking the halls; it was dimes everywhere.

## The green-eyed monster in my closet

Lunchtime was cafeteria style, with picnic tables and supposedly open seating. Open as a nailed coffin! Only Priscilla and her Cool Clique sat at the table by the window. Every day, as she approached the end of the cafeteria line, several of her Cool Clique groupies would race ahead to 'Prissy's' table to scramble for the bench position next to where they predicted the Princess would place her most prized posterior.

Was this being liked? I thought so then.[39] But no, this was the enigmatic love–hate envy syndrome that people feel toward the Priscillas of the world. It's not just high-school snobs – it's grown-up dictatorial bosses, the arrogant rich or conceitedly beautiful. It first rears its ugly head when we're least able to understand or cope with it – in secondary school or the sixth form, where 'coolness' or 'toughness' play a brief but significant role in our lives.[40]

At lunch I always sat with my best friend, Stella, and six or seven other members of my 'Potluck', a younger version of a high-school sorority. On Friday nights we'd have Potluck parties at a member's house, where we brought food and gossiped until we heard our exasperated mothers honking their horns outside waiting to take us home. What did we talk about? Everything, but our favourite topic was Priscilla and her faithful followers.

On the school bus, the unspoken seating arrangement was very formalized. Prissy *always* sat in the second row back, window seat, on the non-driver's side. The entire first three rows were tacitly 'reserved' for members of Prissy's Cool Clique. It was even considered bad taste for one of the 'outsiders' to sit in the fourth row. That was tantamount to brazenly 'auditioning' to be part of her elite circle. The only path to Prissy's prestigious entourage was to be befriended by the Princess or one of her closest ladies-in-waiting.

One windy, rainy day, Prissy was absent. The Cool Clique looked temporarily lost and leaderless. They didn't speak to each other much, or to anyone else that day. It was if they were in mourning. Due to the torrential rain, the school bus was more crowded than usual on the trip home. A few standees were already huddled together and I was the last to board the packed bus. I was wet and tired, and only one empty seat remained: second row back, window seat on the non-driver's side – Prissy's seat. One of the Cool Clique mob sat next to it jealously guarding it and smugly aware that she held this number-two position, even in Priscilla's absence. For a fleeting moment I flirted with courage. I looked first at the seat, then into the stony face of Prissy's seat guard, then up at my Potluck friends at the back of the bus. Did I imagine I heard Stella whispering 'Go, Leilie, go!'?

Looking back at history, I have renewed respect for Rosa Parkes, that courageous black woman who on another windy rainy day, on Thursday, 1 December 1955, refused to relinquish her seat to a white man in the front of the bus. Looking back at my bus incident, I wonder what would have happened if I or one of the other outsiders had sat in Prissy's seat and refused to budge. Would the rest of us nerds heroically band together and refuse to ride the bus to destroy the power grip of the clique? I think not. But we sure would have never forgotten the kid who had the guts to sit there.

> Rosa Parkes did it. Joan of Arc did it. Julius Caesar did it. We all have the opportunities to be heroes or heroines in small ways by being first to do something we believe in for our friends and loved ones – our people.

I kept walking towards the back of the bus. A small part of me still regrets that moment.

**CLAUSE 24 ♂ ♀**

## My Personal Principles Clause

When I *know* in my heart that something is right, especially when it's for My People – whether they are the minority or suffering majority, I will go for it. Whether it's as important as racial relations or as insignificant as cracking a clique in one high school, I'll be the first to stand up – or sit down – for my folks. Yes, they'll like me for it. *But, most of all, I will like myself.* (And that's the first step to making everybody like me.)

# Chapter Twenty Three

# Planting seeds for new friendships

L ast year I made a trip to my old home town because I had to take care of a small financial matter there. Three members of my old Potluck still lived in town, so we all planned to buy a few munchies for everybody and then get together that night, just like we used to so many years ago.

I went to the grocery store to pick up some fruit and cheese. I got in line with my goodies behind a big woman dressed in a cheap cotton, wrinkled housecoat. She's the kind of woman that my country Uncle Charlie would say 'looked like she'd be plenty warm in winter, and provide plenty of shade in the summer'. Pushing her cart filled with food and two screaming kids, she jiggled forward a few shuffling steps every few minutes as the line got shorter.

One of her boys must have grabbed a bar of chocolate from the checkout display, because suddenly she lifted a hefty arm and cuffed him, slapping it right out of his hand and on to the floor. I immediately made a nose dive to pick it up to save her what I knew, for her, would be a formidable undertaking. 'The brat's up to his old tricks again,' she explained as I handed it to her. 'Thanks.'

That voice! I'd never forget it. To confirm my suspicions, I looked into her face and there she was – a few more chins, but the same woman. It was Priscilla! Princess Priscilla who had ruled my high school with the same slightly sarcastic smile she was giving me now.

This time I looked at her, not with envy but with sympathy and sadness. Not because of her weight. Not because of her rowdy kids. But because we just assume our superstars will go on and be superstars in everything they do in life. Priscilla's careworn face and crumpled clothes told me this was not the case.

My green-eyed monster died a quiet death.

 ## Prissy's present

That evening at Potluck, I told my old friends about my brief encounter with Prissy that afternoon. One of my Potluck pals had worked at the same insurance company with her after graduation. I asked Gina what happened. She blinked, obviously not having thought about Priscilla in a very long time.

'Well, after we graduated,' Gina said, 'I guess everyone sort of forgot about her. About half the girls in her clique went off to college. And to my knowledge, they didn't stay in touch. At least she didn't talk about it much.'

'How long did Priscilla stay at GEICO?' I asked her.

'I don't know exactly,' Gina continued, 'because little by little the rest of us got promoted out of that department or moved on to better jobs. And Prissy just sort of stayed in the same position. Nobody really liked her at GEICO.' At that point Gina laughed and said, 'Her terror tactics didn't work in the real world.'

Gina continued, 'She started dating George, you know, the guy who owned the auto body shop next to Pop's drugstore downtown. Then, I guess she got pregnant or something because they got married and pretty soon they had a baby. She quit GEICO and that's the last I heard of her. You said she's got two kids now?'

Gina asked the question quite dispassionately, a far cry from the reverent tone of voice we used whispering about the 'Princess' in the halls. As we munched on our goodies, I found myself feeling a little sad for Priscilla.

## You can never go back (and would you really want to?)

The subject soon changed to more pleasant subjects. I was thrilled to hear that Gina was now a senior rep at GEICO. She attributes her promotion to a friendship she formed at the company, a woman named Pamela whom she called her 'mentor'.

I begged Gina to tell me the story. She said, 'Well, there was this woman that I always smiled at in the company lunchroom. She sort of reminded me of my mom. Anyway, one day when the cafeteria was full, she came over and asked if she could share my table. We had a really nice time and took to eating together practically every day.'

'Well, I had no idea,' Gina continued, 'but soon I found out Pamela was married to a bigwig at the company, the head of personnel. Gradually she felt more comfortable with me and she opened up and told me a lot of company inside dope [info].'

## You made my day!

'For example,' Gina continued, 'we had this system at GEICO, where if you did something nice for someone – you know, covered their phone for them while they were out, or stayed late to help them finish a report – they'd give you a cute little blue card the company printed up that said, "Thanks, you made my day!" and then they'd write the nice thing you did.

'It was good because it made us realize that people really appreciate the littlest things – like if you're rushed, letting them ahead of you in the cafeteria line, or asking if they'd like to borrow a novel by an author you know they like.

'Anyway, at the end of the day, we were supposed to drop it in the "You made my day!" box which, I assumed, was just for recycling purposes.

'But Pamela later told me that the cards were a big deal to the company. The personnel department emptied that box every week and put the cards into the employee's personal record. She then proudly added that her mentor told her that she had 120 "You made my day!" cards in her file.'

Gina then said, 'Leil, you were asking about Prissy? Well, after she left, Pamela was clearing out her files and told me, confidentially, that Prissy didn't have even one card. That's probably why she never got promoted.'

## ✵ Now, about your promotion ...

Pretend that you are angling for a promotion. (Of course you are. We all are, in everybody's eyes!) Every time you do a tiny favour for someone, no matter how small, a 'You made my day!' card is going into your personal file. The more 'You made my day!' cards you have in your personal file, the more people will like you. And isn't that what we're talking about here?

Since every workplace is different, every list will be different. List 10 thoughtful things you can do for colleagues in your place of work that would earn you a card that says:

Thanks, you made my day for ...

1 _____

2 _____

3 _____

4 _____

5 _____

6 _____

7 _____

8 _____

9 _____

10 _____

**CLAUSE 25** ♂ ♀

## Thanks, You Made My Day!

I will keep my eye out at work and attempt to do some of the thoughtful things above for my colleagues.

# ou want to be popular, or do you want to be liked?

Was 'Princess' Priscilla in my high school popular? Most definitely 'Yes'. Was she genuinely liked? Most definitely 'No'; certainly not by the majority of students. I sensed it then, but was too young, too naive or just plain too stupid to say it, even to myself. Decades later, when I started working with companies and exploring elements of charisma and authority, I realized that I should have trusted my instinct. People genuinely liking you is a far cry from the Priscilla-type popularity that pervades many schools.

It wasn't until almost the turn of the millennium that researchers started studying popularity and cliques. Perhaps some of it was in response to a spate of high school tragedies and violence in response to social ostracism and unforgiving hierarchies in schools.

Teens on-line often bemoan the unfair rejection they get from the 'jocks' and 'cool kids'. I've read anguished messages such as 'The popular conformists need to learn to accept every-one else. Why would they shun people who are different?'

'I can't even begin to say all the problems with cliques. I am seen as an outcast and dork by all of the popular people ... It hurts so much to be different.'[41]

Reading messages like this, I found myself conjuring up painful pictures of being snubbed by the 'in-crowd' in my school. In those years, I saw my classmates as a microcosm of the world. And my acceptance or rejection by the Cool Clique seemed to me to be a harbinger of my acceptance or rejection in the real world. If only one member of the Cool Clique had been warm to me. If only one Cool Clique had casually chatted with me while walking to class, or invited me to sit beside her on the bus or joined our group at the lunch table, then I wouldn't have felt like such an outsider.

Did the teens who turned to savagery feel that they were doomed to be failures in life because the 'jocks' and 'cheer-leaders' didn't accept them? Was the pain so great that they had to become violent? It will be a long time before we have answers to questions like this. But the important thing is, impor-tant people are starting to ask important questions.

And you and I can do important things, right now, in response to this ghastly wake-up call. As teenagers, as adults, as senior citizens, we can break the clique system, the caste sys-tem, the social snob system. Those at the bottom can't bust it except by headline-exploding violence. But, if you are at the top – say, a cheerleader, a jock, a corporate giant, a member of 'high society', a celebrity, or a notable star in your galaxy of friends – then you can crack the clique system that exists at every level of life.

Look around your world, your company, your neighbour-hood. Don't you see someone who would value your friend-ship? Someone who you (perhaps the world) would call 'unpop-ular', 'a dork', or 'a freak'? Someone who is a little different from your other friends, and whose life you could light up by shining on them. No one can honestly answer 'No' to this question.

And, hey, you never know ... The dorky-looking guy with glasses and tousled hair whose nose is always pressed up against a computer screen? The girl with the big nose and stringy, long dish-water blonde hair who goes around singing to herself? The chubby teen who always had a clever, cutting snide remark for everyone? Wouldn't it be great to have befriended *those* kids, and now to be able to count Bill Gates, Barbra Streisand or Roseanne among your galaxy of friends?

> Crush the old 'popularity' or 'unspoken social class' system. It's outdated and outrageous, and should be outlawed. We can regulate racial prejudice. But, since 'popularity prejudice' is so pervasive, people just close their eyes and pretend it doesn't exist. Unfortunately, it does.

**CLAUSE 26** ♂ ♀

## Befriend a Nerd

I will open my eyes, look around, and find someone way less 'cool' than me (or someone who is not as accepted by my peers as I am). Then I will reach out and genuinely befriend them. I'll let some of *my* stardust rub off on *them*.

And you know something? You'll find that the 'nerd' enriches your life in many ways. You may not fall in love with your 'dweeb'. But remember – legend has it that inside the frog is a handsome prince or beautiful princess just waiting to be freed by your kiss.

# Chapter Twenty Five

# What if I only feel those butterflies when I'm talking to him or her?

Ah, now we're talking about a different puppy, a different diversity, yet another kind of minority, and it can be a very lonely one at that. We're talking about the drop-dead gorgeous people, the 10s, both male and female.

'Ohh, poor things!' I can hear you say sarcastically.

No really, I have had several jobs where I had the good fortune – or miserable luck, depending on how you look at it – of working with gorgeous people. There was a day in our not-so-ancient history when flight attendants had to meet a strict height, weight and age (read 'beauty') requirement. Pan Am hired some token non-Scandinavian women such as myself, but obviously the recruiters preferred the tall, sexy Swedish beauties.

I became close friends with one of them, a knock-your-socks-off Swedish beauty from Stockholm. We flew together often. I witnessed men dropping coffee cups when they spotted her coming down the aisle. I saw twisting male heads one by one fall into the aisle like dominoes as she passed. I heard grown men – managing director types – rendered speechless when asked by Ulla to make the mind-boggling decision of whether to have coffee or tea. (She didn't say, 'Or me ... ,' but you know they were thinking it.)

One would assume Ulla was deluged with dates, right? I know *I* did – until she told me the truth. Because she was so gorgeous, she intimidated men. No man likes to be turned down and, to avoid that humiliation, very few had the courage to ask her out.

Ulla was not an isolated example. Years later, when I ran a modelling agency, I heard the same thing repeatedly. The most beautiful women were often lonely because no one dared approach them.

Mother Nature played a dirty trick on us. The more we're attracted to someone, the more butterflies we'll have in our stomach when talking to that terrific him or her. That unfortunate fact was proven by a study called 'Shyness and Physical Attractiveness in Mixed-Sex Dyads' (Just a fancy way of saying 'man–woman twosomes').[42] Researchers and self-appointed experts on how attractive someone is ruthlessly gave a control group of people who didn't know each other a rating on their looks. The men ranged from matinee-idol handsome all the way down to a few who ... well, if you looked up 'ugly' in a dictionary, you'd find their pictures. Likewise, the women ranged from drop-dead gorgeous all the way down to some who were critically beauty-challenged.

Then the researchers went about their work of introducing each man to each woman, meanwhile registering their heartbeats, sweaty palms, breathing rates – in other words, counting the butterflies in their stomachs. The results? The more attractive the partner, the more shy and flustered the opposite-sex stranger who was meeting him or her was.

Conversely, the subjects were cool, calm, collected, and the butterflies didn't flap a wing for either men or women when they met the less attractive opposite-sex subjects. Who said life was fair?

##  Great, so I know why; now how can I get rid of those butterflies?

Unfortunately, there's no Raid or Roach Motel (like the ad sadistically says, 'They check in, but they don't check out') for the butterflies in your tummy. However, armed with a little knowledge, you'll feel a lot more confident becoming a friend or lover with a '10'.

It has been said that it is not our actual attractiveness, but our perception of our own attractiveness that plays the major role. In one study, 99 people were told that they were being rated for attractiveness.[43] Then researchers gave them totally incorrect information. They told some of the less attractive people that they had rated them very highly, and vice versa. (What a blow to your ego to think you're attractive and then hear that you're a dud! However, far be it from me to argue the ethics of science.)

Then, in a supposedly unrelated experiment, the researchers told everyone to choose a partner for a task. Practically everyone chose a partner whom they thought was essentially just as attractive *as they judged that they were*, not as they really were. In fact, results showed that the opinion they had received about their own attractiveness was the *primary* factor that determined who they chose, especially when it came to choosing someone of the opposite sex. Even in this small microcosm, the adage 'We are what we think the world thinks we are' seemed to reign.

Especially in dating, if a man or woman only feels like a '5', he or she is going to be uncomfortable making overtures to the '10s'. The typical thought pattern of a man afraid of rejection is, 'Oh, gosh, she's so beautiful. I bet every guy tries to talk to her. She'll think I'm just another one of those jerks if I try to make the approach.' Women also hesitate falling into a relationship with an extraordinarily good-looking man because they assume, given all his opportunity, that he would be a womanizer.

Research has proven that people usually wind up with someone who is within a two-point range of themselves in attractiveness. That could be because most people are afraid to approach the extremely handsome men or beautiful women. Ulla told me – but it took the results of the studies to prove it to me – that '10s' can be very lonely people indeed.

Studies prove the '10s' can be pretty lonely people because no one figures they measure up. So take a shot. If you are attracted to the '10', let him or her know. Your chances are much better than you think. If nothing else, it will destroy the butterflies you have when talking with the 'normal-looking' folks!

**CLAUSE 27** ♂ ♀

## I'll Talk to the '10s'

I'll go for it! I will never again think that I don't have a shot at friendship or love with the most attractive people. I'll make a special point to talk to the '10s'.

## Chapter Twenty Six

# Have you ever had a friend ...

*Who changed your way of looking at life for ever?*

I mean *really* changed it – the way you see certain people and situations for ever? I've been fortunate enough to have shared moments with two and, tragically, they had something in common. Devastating accidents had left both with major disabilities.

Soon after I moved to New York, I attended a concert, and happened to sit next to a striking young woman named Leslie who was also there alone. She and I started chatting and hit it off instantly. The band was not that terrific and we joked about getting together and starting our own all-girl group. We weren't serious about that but, since we were both new to New York and had few friends there, we were serious about wanting to get together.

When the concert was over, our chatting wasn't, and we found ourselves the last ones in the theatre. I invited her over to my place the following week and happened to mention that she'd better do her exercises, because I lived in a three-flight walk-up. She laughed and suggested we meet at a nearby coffee shop that she happened to know instead.

I jumped up to grab my coat and it was only then that I noticed Leslie wasn't standing. Instead, she was deftly lifting herself from the theatre chair to a wheelchair, which I hadn't seen parked in the aisle. I wanted to die inside about my three-flight walk-up comment, but it apparently hadn't affected her.

The following Saturday morning, I arrived early at our appointed place and, right on time, Leslie wheeled up. We laughed and joked all the way through our breakfast. When the bill came, she dived into her bag with one hand and said, 'Oh, please, let me.'

'No, no,' I said reaching across the table and grabbing her other arm which felt – like rubber! She must have noticed my astonished expression because she just smiled and said, 'Don't worry, Leil. Now you've discovered *all* my false parts.'

Very matter-of-factly, she went on to tell me about the accident that had severed her right arm and rendered her right leg practically useless. She told me that she and her (then) boyfriend, who had a small Cessna 150 plane, were going for a Sunday outing. Just as he was about to rev up the engines, she remembered that she'd left her handbag in the tiny terminal in front of the plane. She stepped down from the plane and ran toward the terminal. Just at the wrong moment, the propellers started and sliced Leslie's lower arm off. The freak accident flipped her over, the plane came around again and sliced through all the nerves in her leg.

The slings and arrows of outrageous fortune had left their mark on Leslie's body – but what had they done to her psyche? How does a beautiful woman adjust to life as a 'cripple', that horrible word some thoughtless people use? I didn't dare ask, nor did she speak any more about her accident or the impact it had on her. She gracefully changed the subject and said that next week she'd love to see my loft if I'd help her up the stairs.

That was the beginning of a long friendship, one that lasted many years. Leslie did fulfil her dream of becoming a singer, at least part-time. During those years we went to countless concerts, movies, plays and social events together. I attended the opening night each time she was booked at a new club. At each, I could view the world through her eyes.

This was before the Americans with Disabilities Act was passed and we had to call every theatre and every restaurant we went to, in order to find out if a wheelchair could enter. We had to ring every club to ask if the ladies' cloakroom was on the same floor. We had to look at every sink to make sure it was low enough for her to wash her hands, or had a mirror low enough to check her make-up before going on stage – or whether she would only see the top of her head. Viewing the world from a wheelchair gives one a very different perspective.

If Leslie had just one wish in the world, it would be to be 'normal'. Once she told me that, without a thought, she would trade places with the humblest 'AB' (able-bodied) woman in the world. Her signature song almost always moved her audience to tears. It was an old Carole King song popularized by Aretha Franklin, ' 'Cause you make me feel, you make me feel, you make me feel like a natural woman' ...

Leslie taught me that people with disabilities hate not being treated 'natural'. They enjoy casual conversation with strangers as much as anyone else. She said, 'Just don't think of us as "handicapped" or "disabled". Think person first, disability second. After that minor brain tune-up,' she said, 'even your language will change. You'll be saying "person with a disability", not "handicapped person". You'll say "visually impaired", not "blind person", or "hearing impaired", not "deaf person". You'll talk about "someone in a wheelchair", not a "wheelchair-bound person".'

I once asked her if people should ignore someone's disability.

'No, it's obvious to us that it's obvious to you,' she said. 'But let us take the lead in talking about it. We will when we feel comfortable.'

Leslie said that one question she despises is, ' "What happened to you? Were you born with ... " But,' she said, 'if you ask the same question in a different way, we're happy to tell you. Just say, "How did you come upon your disability?" or "Have you had your disability since birth?" This treats the disability as something we wear or have, not as an integral part of us.'

Leslie gave me one of the most beautiful compliments I've ever received – one, unfortunately, I knew I didn't deserve. One evening in a little club where she was singing, as she finished her signature song, she looked at me and said into the microphone, 'I want to dedicate that song to my friend Leil. Because she makes me feel like a natural woman.'

I didn't keep many secrets from Leslie during the years of our friendship. However, I never told her that, had I known when I first met her so many years ago that she was in a wheelchair and had only one arm, I probably would not have been as comfortable chatting and joking with her. I would have been frozen like so many others when confronting someone with a disability. And our beautiful friendship never would have happened.

The Leslie in New York story ends happily. She fell in love with a man who played the piano for her at one of her club acts. Within the year, they married and moved to St Thomas together, where Leslie and her husband are one of the most popular club acts on the island.

Having a 'PC' (physically challenged) friend will open new worlds within for you. Your PC pal may become the most wonderful friend you'll ever have because they've had to travel so much further than most. You'll never see the world in quite the same way again. You'll experience emotions you never thought possible.

**CLAUSE 28 ♂ ♀**

## My Physically Challenged Pal

If I know someone with a 'physical challenge', I will become closer to him or her. Also, I will actively seek out the friendship of other physically challenged pals.

My friendship with Leslie paved the way for a light flirtation I had with Richard, a studio engineer working on some of my audiotapes. The receptionist had already taken me into the recording booth when his voice came through on my earphones, welcoming me and asking me if I was ready to start.

I made the usual number of recording bloopers and Richard gently guided me through all of them. I liked his voice and, although I couldn't see him too clearly through the double recording glass, I could see that he had some facial scarring. His silhouette intrigued me. He had long hair halfway down his back and, in the distance, he looked like – don't laugh – Flavio, the heartthrob on the cover of so many Mills and Boon romances.

After the session, I went out to meet him and I could see that it wasn't just a few scars. His entire face was badly scarred and distorted. Obviously he had undergone many plastic surgery operations to try to construct an almost entirely new face, which looked like it had been badly burned.

We chatted for a few minutes and I asked Richard if, after the recording session, he happened to be driving in the direction of my hotel. He was, and on the way I suggested we grab a bite at a restaurant we were passing. He seemed surprised at my invitation and haltingly agreed.

During dinner, struggling to sound as though his question were casual, he asked why his distorted face had not turned me off. I told him, truthfully, that I wasn't. In fact I saw tremendous beauty in his eyes.

Then, when I mentioned that someone I had come to admire deeply was a man who not only had worse burns than he, but was also in a wheelchair, he asked in awe, 'Do you know W. Mitchell?' I said that I had been fortunate enough to meet him several times at a National Speakers' Association conference.

A flaming motorcycle accident had taken W. Mitchell's face, his fingers and nearly his life. Later, in an emergency crash landing in his private plane, he was paralysed and confined to a wheelchair.

Now, W. Mitchell is tougher on his wheelchair tyres than he is on himself. He travels the world delivering his inspiring message that (as one of his books is titled) *It's Not What Happens to You, It's What You Do About It*.[44]

W. Mitchell was Richard's hero, and my connection with him, however slight, was all he needed. His emotional and verbal floodgates opened. The fact that I knew W. Mitchell somehow 'gave him permission' to pour his soul out on a subject he rarely, if ever, spoke to anyone about. He told me the story of the car crash that killed his mother and burned 90 per cent of his body when he was only three years old. He told me of his years of suffering as a child, and the gradual and ghastly realization that he looked different from everybody else. He told me how he knew 'people were repulsed by the monster', and how they would point and stare. He detailed dozens of painful incidents – how his father beat up a man in a grocery store he overheard whispering to his kid about the 'freak' in the next aisle; how his own brother didn't want to be seen walking to school with him; how, in his entire life, he'd only had a handful of dates and he knew those were sympathy dates and the women felt sorry for him.

I tried to convince Richard that he had a very special quality and that many women, including myself, found him very attractive. But Richard's pain was too great and his experiences too poignant, ever to have a relationship with a woman unless separated by the double glass at the studio. Maybe, if Richard someday hears W. Mitchell tell his story, 'The Man Who Would Not Be Defeated',[45] he will.

Or perhaps his mind will travel back to my descriptions of the gorgeous women I've seen wheeling W. Mitchell around the National Speakers' Association conference. I hope he remembers the picture I painted for him of the gorgeous blonde in a bikini sitting with W. Mitchell around the swimming pool, lovingly and sensually massaging suntan lotion all over his scarred body.

# Chapter Twenty Seven

# If you've got it, flaunt it!

After the dark dungeon that imprisoned me for four months mysteriously dissolved, I was able to peek back through the bars and see that I would not have survived, had it not been for my two dear friends, Giorgio and Phil. It was at that moment I resolved to meet more people ... all types of people.

Phil and I decided to give a series of 'Bimonthly Meet New People Parties'. We invited a dozen or so friends and invited each to bring someone along – the more unusual, the better (although we didn't say it in precisely those terms).

To describe the first bash as 'diverse' would be an under-statement. A 70-year-old retired corporate giant chatting with an orange Mohawk spike-haired kid wouldn't turn any of the other party-goers' heads. Conversation ranged from the stock market to the flea market, rock music to muzak, jogging to logging.

People often ask me, 'Who was the most unusual person at the party?' It was a close call, but I'd have to say that 'Nicky the Nose' would get the dubious honour. If ever you hear someone attacking insurance salespeople as being 'uncreative', you can counter with the fact that they have come up with every kind of insurance policy imaginable. Insuring people's houses, cars and health is nothing. They offer doctors and lawyers malpractice insurance, of course. They sell companies 'bad rumour' insurance. Virtuoso insurance agents determine what esoteric value entities have to certain folk, then agents offer expensive personalized policies so those paranoid people can sleep at night. For example, surgeons who don't even like to shake hands (for fear of finger-crunching) take out policies on their hands. Betty Grable was a trendsetter, being the first of many actresses to insure her legs. My actress friend Pam brought along to our party a fellow performer who had a two-million-dollar policy on his nose.

So why Nicky's nose? Because this particular performer makes his entire living on his schnozzle. Nicholas is one of the few (if not, the only) actor who can – right on cue – let out a huge a-choo, a medium honk or a little toot. His clients can choose 'with sniffle' (signifying the common cold) or 'dry' (to indicate the beginning of a cold). In fact, one cold-remedy company tried to sign him on as an exclusive. But, as my friend likes to tell it, 'The nose knows.' He turned up his well-trained one at their offer. Instead, he sneezes on command with just the right tone and nasality for the highest bidder's price.

Nicky the Nose's nasal talents don't end there. It is as though his proboscis is double-jointed. He can turn it up, down, right or left. He can flare his nostrils so he looks like a pig, or squeeze them so tight that he looks like he was born with a silver pince-nez on his schnozzle.

It was very cold the night of the party. Pam arrived with Nicky, who had a cashmere scarf around the lower half of his face, guarding his sole source of income from the elements. I put out my hand to welcome him to the party. Instead of shaking hands, however, he gave a respectful little bow and was seated. Pam, seeing my puzzled look, explained that Nicholas never shook hands, for fear of cold germs, and always protected his nose from the elements.

I asked Nicky what movies and commercials he'd be in, and he promptly listed an impressive array of pharmaceutical companies who make cold remedies. He said those were just for his sneeze, his sniffle and his wheeze. (He seemed to know the difference.) He had also done commercials for nose drops, nose-hair clippers and a nose clip for swimmers that conforms to the shape of any nose. He continued telling us one of his favourites was a TV spot for a national newspaper. While the announcer asked, 'Do you have a nose for news?' Nick's nose-tip travelled left to right, appearing to read.

By this time, a small group of party-goers had gathered around this masked storyteller. Then, slowly unveiling his treasure, he announced that it had finally broke into the fragrance industry. He seemed quite fond of one suggestive TV ad he had filmed the week before. The commercial opened with a close-up of his nose only a few millimetres away from a shapely female bosom overflowing from a white silk evening gown. As the voiceover said, 'Don't wear just any perfume', Nick's nose-tip took a downward dip. The voiceover continued with 'Excite him with ...' and here was the product name. At this point, the tip of Nicky's nose stood tall, virile and erect. When the camera pulled back, the gorgeous female winked at the camera as the handsome sniffer's strong arms encircled her and he buried his face in the valley of her hilly terrain.

Except that now Nick wasn't the male. They used a hand-some actor who happened to have a similar-looking nose. In fact, Nick didn't seem the least bit sensitive to the fact that they used another actor for the full-body shot.

You see, Nick didn't consider himself the 'stand-in nose' for the handsome actor. In fact, he referred to the final shot with the actor as being a stand-in for his significant sniffer.

Nicky then began to give us an unsolicited tour of his notorious nose, pointing out the nares, dorsum and philitrm along the way. I decided it was crossing the bounds of good taste to let us hear his famous sneeze. After all, if you were to meet Maria Callas at a party, you would not ask her for an aria. Meeting Gregory Hines, you wouldn't ask him for a little tap dance.

But Nicky the Nose must have sensed my desire because, just then, he began a long wheezy three-second inhale, and then let out a thunderous AAAAH-CHOO, which sounded as though it could blow all the windows out of the loft. Everyone at the party froze. It was as though a huge freight train had just come through the loft. Never again will I think of those insipid little noises we mere mortals make when we have a cold as a sneeze. In fact, Nicky did carry a two-million-dollar disability policy on it – 'disability' defined in his policy as the inability of his nose to 'perform'.

When baby-boomers were little more than babies, they sat in schoolroom classes watching a series of films on how to 'fit in' and 'be like everyone else'. Nowadays, the man or woman who has the courage to stand out and be different is the one we respect and admire. The man or woman who nose – er, sorry, knows – his or her assets and plays them up wins our hearts. Like Nicky's nose, something about you can stand out.

CLAUSE 29 ♂ ♀

## Dare to Be Different

I will actively seek my differences and cultivate them.

# Chapter Twenty Eight

# Diversity, it's not just for the workplace

In 1945 or so, St Peter, hearing a ruction on earth, looked down from the heavens on high, then turned to Jesus and said, 'My Lord, listen to all that bawling, bellowing and booming down there. They're multiplying like rabbits!'

And Jesus replied, 'Yes, Peter, let them be known as baby-boomers.' And so they were.

Then Jesus continued, 'And, Pete, I want to warn you. When they get to your gates, they're going to have a lot of stories to tell. Those boomers are going to behold more of life as a group than any of their brothers and sisters before them. Some of the things they'll see are good – and long overdue, I must say. They'll give the good ones names like "civil rights movement" and "womens' liberation". They'll also see some stuff that has a good side and a bad side. They'll call them "student activism" and "sexual revolution". A couple of them will even take a few small baby steps toward us up here, with the rest of them watching on TV. Of course they'll call them "giant steps" for mankind.'

'All these happenings the boomers will experience together will create a fantastic fellowship among them. But, I'll tell you,

Pete, in my eyes the biggest step was not that guy Aldrin on the moon. It was when they started appreciating the incredible diversity I gave them.'

In the eyes of God, diversity was the biggest step that mankind has ever taken.

##  Guess who's coming to dinner?

Until the early 1950s, that phrase, 'Guess who's coming to dinner', would strike fear in Mummy and Daddy's heart. Many baby-boomers were the first in their family to bring home a friend with a different skin colour.

But now that baby-boomers are parents, many look forward to their teenager playing the 'Guess who's coming ...' game. They know that whoever shares their table that evening will probably be able to broaden their understanding of the world. Many of their own friendships, some of which have spanned three decades, are crosscultural.

Sometimes we become confused and, instead of listening to our hearts, we listen to the heartless. I was on the front end of the baby-boomers, and the world was a very different place then. Civil rights was in our recent history books, but it wasn't flowing through our veins yet.

In my high-school class, there were six African-American girls. One of them, Lacey, had been sent by her family in Bermuda to study in the States. Lacey's locker was next to mine and, daily, as we crammed stuff into (and yanked stuff out of) our lockers, she and I would talk non-stop. I spent summers in Bermuda because my mum, a speech pathologist, worked there tutoring a little girl who was the daughter of a member of the Bermudian parliament and his wife. Whenever we talked about Bermuda she'd get homesick, and I'd get nostalgic. Sometimes we'd talk about how we missed Bermuda until we were almost in tears, and then we'd break out hugging each other and laughing together.

One day, as we were chatting by our lockers just before lunch, it came up that Lacey knew the man whose daughter my mom tutored. She said there had been some heated debate in the Bermudian parliament recently because some of the MPs thought ' "Negroes" should not be hired as sales clerks in the Front Street shops.'

'Why not?' I asked her naively.

'Because they think it will turn tourists off.'

'That's strange', I remember thinking. But we both laughed it off and then I didn't think much more about it.

Far more interesting to me, in those days, was Lacey's description of the dating scene in Bermuda. She gave me the names of some places where the locals went to meet each other. We continued girl-talking about this all the way to the lunchroom. I wanted to write down some of the names of the Bermudian hotspots she'd mentioned, so I invited Lacey to join me and some of the girls in my Potluck (junior sorority) at our table.

She smiled, politely declined, and said, 'No, but you're certainly welcome to sit with us if you like.' Without thinking anything about it, I went and sat with Lacey and several of her black Bermudian friends. We launched into a hot discussion about places like The Swizzle Inn, Baileys Ice Cream Parlor, The White Horse Tavern, and several I'd never heard of.

Just as I was scribbling down the names, one of my Potluck girls came over and whispered something in my ear. I was stunned. My Potluck mate had said, 'Leil, everyone in the lunchroom is looking at you. You shouldn't be sitting here.' Feigning unawareness that I was being chided because I was sitting at 'the negroes' table', my Bermudian friends started talking among themselves. Behind my hand, I said to my Potluck mate, 'Why?'

She just rolled her eyes and said, 'Leilie, you know,' and went back to 'our' table. Finally it dawned on me. I smiled at my Bermudian friends and tried to pick up the discussion where it left off. But I could tell that things were different now. Conversation was strained.

Another moment that I am now ashamed to remember is that I never joined Lacey and her friends at the lunchroom table again. Lacey and I remained fast-locker friends, but that was it.

However, a few weeks later, Carolyn, not exactly one of the Cool Clique (but close to it), made a move that astounded the whole school. She started being seen walking the halls with Lacey, and standing outside the school on warm days chatting with her and her black friends. At first, many of my schoolmates whispered, in that tone usually reserved for scandals, about their friendship. But, as Carolyn and Lacey were seen together more and more, even sitting next to each other in the study hall – people stopped talking. Deep down, I think everyone realized that what Carolyn was doing was really cool, and the rest of the students were very wrong to think anything of it.

Little by little, people's opinions started reversing themselves. And by the time Carolyn found herself once or twice a week sitting at Lacey's table, the rejection of Carolyn had turned openly to respect of her.

I, too, admired Carolyn. But I had a sadness and a shame mixed with my admiration. *I* should have been that girl who broke the insidious unspoken rule. *I* should have been the girl to make the first obvious and flaunted cross-racial friendship in our school. *I* should have known that my friendship with Lacey was far more important than what a few misguided people thought about me.

Since then I have made many crosscultural friendships. I've learned how to cook couscous from a Tunisian friend; and been taught by a Japanese friend how to take nearly three hours to pour and drink one cup of tea. I've gone to a jai alai match (a game similar to pelota) with a Mexican friend; I've watched grown men hyperventilate over throwing a metal ball around in the sand (the game of petanque) with an Italian; and I even saw a guy catch a cow with three pieces of twine and a ball (a bolas) with an Argentine friend. What have I done for them? Well, I've introduced them all to McDonald's hamburgers, country music and Thanksgiving turkey.

Most people have no idea of how lonely someone feels when the majority of people around them are a different nationality or a different colour. No matter where you live, the 'Black Experience', the 'White Experience', the 'Asian Experience', the 'Hispanic Experience' and the 'Your First is My Second Language Experience' are very different. Fortunately, if you make friends with someone who has a thick accent in today's world, nobody will whisper. They'll just admire you for walking what (unfortunately) most people just talk.

**CLAUSE 30** ♂ ♀

## Multicoloured Chums

No matter if my skin is black, white, black, brown or yellow, I will consciously seek out friends and lovers of other colours, and from other countries.

# Part III

# Cupid's secrets

*Sexy schemes for luring lovers – and keeping them*

# Chapter Twenty Nine

# Cupid's got LOTS of secrets!

See if you can answer this riddle:

It's impossible to describe.
It's more common than the common cold
(and sometimes can be more of a nuisance).
It comes and goes with no apparent reason.
We have no idea what brings it on,
And when it goes, it's almost impossible to get back.
We have no idea of why it happens.
Lots of times you expect it and it never happens.
Other times it happens and you didn't expect it.
Sometimes you welcome it.
Sometimes it gets in your way.
There is no predicting when or where it will hit,
But it usually comes in a flash –
Then it disappears just as fast.
Or sometimes it dies an agonizingly long, slow, painful death.
It's one word. What is it?

If you guessed 'love', some people would say, 'You're close.' Others would laugh and say, 'You're way off base! It has nothing to do with love.' Since this perplexing phenomenon is so common and hits everybody at some time or another, linguists had to give it a name. But nobody could pin it down. So they wound up giving it a name that seemed virtually worthless at the time. They called it 'Chemistry'.

##  Cupid, please tell me – Why him? Why her?

We've all asked ourselves the same question. 'It seems crazy. Of all the people in the world, why do I find this one person so attractive? Why do the sparks fly when we're together, and not when I'm with anyone else – even though that "anyone else" is much better-looking?'

For women, chemistry seems even crazier. Imagine that 10 men are standing in a row like in a police line-up. Instead of having to choose which one is guilty of burglary, you have to choose which, if any, is guilty of a different type of robbery – stealing your heart at first sight. You look at each, one by one. They're all good-looking guys, but no suspects yet. You're getting near the end of the line. The police officer in attendance is about to dismiss the men because nobody would ever believe that funny-looking, lanky cowboy at the end of the line with the smiling eyes, the sarcastic smile and the lock of hair falling in his face could be the one.

Then you take one glance at him and, BLAM! There goes your heart. Why?

##  When two of Cupid's arrows cross

Before we look at that, we should probably discuss some fantasies, falsehoods and facts about love at first sight. Suppose the cowboy looks at you and finds you pretty as a little red heifer in a flowerbed. His big goofy heart skips a beat, too. Before a word is spoken, you both know you are destined to ride off into the sunset together.

Is it possible? Does love at first sight exist? What do you think?

Let's put it this way. It exists if the two of you agree that's what it was. It exists if, six months later, you're sitting on the couch together holding hands and cooing to all your friends, It was love at first sight. Nobody – not even those cold-hearted scientists I cite – want to burst your balloon.

All of this is just to say that 'love at first sight' is merely a semantic term that covers that delicious serendipity when two people look at each other and feel a simultaneous BLAM. Then the DOUBLE-BLAM turns into a serious relationship.[46]

Nothing beats love at first sight ... *except maybe love with INSIGHT.*

##  Some Cupids who crashed and burned

Back to 'why'? Starting with Aristotle and Plato, right on up through the heyday of psychoanalysis (with Theodor Reik telling us that love is filling a void in oneself, and Sigmund Freud not *really* believing that sometimes a cigar is just a cigar – it's *always* sex!), there have been countless theories why our little hearts go pitter-patter when we look at one individual and not another.

The most recent theory to bite the dust is Margaret Mead's. This superstar anthropologist, observing the mind-boggling antics of males and females the world over, told us all that this sex stuff was learned. It's the old nature versus nurture argument, and she cast her vote on the nurture side.

'We may safely say', she wrote, 'that many if not all of the personality traits which we call masculine and feminine are as lightly linked to sex as are the clothing, the manners and the form of headdress that a society at a given period assigns to sex.'[47]

Her colleagues proved good ol' Margie factually wrong later, but she had been 100 per cent *politically* correct, because the times were ready for such a feminist theory. It benefited our fair sex for the world to think there was little difference between *Homo sapiens* males and *Homo sapiens* females. (At least, it helped women to smash a few glass ceilings and take the wind out of a few old windbag politicians.)

Before the argument got too lodged, however, some vehement scientists hopped aboard the loveboat and found that a large body of research on specific behaviour could not possibly be traced to learning, as Mead had proposed. Even when children are brought up in identical isolated environments, little boys will still bop each other on the head and little girls will still try to put a nappy on the cat.

Upon further examination, the scientists found that there were, indeed, biological factors that contributed to these behaviours. There were differing levels of sex hormones, and even sex-specific differences in the human brain.[48] The prevailing theory now was that men and women are very different. (*'Mais bien sur,'* say the French. 'But of course. *Vee have known zat all along. Vive la différence!'*)

Speaking practically for a moment, it's unfortunate that, when the good Lord gave us male and female brains respectively, He didn't include an information kit for the brain we didn't get. I'll try to make up for some of that here.

# Chapter Thirty

# Finally science captures Cupid

At last the world of science has found *the* explanation of love that is tough to refute, because (like pieces of a tight puzzle) it squeezes in all disciplines from Anthropology to Zoology.

Scientists have isolated chemicals in our brain called neurotransmitters. They are responsible for that wonderful, wacky feeling of being in love, wanting to shout it from the rooftops, sing about it the rain and do a variety of loony things dangerous to life and limb. The neurotransmitter that really causes grown men and women to come unglued and want to swing from the chandeliers can be traced specifically to the one called phenylethlyamine (PEA).

Our PEA-soaked lovesick brain causes grown men to talk baby talk and grown women to count the hairs on their lovers' chests. It causes us to think the love object is the centre of the universe and that even the most mundane and trivial characteristic of the magical other is a source of utter fascination.[49] (I once went absolutely ape over the bushy hairs on a boyfriend's chest. There were 3042 to be exact. Six months later, when the PEA disappeared, I disdainfully thought of him as a real ape.)

##  Cupid does drugs

Now, this PEA substance, along with the two other natural amphetamines – dopamine and norepinephrine, which flood our lovesick brains – has some other debatable side effects. We feel giddy, optimistic, wonderfully alive, full of extraordinary energy, and we want to dance or make love all night in a euphoric trance. In other words, we're stoned out of our minds!

'Hey, what's so bad about that?' you ask. Well, nothing – for a short period of time. However, like any drug, it takes its toll. You'd crash if you were constantly high. Not only that, but (like any drug) you can become addicted to it. In fact, some people are. They get comfortable in a really good relationship but, unfortunately, the newness, the excitement, the PEA, wears off. So these folks blame it on the relationship and think it's going stale.

They deserve your sympathy. They are uninformed and sick. We call them 'love junkies' because they jump from one relationship to the next in an attempt to keep that initial high going all the time. Or they keep the excitement going by continually getting themselves embroiled in bad or abusive relationships.

##  Why do so many women go for the bad boys?

A constant quandary for men is why some women are attracted to the tough bad boys. It isn't just women. Many men also find themselves getting entangled in costly relationships. Admittedly it is confusing, because people profess to wanting a nice partner but continually get themselves involved in destructive relationships. Why?

There are several theories. The most plausible is that they find a perverse kind of pleasure in this type of liaison. Many women find the abusive men attractive because, to all outward appearances, they seem confident. They give off the air of knowing what they want, and pushing others around to get it. Usually it covers up a deep insecurity, but many of these 'tough' guys keep it deeply hidden.

It also could be that the tough guy reminds her of a time when she was a little girl. Daddy may have pushed her around, but she knew that deep down he loved her. Thus she connects the being pushed around with being loved.

Additionally, as they grow up, many people feel their life lacks drama. They remember the pain, the pleasure, the discovery, the being on the brink of disaster of their first love. Later, they develop a 'been there, done that' attitude with relationships, and they have a higher and higher threshold of what it takes to get that PEA juice flowing again. For some, it gets to the point where they have to be abused in order to recapture those melodramatic moments and get their PEA jolt.

The results of a massive study of women who continually chose abusive partners revealed that they suffered low self-esteem. The relationship only aggravated it. The verbal aggression and violence they endured caused depression and a myriad other symptoms. Yet they stayed. Many were love-dependent, feeling that they could not survive without the partner's love.

It is very common for women who love a bad boy to have a nice guy waiting in the wings – a soft bed to fall on if the tough guy gets too tough. They keep stringing their nice boy along as an insurance policy.

Researchers call this phenomenon of being attracted to the bad boys, the 'Stockholm Syndrome' and it is very difficult, if not impossible, for a 'nice guy' to pull her out of it. Many 'nice guys' in my seminars ask me if they should stay in the wings in the hope that she'll 'see the light'?

I answer, 'Your choice, but the statistics are pretty bleak. It must be her desire to escape the repetitive destructive pattern herself and, deep down, she probably doesn't want to.'

## ✿ Cupid grows up!

The hot passionate kind of love – in other words, the state of abnormality caused by PEA – promotes mating. However, after this, remaining this high is not evolutionarily advantageous. It's bad for the eventual offspring. Given the crazy things lovers do, that could threaten survival of the kids' parents. (They could fall off the roof while shouting their love from it, or catch pneumonia while singing in the rain about it.) Speaking biologically, unless unusual circumstances intervene (three of which we'll soon discuss), the PEA subsides.

Bye bye PEA, bye bye love. So goes the PEA, so goes the relationship – in many other cultures as well. Anthropologist Helen Fisher found that in societies as varied as Russia, Egypt, South Africa, Venezuela and Finland, divorces generally occur the year after the PEA disappears from their system, and the reality of two very different biological animals (male and female) having to deal with each other sets in.

##  So how long can I enjoy this legal high before I come down?

Here's the answer you've been waiting for. The normal lifespan of PEA is one and a half to three years.[50] Sorry, but it's true. The first happy, happy days and hot, hot nights last (on average) only up to three years.

Still, it doesn't make sense that couples split just because of a PEA drain. It does NOT mean anything is wrong with the relationship! It just means that nature is taking its natural course for propagation of the species. The great PEA loss is much better for the kids and the long-term good of you and your partner.

Since parents must care for children well into their teen years, Mother Nature doesnt want you to separate and have the kids shuttled back and forth. But, if she leaves you with a PEA-filled brain, you might be copulating around the clock when you need to take the kids to the doctor or get them ready for school. Or all the couples in the neighbourhood would be shouting their love from the rooftops all night long and the kids wouldn't be getting any sleep.

## Chapter Thirty One

# A better, deeper kind of love sets in – really!

So Mother Nature gives us another gift – one that, unfortu-nately, many people don't appreciate. The brain compensates by increasing the levels of morphine-like substances, endor-phins.[51] These create feelings of calm, security, well-being – that family kind of love. Wait, there's more good news. If you open your heart to this new kind of love, it will give you the deeply satisfying lifetime of love that we all crave.

Passionate love turns into companionate love. Eros goes from illogical need and obsession, to mutual support and acceptance. Any way you look at it, it's a much classier pooch than puppy love.

 ### What if I *still* want the 'can't wait to jump your bones' kinda love?

Well, for those of you who just have to have it, there is one way to keep the hot puppy barking. But not with your partner.

The first is having the spouse for the for-ever kind of family love – and the occasional lover on the side for the hot'n'heavy stuff. However, that would make you a two-timing, sneakin' deacon, double-crossing, two-faced, hanky-panky philanderer who risks losing the long-lasting kind of love that nature intended you to have, and is proven to give you the most happiness over time. If that's what you want, that's *your* business, but I don't recommend it.

By the way, here's a statistic for those of you who think you're missing out on something that everybody else has: Based on interviews with a random sample of almost 3500 people, aged 18 to 59, the Social Organization of Sexuality found that the average male has sex with six women over a lifetime, and the average woman has only two lovers.[52] When they counted noses on hanky panky, 75 per cent of married men and 85 per cent of married women had never put theirs on the same pillow with anyone apart from their spouse.

Is there a way I can keep the passion flower blooming with one partner? Yes, but it may not be worth the effort. Let me tell you about a friend of mine, Cindy, who has managed to keep her marriage hot and sexy for almost four years now. That's almost a record for PEA duration.

##  How Cindy keeps the sex cinders hot

Cindy (who also features in my *How to Make Anyone Fall in Love with You*) was my nail technician (I still have trouble not saying 'manicurist') and was always complaining that, in her line of work, she never met any men. After a long day of nail filing, buffing and clipping hangnails, she was too tired to go out and socialize, she said.

Although Cindy didn't have a boyfriend, she did have a platonic male friend, Victor, a carpenter who occasionally helped Cindy when she needed some repairs around the salon. I could never figure out why she let him hang around because, every time I had my nails done, Cindy regaled me with some new horror that Victor had committed.

Once she told me that, the previous week, she stayed after hours to give him a manicure. He's always bragged how 'tough as a cactus' he said he was but, when clipping his hangnails, she happened to give him a teensy cut.

'You should have heard him squeal,' Cindy said. 'Then, he had the nerve to call me clumsy! I was furious, I suggested he finish his own %#£@ing manicure.

'So, instead of saying he's sorry for snapping, he gets up, goes over and turns on the TV, and clams up. Typical male,' she muttered.

Another time, Cindy said, 'Victor came into the salon at one of our busiest times to repair a broken light fixture. All the girls and I were rushing around taking care of our clients. So Victor works on the light in silence for about 15 minutes and then, as he's leaving, instead of saying something nice to me, he says to us all with a great big grin, "Boy oh boy. You gals can sure talk up a storm. I think you all were vaccinated with phonograph needles. Hardy har har." And that, in front of my clients. I could've killed him.

'The following summer I didn't see Cindy because I was away. When I came back in the autumn with my sorry-looking set of split nails and overgrown cuticles, I started with my usual, 'So what's new in your life?'

She smiled and said, 'I got married in July.'

'You're kidding. How great! Who's the lucky guy?'

'Victor.'

'You met another Victor?' I asked.

'No, the same Victor.'

'Whoa, Cindy,' I thought. I knew I had to proceed very gingerly here. 'I thought you said you we're always fighting.'

Cindy laughed and said, 'Yeah, I couldn't take him as a friend. As a lover, that's a different story.'

If my hands weren't soaking in her bowl of soapy water, I would have scratched my head in confusion. However, after having read the multitude of studies on male–female relationships, it starts to make more sense to me.

One of the reasons there are fewer male–female platonic relationships than same-sex friendships is because the hierarchal male nature comes up against the solidarity-striving female nature, and causes a clash.[53] Men and women view relationships and life in a different way (so what else is new?) and, in love relationships, this can be exciting. Also, in romances, other factors keep the boat afloat.

Another reason is, of course, men's and women's friendship styles are very different. It is common knowledge that men bond by doing things together, but women bond by talking. It's hard for a woman to imagine having a close friend, male or female, who didn't bare his or her soul. But a man being asked to bare his soul is tantamount to a woman being commanded to bare her bottom. He'd consider it tantamount to rape if you insist!

Likewise, how many times do you see a group of women bonding at a baseball game or wrestling match, unaccompanied by males, yelling, 'Kill da Ump?'

I figured that, now that they were married, Cindy and Victor wouldn't fight so much. But still, she talks about the Victor vs Cindy skirmishes. Additionally, they have the challenge of growing the business together and are constantly fighting on which way is best.

They have been married for four years now, so I just had to ask her, 'Cindy what keeps you two together, if you're always fighting?'

'Well, it's not *always*,' she said with a little smile on her face. 'What keeps us together ... I guess it's the sex – every night, sometimes twice a night.'

'Sex, after four years, is still going strong?' I asked (with renewed respect for Victor!)

'Yeah, we fight like a rattlesnake and a cat.' She looked up with a big smile and made a clawing movement with her hands. 'I keep my nails filed nice and sharp now. They come in pretty handy. Then, about the time I draw blood, we know it's time to make up and we make fantastic love.'

While I was soaking this all in, she continued. 'Sometimes we even fight during sex.'

'OK, Cindy. If that works for you. You're the world's expert on what turns you on.'

# Chapter Thirty Two

# What about turning a friend into a lover?

An oft-asked question in my seminars is, 'Can you turn a Platonic friend into a lover?'

'I haven't run into any studies on this,' I tell participants. 'But my friend Annie did it. And, whether it was accidental or on purpose, I'll never know. And she'll never tell.'

Annie is a beautiful, brilliant and accomplished woman, who lives in California. We were introduced about six years ago by her uncle, whose company I do various audio projects for. He had planned a small luncheon party and I was to ride to the restaurant with Annie.

By the time we got there, in typical female style, we knew each other's life story (the ride was 20 minutes long) and we were fast friends. One of our big bonds was that Annie also had a PMR (Platonic Male Roommate) named Tim.

'Would either of you prefer not to be so Platonic?' I asked her.

'Oh, no,' she assured me. 'It works well this way.' I detected a trace of a faraway look in her eyes as she answered, but I didn't know Annie well enough to press.

I've now seen Annie about four times, once each year when I visit her uncle's company. Nothing changes except Annie's job title and the ever-growing size of her office. I always ask about Tim. Still roommates, still Platonic, and still a sweet smile on Annie's face whenever she talks about him.

My last visit was just a few months ago. This time Annie's reaction was very different when I asked about Tim. She stood up from her big mahogany desk, closed her office door, and said, 'I moved out.'

'Oh, no, I'm sorry. You were such good friends.'

'No, it's good news,' she said. 'We're engaged!'

'You are what? Tell me, what happened?'

Those of you who saw *Terms of Endearment* (1983) can probably guess. Do you remember when Shirley MacLaine and Jack Nicholson, platonic next-door neighbours, got rip-roaring drunk one night, danced in the ocean, and wound up in bed together. They had succeeded in holding on to their nightcaps, but didn't do so well with their nightclothes.

Well, it wasn't quite that raucous with Annie and Tim, who are both teetotallers. But one tiny drink at a holiday party had its effect, and the next morning they could no longer call themselves 'platonic' roommates.

What happened next? Annie moved out. Tim went crazy missing her. He invited her on a ski vacation to Austria – separate rooms, of course. And in a charming little restaurant in the Alps, he got down on one knee, brought out a beautiful engagement ring, and proposed.

Important note: I am not – I repeat NOT – advocating battling like Cindy or tippling like Annie to make him or her to take the Platonic out of your friendship. However, there's a reason they say, 'The course of true love never did run smooth.' As in Cindy and Victor's case, a touch of inflammatory action can fuel the flames of passion. And, in Annie and Tim's case, if you have very strict morals, a little libation can mean liberation.

# Chapter Thirty Three

# Cupid's last words

So, Cupid, what's the last word on keeping it hot? Well, first the good news. Yes, you can keep the passionate kind of erotic love going. Now the bad news. The three ways to do it are:

**1** be constantly faced with adversity (like Cindy and Victor growing the business together and fighting with each other);
**2** have the relationship forever threatened and be in fear of losing your partner (like Tim's fear of losing Annie, and Annie probably wondering if her moving-out gambit would work); or
**3** be separated most of the time.

Concerning 1 and 2, there is hardly a love story, play or movie which doesn't portray lovers whose relationship or lives are not threatened. It's the stuff that love feeds on. In fact, many studies have shown the direct relationship between danger and sexual passion. Who hasn't had the old excitement of the 'getting caught' fantasy?

One study called 'Some Evidence for Heightened Sexual Attraction under Conditions of High Anxiety' proved the linkage.[53] In fact, since the beginning of recorded time, people have sensed that danger and hot love go hand in hand. Publius Syrus said, 'The anger of lovers renews the strength of love.' (Who? I don't know who he is, either. But he sounds pretty Roman to me and he's quoted a lot in dusty old books.)

Concerning number 1 – being separated – everyone agrees that 'Absence makes the heart grow fonder.' This is true, for a while. Then you get so fed up with being alone that you look for some 'consolation'. Often consolation turns to adulation of the consoler. And that spells tribulation for the absentee lover.

'In summation', as the lawyers say to the jury, 'you must decide the case.' If the loneliness of separation or the fear of losing your lover or your life is worth it, OK. But, that's a pretty steep price. I'd vote thumbs down on the constant PEA urge, and go for that other kind of endorphin-based for-ever love.

##  Can you have the peaceful for-ever kind of love straight away?

It depends. A relationship can begin with the more endorphin kind of love when, due to age or other factors, sex has taken a back seat. It is very common between much older couples, who are marrying more for companionship than sex. However, younger couples usually need the PEA to kick-start their relationship.

A college friend of mine, Maria, lived with her boyfriend for six years. She said that the minute they met on a tennis court they felt like old friends. They were perfectly matched in tennis and in the game of life as well. Sometimes I would double-date with them and I saw how beautifully she and Michael got along.

Maria once told me, 'I'm so grateful that Michael is such a nice guy. He's one of those rare men you can talk to. And he actually listens! I always feel like my opinion counts with Michael.'

In fact, if there were a nationwide £1,000,000-prize contest for the world's most compatible couple, and it cost £100 to submit a couple, I'd have no hesitation about submitting the M&Ms (that was their nickname with all their friends). Whenever any of our friends were giving a party, they'd put the M&Ms on the top of the list because they were so pleasant.

Well, here we go. Astonishment time again. I called to invite the M&Ms to dinner one evening and discovered they were separate Ms now. I was as surprised as you'd be going into a store and asking for a packet of M&Ms and discovering that they were selling the Ms separately now – the centres in one bag, and the chocolate covering in another.

Maria told me she broke up with Michael because, 'We were more like roommates than lovers. Oh sure,' she said, 'we had sex, but it was like having sex with your brother. It was a warm and comfortable relationship, but never sizzling hot.' And that's what Maria craved.

## ☀ So what's Cupid's secret? What really keeps couples together?

Powerful stuff, that PEA. So can love exist without it? Yes, the permanent, more serious, kind of love can (and usually does) last a lifetime. That love incorporates love, not only of each other, but love of some principles of love.

Six massive studies were conducted to find the answer as to why people stay together. It may not sound like as much fun as getting drunk and dancing together in the ocean but, for better or for worse, here they are. The happiest married folks are:

- the ones who believe in the institution of marriage, either as a social or religious force in their lives;
- the ones who also have a touch of fear of the emotional, financial and social costs of calling it quits; and, above all,
- the ones who have a devotion and deep respect for the one whom they have chosen as a life partner.

The hot sexy part? *Enjoy it while it lasts!*

**CLAUSE 31** ♂ ♀

## I Won't Toss the Person with the PEA

I do understand – when our wild, wet, wiggly all-night love-making seems to be history – that it won't mean our love is. It is with that in mind that I will continue reading to learn how to capture or recapture my lifelong love.

# Chapter Thirty Four

# Mirror, mirror, find me a mate

Now, if you are not currently in a relationship, and masochistically decide you'd like to trade in some of your loneliness for the lunacy of love, this clause will astronomically increase your chances of making someone fall in love with you. It invokes what science tells us about why our hormones dance a jig on our backbone and our knees go to jelly when we look at one person and not another.

Without getting too technical, the organization of neurons in our brain from birth through our difficult teen years is determined by what we see, hear, touch, smell and feel. That interplay of neurons constitutes our *subjective reality*. Within that maze, there are patterns associated with the opposite sex. When little girls see Daddy or some other male family figure, it forms her definition of 'maleness'. When little Jimmy sees Mummy, or Aunt Ellen, or another female family member, his little brain says 'Ooh, female!' Sort of an instinctive 'Me Tarzan, you Jane' reaction.

For children who are fortunate enough to be loved by these opposite-sex family members, it's very comforting indeed. The pattern gets reinforced by other (usually) opposite-sex individuals in the family such as aunts and uncles. The boy or girl next door can be a secondary source of these images, but the primary source is usually related individuals.

Now, considering that half of these family folks share half our genes, they look a lot like us. And, since our love map gets formed early, it begins to make sense that *people are attracted to people who look like themselves!* (Therapists prefer a fancier term – people who fit our early 'Gestalt image'.)

In a fascinating study, researchers found that married couples resembled each other, as expected, in age, ethnic background, religion, socioeconomic status and political views. But they were blown away when, *four times higher on the scale*, were similarities in appearance right down to length of earlobes, lung volumes, circumferences of wrists and ankles, distances between eyes, and even length of middle fingers.[54] In other words, we are pre-programmed, from childhood, for 'BLAM' with the proper stranger.

> Far be it from me to tell you to carry a ruler around with you at parties and measure the earlobe, middle finger and distance between the eyes of a potential mate. But let me momentarily push aside my own mission statement on friends, love and diversity, and simply offer you this proven scientific fact: If you go out with someone who looks like you, they are four times more apt to fall in love with you.

🌼

**CLAUSE 32** ♂ ♀

## Look for a Lookalike

If I'm desperately desiring someone to fall in love with me, I will seek someone who looks just like me.

🌼

An interesting postscript to this study ... It seems that in societies where there is a very high social stigma on being cuckolded, there is a higher frequency of lookalike mating. The men choose women who look like them so that it will leave absolutely, positively, definitely no doubt in anyone's mind from whom their offspring sprang!

# Chapter Thirty Five

# Get off my bottom

Now, for a more practical approach. How do I get the love juices flowing through someone's veins if this person doesn't have the phenomenally good fortune to look like me?

Well, at the risk of sounding sarcastic, 'You have to meet them.' Why do I even have the pluck to put something so obvious in writing? Because it's a minor detail that escapes so many wannabe lovers' attention. Sitting home watching TV or talking with their same-sex friends on the phone, they are constantly complaining, 'Why don't I ever meet Mr or Ms Right?' Since surely you're not one of those many who must assume their dream lover will ooze through the telephone wires or come leaping out of the television screen, let's construct a game plan.

Before continuing to read, please list five outside activities you truly enjoy. By 'outside', I simply mean outside your *own* home. It obviously can be indoor, like handball, or even in a cave, like potholing. Going to lectures on a subject that interests you also counts. The only unifying factor of the five activities must be that each is something that you sincerely enjoy.

1 _____

2 _____

3 _____

4 _____

5 _____

Several months ago I was giving a talk to a singles group, and a woman came up to me after the seminar and said she was having a horrific time meeting any cultured men. I asked what her definition of cultured was.

'Oh, you know,' she said. 'Someone who likes the finer things in life – opera, art, classical music. A man who enjoys dining at fine restaurants, who knows his wines. All the guys I meet are jerks,' she complained.

I asked if she belonged to any opera societies.

'No,' she responded.

Had she gone to any art galleries lately?

'No.'

'What about classical concerts?'

'Well, no.'

'Have you ever sat alone at the bar of a fine restaurant or hotel and had a drink?'

'Uh, no.'

'What about some wine tastings?'

'I guess not.'

I hope her own series of negative responses gave her the obvious answer. You want to catch trout, you go to the stream. You want to trap bears, you go to the woods. And, if you want to find cultured man, you go to the places where cultured men go.

The problem I could foresee for this woman was, if she wanted a cultured man who liked some of the finer things in life as she described them, she'd have to start experiencing and appreciating them as well. If she didn't, after one date (provided she could wangle that), he would be bored realizing how little they had in common.

Therefore it doesn't pay in the long run to go somewhere to bag the kind of bear whose interests you won't share. Obviously, the only way to meet Mr or Ms Right is to go where the folks with the right stuff for you go.

Take a look at the list of your hobbies and interests you wrote while you were happy and unaware that you would have to sign the following clause. Once signed, you are committed to attending the event or going to a gathering of like-minded people once a week, and *alone* (preferably twice this if you are seriously seeking love in all the right places). When you go to an event alone, your chances of meeting someone new increase astronomically.

Women, this clause is especially important for you, since similarity of interests is high on the male wish list. It has been proven that a woman's interests are a hot relationship igniter for a man.[55] Men want women they can have fun with, can go to movies with, go hiking with, maybe (if he's lucky) even a woman who will go to baseball games with.

My PMR Phil loves the theatre. He's one of the few men I know who will buy a ticket and go sit in the audience all by himself. Being a healthy red-blooded male, instinctively his eyes (like a pilot's) scan the horizon of the audience. If he sees a woman who seems to be sitting by herself, unencumbered by a husband, boyfriend or girlfriend, he makes a mental note to catch up with her during the interval.

'Sure, I know I should go to events alone to meet people.' But, until you sign this clause, you're going to make excuses like being dog-tired after work and just wanting to put your legs up and sleep. Well, if you let those sleeping dogs lie, you'll never get any bites. Get up. Get out. Get loved.

**CLAUSE 33** ♂ ♀

## Weekly off-my-bottom promise

To meet the type of love I want, I will go to an event that interests me once a week – *alone*. (And that's if it's only a half-hearted hunt.) If I'm really serious about finding love, I'll go twice a week.

## Chapter Thirty Six

# If you want to date, you must initiate

Is it enough just to show up? To attend? To make the scene? To punch the clock? To breeze in? That's where most love-seekers stop thinking they've done their bit to find love. They go to an event with some of their same-sex friends and spend the whole evening shooting the breeze with their buddies. Oh, occasionally, they cast furtive little glances at interesting potential partners (trying to look like they didn't) and then expect the other party to take the initiative.

Do you remember how Johnnie Cochran won the OJ Simpson case? He probably did it with one line alone: If it doesn't fit, you must acquit.

Here's your line for posterity: *If you want to date, you must initiate*.

Once initiated, you must then perform a highly choreographed dance called the 'Dance of Intimacy'. This is a term coined by Dr Timothy Perper, a dauntless researcher who spent thousands of hours in his laboratory observing animals' mating rituals.

His laboratory? A singles bar.

His subjects? Human beings.

His observations? Who cast the initial glance, and how? Who made the initial move, and how? Who lost interest, and why? Who left together, and why?

In other words, Dr Perper took careful note of how they met, how they went off to date, and possibly eventually to mate. Over and over, he saw the same pattern.[56]

##  The dance of love

It is absolutely riveting to see videotapes of women giving signals to men, and men approaching women, to see how far they will get in the Dance of Intimacy. Sometimes they don't last one song. Other times, they become a couple for the evening and, who knows, perhaps a lifetime.

Once begun, the unspoken do's and don'ts in the Dance of Intimacy are so rigid that, if you accidentally step on your partner's toes, you are immediately eliminated. There are lots of folks who are great dancers. They know all the old dances – the cha-cha-cha, the Charleston, the conga, the clog dance, the hootchy-kootchy – but when it comes to the oldest dance of all, real hootchy-kootchy (more commonly known as courtship), they fall flat on their faces.

We will detail the steps which are as carefully choreographed as the most graceful *pas de deux*. A woman's smile is often the 'curtain cue' that begins the dance. Then, the actual body movement begins with our ballet prince taking one step – it must be adagio (slowly). The ballerina responds with a tiny 'pirouette' toward him. If she approves of his *placement*, she shows a bit of reverence, such as a smile. This encourages him to do a tiny *divertissement*, to make her smile again. If she does, he can proceed a bit more allegro (quickly). However, his timing must be impeccable. At this point the ballerina must perform some sort of *en avant* (forward motion), to encourage him. If not, the whole dance collapses and each is left to dance *pas seul* (alone)

Sound complicated? It is. But then, would we really want to return to some early native customs? For instance, the Crow

Indians of North America did have a more direct approach. The male pursued a female by crawling up to her tent at night, putting just his hand inside and, if he was lucky (in other words, if she positioned herself just right), his hand found her genitals. He would stimulate them and, if he did a good job, he could follow his hand into the tent and persuade her to have intercourse.

Today, I think most of us would prefer the whole-person approach to auditioning each other for love.

##  Inviting someone to the Dance of Intimacy

There isn't going to be any love dance if it is not advertised, or if no invitations are sent out. Therefore, the woman who wants the dance to begin must either advertise or send out a private invitation. The latter is far preferable, because you'll get a much better class of men responding.

Advertising (not recommended) is going to a bar wearing either a peek-a-bosom dress or one cut up to 'see' level. A private invitation (highly recommended) is smiling at the gentleman you would like to meet.

I'm sure it's happened to you dozens of times across the proverbial crowded room (or, more likely stuffing 50-pence pieces in the dryer at the laundrette, or shopping for socks at the shopping centre). You spot that special person and BLAM! He got you. Cupid's arrow is sticking right out of your heart. You feel unsteady on your feet. Your palms get wet and your throat gets dry. Your mind races for a way to make the approach. While trying to get up the courage, you are reduced to lurking around and furtively looking at the man or woman whom you know is destined to be your mate.

It happened to me just last week. There was an adorable man buying socks in the men's hosiery section of the department store. Did I do anything about it?

No. (I'm still kicking myself.)

Why not? Well, my thought process went something like this ... 'Uh, he looks busy. After all, he's making the monumental decision of which socks to buy. Bet his feet are cute too. Wish I could see his left hand, ring finger but it's inside the socks. Oh he's probably married anyway. Besides, what would I say? "Excuse me, but I think the brown socks would go best with your skin colouring?" '

I finally settle on a courageous and clever comment 'Excuse me, do you know where the men's shirts are?' But, before I take a step, he's purchased his socks and is on his way down the escalator. Bye bye love.

For the rest of the afternoon my fantasies run rampant. I see myself in soft focus, gracefully lifting the most luxurious pair of brown socks on the table, running them sensuously against my cheek and, looking up at him through my lashes, saying seductively. 'Ooooh, try these. They're soooo soft.'

He, immediately captivated by my beauty, my perception, my ... Oh, cut it out, Leil! It's just another possible love who got away. And all because I didn't initiate.

If you want to date, you *must* initiate.

> Thousands of variations on this scenario are happening at this moment all over the world – the mating game, aborted in its incipient stages. Love with a proper stranger seldom gets beyond the looking stage because we are all reduced to shy children when we spot a potential love. Women, in all the animal kingdom, we are the ones pre-ordained to initiate encounters with the male of our species. Go for it!

Women, do not be embarrassed about making this first move, i.e. smiling. Your smile is helping to populate the universe. In fact, the earth would have only one-third the number of mammals, marsupials, reptiles, birds, fish, primates *and* humans if it weren't for the female initiation of courtship.

Even though two-thirds of all liaisons are initiated by the woman, I promise you that less than 10 per cent of the men realize it. Women, you may be infuriated when the man who works in your office actually thinks one of your good ideas was his and tries to take credit for it. But the good side of this is that, in love, no matter how blatant your approach is, the male will also think the idea of meeting you was his, and will claim credit for it.

Sisters, take my word for it. You are many, many times more apt to meet the man of your dreams if you can master the simple smile. It's all a matter of attitude. If you happen to be at the prototypical meeting spa for men and women – a pub – don't think of it as smiling at a man in a bar. Rather, think of your smile as sending this message:

'With this smile, I hereby present my compliments to you, and will feel much pleasure if you should choose to grace me with your company at this moment on the stool next to mine. I regret that decorum dictates that after I have delivered this favour of my smile, my modesty decrees I must demur and not allow my eyes the pleasure of continuing to remain on your person. It is my sincere wish, however, that you have understood my intent, and that you will permit us the pleasures that I know that we shall both experience in each other's company.' Or, in other words, 'Hi, c'mon over!'

---

**CLAUSE 34 ♀**

## If I Want to Date, I *must* Initiate

I will definitely smile at EVERY man whose looks I like. And be secure in the knowledge that, if he then chooses to speak with me, he will think it was all his idea.

For women only

# Chapter Thirty Seven

# Don't think lines, think lyrics

Because I'm constantly on the road, I dine alone in hundreds of restaurants around the country. And, being a shameless people-watcher, I'd like to offer my own observations. They are, I discovered, thoroughly in accord with the sobering research conducted in bars by the dauntless researcher, Dr Timothy Perper. He received a two-year grant from the Harry Frank Guggenheim Foundation to hang around singles bars and observe. (Nice gig if you can get it!) Dr Perper postulates and proves that the response of the woman must mirror almost precisely in energy level the approach of the male, or else the meeting usually aborts before it ever has a chance to take off.[57] Regrettably, since I decided to undertake my own study, I had to pay for my own drinks (or let one of my unsuspecting subjects pick up the tab).

Often I would have to sit at the restaurant's bar while waiting for my table, and occasionally someone sitting on the next stool would make contact. Whenever the gentleman said 'Hello', 'Howdy' or 'How ya doin'?', and I responded with *equal* (not more, not less) warmth, things seemed to progress well. If my reciprocal greeting was less warm (as often was the case if his opening salvo was 'How ya doin'?') he would soon retreat. If my reciprocal greeting were much more enthusiastic than his, he was usually the one to stop talking. I realized, after reading Perper's research, that he was probably thinking, 'A pushy chick? Hmm, desperate, I better run.'

Now, if his opening salvo was not superfriendly and warm ... let us say his personality was more reserved and he opened with, say, 'Hello, er, would it disturb you if I sat here next to you?', it was best if my response matched his politeness. The enthusiasm and the melody of our voices are crucial if we want to fan the flames of any encounter.

For this gentleman, the best response would be an equally gracious, 'Not at all', or 'My pleasure'.

## Rule 1 for women

Match *precisely* the enthusiasm, warmth and energy of the gentleman's greeting.

Dr Perper also observed that, once two people have fallen into conversation, each subsequent step must be an advance of sorts, not a falling-back. Or, if a backward step is taken, it must be quickly compensated for by two in advance. In other words, there has to be a logical progression towards coupling. The steps can be verbal or non verbal.

For example: He comes up to the bar where She is sitting.

*He* (turning toward her, immediately asks, a tad nervously): Hi, mind if I buy you a drink?

*She* (a little startled because he sat down on the next stool and immediately asked her the question, turns just her head toward him and thinks, 'Hmm, I do like his looks but, if I let him buy me a drink, I'll have to talk to him the whole time I'm drinking it, and he might turn out to be a jerk. I'll stall it just a little and find out'): Oh, no thanks, I haven't finished this one.

*He* (thinking, 'She doesn't like me'): Oh, well (embarrassed smile). If you get thirsty, you know where to find me! (Gets off stool and walks away)

*She* (thinking, '*Wait a minute*, he seems kind of sweet. I wish he wouldn't go away')

But now it's too late.

What went wrong? Who was at fault?

They both were. He, because his sense of timing was off. He should have waited until she had seen him and observed a little of his behaviour before making her decide about the drink. She was at fault as well, because she did not meet his enthusiasm with equal energy.

Women, think music, not words. Remember the pitch pipe your music teacher used? When the gentleman first speaks to you, match *precisely* the amount of energy and enthusiasm in his voice. Too little, and you lose him. Too much, and you spook him.

---

**CLAUSE 35 ♀**

## Think Lyrical, Not Lyrics

I will listen very carefully to the first words a man I like says to me and then match *exactly* (not more, not less) his zeal.

For women only

# Chapter Thirty Eight

# Men 'pick her up', gentlemen 'make her acquaintance'

It is a delicate art these days to make a woman's acquaintance without the benefit of a third-party introduction. First let's talk about the rudiments; we'll graduate later to more advanced techniques.

Gents, whether you are a Beginner, Intermediate or Advanced, your approach begins with eye contact. (Note: Women do NOT like you to call them 'girls' – unless they are over 40, in which case it is a compliment.) Here is how to use those grenades placed above your nose to captivate the woman.

Positioning is extremely important. When you first spot the woman you would like to meet, jockey yourself into position so you are in her *direct line of sight*. Then, keep a gentle but fixed gaze on her. Soon she will feel your eyes and look up at you. At this point, you give a respectful small nod, accompanied by a smile.

She will, naturally, look away. It is part of the courtship ritual for women the world over. (Even female rabbits do it, and you know what they say about rabbits.) However, you can judge by the *way* she looks away whether she likes you or not. Here is the Aversion/Assertion eye-contact test which I have found to be 100 per cent accurate. She first averts her eyes, and, if she looks back within 45 seconds, she is asserting her interest in you.

It is a tad more complicated, however, because you must observe how she looks away. It is a true barometer to her feelings.

*She likes you if* ... she looks down towards the floor and away, sweeping the floor as it were with her eyes. The woman who looks away in this fashion probably welcomes your approach. Sometimes a tiny suppressed smile accompanies this downward look. All the better.

*She's not sure she likes you if* ... she looks away, horizontally on a flat plane, as in sweeping the walls. This means her internal jury on you is still out. We don't have the verdict yet.

*She probably doesn't like you if* ... she looks towards the ceiling and away (in essence rolling her eyes). If she does that, the following test is hardly worth the effort. Other possibilities are, of course, that she finds you attractive but she has a husband or boyfriend and is discouraging you.

Now, presuming she has looked away either horizontally or down, quickly check the second hand on your watch. You are measuring the time it takes her to look up again. If she looks at you within the next 45 seconds, she wants you to make the approach. This is as good as an engraved invitation reading, 'You are cordially invited to come talk to me.'

*Step One:* You give her a second smile.

*Step Two:* Now you walk towards her and stand close enough to talk, but not too close. Keep a respectful distance, yet one that permits easy conversing. The precise distance will vary depending on the room size, the crowd, the situation and certain other variables.

At this point, you can test her interest again by her body movements. Does she partially or fully turn away? (Bad and very bad signs.) Does she stay in the same position? (Jury is still out.) Does she turn partially or fully towards you? (Good and very good signs.)

*Step Three:* Now you say something to her which is neutral and courteous, but not personal. If it's a private party, you can ask how she knows the host. If it's at the theatre, you can ask her how she is enjoying the play. Try to ask what is called an 'open-ended' question – one that she cannot answer in 10 words or less.

You may remember that in Part I I mentioned that someone's first impression of you is 50 per cent visual, just what he or she sees; 30 per cent auditory, just the sound of your voice; and only 20 per cent your actual words.

For that reason, pay special attention to something that you are not used to being aware of – the sound of your voice. Women are far more sensitive to this than men. What kind of voices do they prefer? One study called 'Voice and Interpersonal Attraction' said that women prefer a voice that is 'bright, low timbre, good variety but not a large range of vocal pitch'. In other words, a voice that is expressive, but not all over the place.[58] Obviously, don't make your voice appreciably different from what it is. But think mellifluous, think warm, think confident. Think 'I like you. I'm interested in you' – as a person.

At this point, if your appearance passed muster, and if your sound is sufficiently lyrical and your words suitably mannerly – in other words, if you have completed the three steps correctly – all augurs well. Now is the time to begin conversing comfortably with her. Say the same things to her as you would to anyone you would like as a friend, again trying to avoid too many personal questions. During this conversation, you can keep your eyes open and judge some of her body language to monitor how you're doing.

**How to know the answer to 'How do you like me so far?'**

Gentlemen, reading body language is not rocket science: for many men, it's far more difficult to grasp than rocket science. Women seem to be naturals at it, so – for men only – I present a basic body-language primer.

A woman gives off hundreds of sex signals every minute you are talking with her. When you learn to interpret some of the subconscious movements in the following, you will have a much more accurate answer to the question you always ask yourself when you find youself talking to attractive women: 'How am I doing?'

A quick review of the three steps in meeting a lady ...

Step One: Smile at her.

Step Two: Position yourself in her line of sight and keep a gentle gaze on her. Gauge her interest from the 'Aversion/Assertion' test. Depending on your score, move within speaking range. Gauge her interest from her movements (see Appendix D).

Step Three: Depending on your score, begin casual conversing, paying special attention to the sound of your voice.

**CLAUSE 36 ♂**

### Step Strategy Clause

Whenever I want to meet a woman I haven't been introduced to, I will follow the three-step strategy outlined above and pay special attention to the sound of my voice.

For men only

# Chapter Thirty Nine

# The failure fallback plan

Now, suppose you make the approach and, alas, he or she rejects you. To take the stinger out of this zinger, gentlemen and ladies, I recommend that you have a few foxy little face-savers in your pocket. You will find the approach much easier if you have a quick and cool complimentary comment to cover yourself in the unlikely event that he or she rebuffs you.

For example, if she says, 'Sorry, I have a boyfriend', you respond with 'He's a lucky man.'

She says, 'I'm not in the mood to talk now.' You respond with, 'That's my great loss.'

He makes it evident that he doesn't welcome your approach. You say, 'Please consider it a compliment.'

She turns away from you. You respond by saying nicely, 'Whoops, I forgot. Let me go take off my invisible cloak and I'll return when you can see me.'

She laughs in your face. You tell her, 'You have a beautiful laugh.'

She moans. You respond by saying nicely, 'I only make the most beautiful women ill.'

When you are armed with a compliment or a respectfully funny line, you'll have more courage to make the move on a proper stranger. A really foxy face-saver, skilfully delivered, often turns an early 'No' into an eventual 'Yes'.

**CLAUSE 37 ♂**

## Foxy Face-Saver

I will prepare a variety of compliments and funny comebacks to cover the awkward moment in case she rejects my advance.
For men only

# Chapter Forty

# Creative courting

Of course, when the competition is rougher, the competitors get tougher and you need to be a bit more creative in your technique. Let me tell you about one of the most impressive feats of winning the fairest damsel's heart I've witnessed. Then we'll discuss the underlying principle and how you can use it.

You don't have to be James Bond to pull this one off. All you need is imagination and an understanding of beautiful and ambitious women's hot buttons.

My friend Phil and I were at a party some years ago which, from the looks of it, was definitely stacked against him in the 'finding love' department. He didn't know anyone there because most of us were members of the same health club; the ratio of men to women was two to one; and the men who 'were' there looked like they'd just stepped off the pages of *Men's Health* magazine. Phil to this day has no idea what the *inside* of a health club looks like. He's more of an *Yachting Weekly* kinda guy than a *Men's Health* reader.

I could tell that Phil was bored with the current discussion. Five or six people in our part of the room were passionately sharing their favourite recipes using wheatgerm, soya beans and buckwheat flour. (Phil's favourite food is pork chops and mashed potatoes with lots of butter.) He turned a little green when a man with Arnie's biceps and a *Baywatch* beach-boy's abs started bragging about his daily brewer's yeast and acidophilus milkshake.

Just then the doorbell rang. The host of the party opened the door and there stood ... nothing short of a goddess, who was gracing the earth with her presence. She was 175 cm tall, with blindingly shiny blonde hair to her waist, and big blue eyes with lashes so long they'd fan flies away.

All heads turned. No highway crash ever rivalled the amount of overt gawping that swept around the party. The electricity she generated was almost lethal, as the men's eyes widened in excitement and the women's narrowed into green slits of jealousy.

Much to the delight of the males and the dismay of the females in our group, the host brought Alexis to introduce to us first. She joined in and the conversation gradually drifted from nutrients, protein and carbs to what all the men were interested in – Alexis. Where was she from? How long had she been living in New York? What did she do? And, of course, there were many comments aimed at finding out if she had a steady boyfriend, so the men could discover if they should start getting their hopes up. So far, Phil had not said a word.

Alexis's answers came smilingly and easily, with that California girl charm. Lexi, her nickname, was from San Clemente, California, and she had been living there for about five years now with a girlfriend in Greenwich Village. She was an actress and had performed in a number of small theatres, the largest being The Public Theatre in New York. She had got a role there soon after she came to New York and, yes, between the lines, she was available.

Now, gentlemen, given this information, what would you have done to stand out and capture Lady Lexi's interest? Here's a hint. You have your laptop in your briefcase in the closet.

You may have guessed it. Phil, in full realization that the cards were stacked against him, excused himself saying that he had to make a phone call. When he came back 15 minutes later, nature was taking its inevitable course. Most of the women had drifted away and the throng of men around Alexis was growing.

Phil patiently awaited his chance. Instead of pouncing, he waited for a lull in the conversation and then casually asked Alexis, 'Incidentally, how was it working with Joe Papp?'

Alexis's head swung around, noticing Phil for the first time. 'Uh, you knew Joe Papp?' she asked.

'No,' Phil replied honestly, 'but I know people who have worked with him and I've heard he's, well, not terribly insightful about the theatrical craft. A lot of performers really didn't like him. But, of course he is unquestionably one of the most dynamic forces in American theatre in the last fifty years. What do you say?'

'Oh, yes,' Alexis said cooingly. Phil's insights had interested Alexis. He gradually let the discussion flow naturally from Papp's raging-bull personality to wondering what Al Pacino, Meryl Streep, Kevin Kline and Denzel Washington – all of whom had worked with Papp – would say about him.

Soon Phil and Alexis had jockeyed themselves in side-by-side position. The other men, not getting a word in, soon began to smell defeat and started drifting away. Alexis and Phil then took a walk over to the bar together to refill their drinks. Before the end of the evening, Phil had a date with Alexis to take her to the theatre the following week.

Now, do you think it was just accidental that Phil knew all about Papp? Of course not. He knew nothing about Papp, but the WEB knows everything. That 'phone call' Phil had to make was to log on and run a quick search on 'The Public Theatre' and 'Joe Papp'. Phil found everything he needed in one book review on *Amazon.com*. Although Phil had enjoyed theatre, I don't even think Phil knew the words 'theatrical craft' before that night, when he let them roll so comfortably off his tongue into Alexis's beautiful lap.

And, of course, before his date with Lexi, Phil went online again and learned all about the play they would be seeing –

details about every cast member, the gossip on the problems the show faced. He started practising words and phrases on me I'd never heard him use before: 'fringe theater', 'Great White Way', 'improv', 'showcase', 'equity waiver', 'straw hat', 'born in a trunk'. He even said 'Break a leg!' to me as I was going off to a speech that week.

Well, Phil certainly did not lack material to engross fair lady at dinner after the show. Obviously it worked. He and Alexis dated for about six months, until Alexis broke up with him because she got a role in a grade B sitcom in California. The one thing Phil forgot to research was what to do when your rival isn't a *Baywatch* boy but a role, on a wannabe *Baywatch* show.

> You've heard the phrase, 'I can't go. I haven't a thing to wear.' It should be, 'I can't go, I haven't a thing to say.' Now you can nibble every morsel of information on any subject in the world right off the Web, so your tongue will be well adorned for every occasion.

**CLAUSE 38** ♂ ♀

## Hunt Down Hot Buttons

I won't leave love to chance. Whenever I know who I want to make a hit with, I'll do my homework beforehand and click on some information so that I am in an advantageous position.

# Chapter Forty One

# Shhh, he's annoyed!

The only time my PMR Phil was truly annoyed with me was a few days after Lexi had broken up with him. The previous evening, he had been moping around and I had resisted saying anything. I figured he'd feel much better after a good night's sleep.

Now it was morning and Phil was at the refrigerator getting his usual breakfast: some Rice Krispies and a glass of orange juice. I asked him what was wrong.

'Oh, nothing,' he replied, taking the milk and orange juice cartons out of the fridge. I knew precisely what was bothering him and figured it would be helpful to get it off his chest and talk to a friend about Lexi.

'Phil, c'mon. I can tell there's something.'

'Leil. I said nothing's bothering me,' he said as he poured the orange juice over his cereal. I pretended not to notice until Phil started eating the soggy Rice Krispies with orange juice.

When he spun around to the sink to spit out the orange juice and Rice Soggies, I couldn't help but smile. But Phil wasn't finding anything funny that morning.

'What's bothering me,' he shouted, for the first time in the eight years he'd been my roommate, 'is your constantly asking me what bothers me.' Constantly? Constantly? I'd only asked him twice.

But, as I learned, for a male that's two times too many. Phil then disappeared into his bedroom with a fresh bowl of Rice Krispies in one hand and the whole milk carton in the other.

> 'Whew,' I thought. 'I can't believe I did that.' I'd read all the good books on gender differences. But what a dummy! I hadn't really drilled it into my head that men hate to be asked what's wrong. They like to think they have everything under control and that nothing shows.

I vowed at that moment that the only thing I would ever do around an upset male is let him know I'm there for him if he wants to talk. I'll never make the common mistake of thinking he's just like us women and will feel better getting a problem off his chest.

Sisters, in the hope that *you* won't either, here is a clause for you to sign.

**CLAUSE 39 ♀**

## Let Him Sulk in Silence

I will never again press a male at home or at work to tell me what's bothering him. If he wants to be a silent, testy, petulant, crabby acerbic old grouch, I'll let him enjoy wallowing in it. The most I'll say is, I'm here if there's anything you'd like to talk about. I'll say it ONCE, and then drop it.

For women only

Now, gentlemen, please do the women of the world a favour. If something is bothering you, try not to be that stereotypical silent, testy, petulant, crabby acerbic old grouch. Don't stonewall the problem. Go to your wife. Go to your girlfriend. Go to your female business colleague. Women *appreciate your seeking their counsel or even just sharing a problem with them* (*except* problems with another woman!).

Why is this difficult for guys? Because, a study found, most men, when they have a problem, either feel embarrassed about it or they kid themselves that the problem is controllable.[59] The few who do seek help are more apt to go to a male friend.

On the surface, going to your *amigo*, your *compadre*, your good ol' buddy, sounds like good advice. But, unfortunately, it's been proven that another male is the *worst* person to ask for advice. Why?

Because good ol' buddy is probably as ill equipped as you to give or receive emotional support. After all, he suffers an equal handicap in this department – he's been brought up male too. He never learned the necessary skills which are almost second nature to women.[60] Little girls in nursery school encircle one of their classmates who is crying and try to dry her tears. Little boys respectfully ignore one of their own and let the other little boy bawl his head off.

Additionally, your buddy might not take your problem seriously, because belittling it preserves your dignity – and that's a higher priority in his mind than actually solving your problem.

Fellas, I know it's hard for you to believe, but you'll gain sensitivity points in a woman's eyes when you share. Especially if you present your problem confidently in a 'Let me run something past you and get your input' kind of attitude. How often? Once a week is enough, given a stiff upper lip or two.

Actually, *not* going to a woman when something is in trouble can mar the relationship. A study called 'Effects of Gender Role Expectations on the Social Support Process' said that 'Males may develop indirect ways of revealing inner hurts and struggles ... in order to escape rejection and loss of self-esteem.'[61] That means you may do some really scatterbrain, off-the-wall screwball things in an attempt to suppress the problem. You may think you're being brave. But women will just think you're stubborn. So, please, talk it out with us. (Once in a while, that is.)

**CLAUSE 40 ♂**

## No More Troubled Clam

When something is troubling me, I'll talk it out with my wife, my girlfriend or even a PFF. I will remember that, unlike us guys, women *love* that kind of stuff. They call it 'deep communication'. For men only

# Chapter Forty Two

# Give me a strong shoulder and a big ear

Now, gentlemen, a warning. If *she* is upset about something, don't assume that, like one of the guys, she wants to be given her space. That's the *last* thing she wants. She yearns for a strong shoulder and a big listening ear – both attached to you. Whether she's the woman who shares your office or shares your pillow, she welcomes your asking her what's wrong.

For women, seeking help is absolutely not a loss of self-esteem. Just the opposite. 'Because females are "expected" to need help in times of stress, men who truly understand women give it to them. They know she both wants and appreciates it.' [62]

**CLAUSE 41 ♂**

## What's Wrong, Lambchop?

Conversely, if a woman friend, close colleague or loved one seems upset, I *will* ask her about it. In fact, she expects me to! If I don't, she may think I'm a cad.
For men only

# Chapter Forty Three

# Go figure!

Now, sisters, it gets a little confusing in the choosing of what to do here because, if he does ask you what's wrong, and you tell him, and he thinks you could have handled it by yourself, there goes his sympathy.

Let me start at the beginning. We were brought up in an atmosphere of nurturing. We played with dolls and gave our little pussy cats nice milk in a baby bottle. Then, when the cat didn't like a baby-bottle teat forced down its throat, and scratched us to signal its displeasure, we could sit on Daddy's lap and bawl our heads off. That's what the researchers call 'emotional expression'. By the very fact of being female, we were permitted.

Our brother, on the other hand, when he messed around with the cat and got scratched, was told he was responsible for his own dumb actions. And, furthermore, Dad said that 'big boys don't cry'.

'So why,' we women ask, 'when we are adults, doesn't our man act sympathetic like Daddy did? Why, just because he feels we could have handled it, does he get angry? It's not fair!' (What we really want to say is, 'Why can't you be more like my Daddy?' but we don't dare.)

One Saturday morning several Aprils ago, I had just finished reading a popular book on male–female communications. At the time I was crazy about a boy named Bill, and one of my New Year's resolutions was to get him equally as crazy about me. The book told how much it pleases Martians (men) to help Venutians (women). Being needed reinforces the Martian's masculinity and can sometimes be just the spark needed to ignite a spot of love. He feels like he's slaying a dragon for his lady. I pictured Bill dressed in full armour, breastplate tight, steel visor down, lance in hand charging forth to help the poor damsel (me, of course) in distress.

Well, I was in no distress at the time. In fact I'd never felt better. Things were great with my work. I'd been able to keep up with my exercises and was feeling good about my body. My love life left a bit to be desired, but I couldn't complain to him about that because I was hoping he'd play a big role there. So I 'dug deep down to the very bottom of my soul', as they sing in *A Chorus Line*, and tried to come up with a problem.

Alas, I couldn't find anything that I needed some help with. So, wily female that I was, I invented a problem. That morning I had just finished reconciling my bank statement on a computer program called Quicken and, as usual, it came out perfectly. 'But,' I figured, 'since Bill considers himself financially savvy, this is where he can really shine.' I opened up Quicken and transposed the amounts on a couple of cleared cheques and deleted the interest and finance charges for that month. Then I closed it down again, and of course it didn't tally with the bank statement. Like cards in a poker game, I then strewed my cancelled cheques out on the table, ruffled the neatly folded statement and laid it on the top as the centerpiece representing my frustration. Then I put on an extra coat of mascara and awaited my modern-day Lancelot.

When I heard Bill's knock at the door, I gave one last sweep of my arm across the table of cancelled checks to put the finishing touch on their random disarray, and took a peek in the mirror to perfect my best sweet-damsel-in-distress expression.

'Leil, what's wrong?' were his first words when he saw my dismayed expression. (So far, so good.)

'Oh, Bill-ee. I'm just having a terrible time with my tax return. Do you suppose you could answer just a couple of teensy questions for me?'

He smiled. (Hooray, it was working.)

I proceeded to show him how I'd entered all the income here, all the cheques there, and even the cash withdrawals. He took one look at it and said, 'Well, for starters, you've neglected to add the interest or subtract the service charges.'

'Hmm,' I remember thinking. He doesn't sound quite as protective and happy as I was led to believe he would be. Well, maybe he was just hiding his deep-rooted satisfaction.

And then, 'Jeez Leil, you transposed numbers in the amount column on two cheques! How could you have done that?' He sounded agitated. 'Do you suffer from dyslexia?'

Then he stood up and, pointing to the columns said, 'Here fix those and I'm sure it'll come out right. I'm going to go down and wait in the car. Come out when youre ready.'

'Bill! Bill!' But he was already gone in a mini-huff. 'Thanks for figuring that out for me,' I called out after him.

'If you'd just be more careful, things like that wouldn't happen,' he scowled back.

Now I was seething. 'You big doof, I wanted to say. Here I go to all the trouble to fabricate a situation where you can play the role of hero, and you get ticked off at me.' I definitely felt he was the guilty party for being angry.

## ❁ You be the judge

If the case went to trial, Bill's lawyer would say, 'The jury – as you can see from the evidence presented here today, Ms Lowndes' crime against my client was premeditated, and she had ulterior motives. Her actions involved lying, tampering with records and attempting to cover it up. My client's anger is completely justified.'

My attorney's summation to the jury would be: 'Ladies and gentlemen of the jury – my esteemed colleague has, indeed, outlined some of the broad strokes in this case. But remember, this is NOT a case about Ms Lowndes' creation of a falsehood. His client didn't even *know* at the time of his anger that Leil had fabricated the story. The only question before the court today is: Knowing what we do today about gender differences, was Bill's fury at her making the mistake really justified?'

Here's where you come in. You have been flown in as expert witness. As a specialist in gender differences, you know how males and females typically react in certain situations.

After being sworn in, under oath, you affirm that men indeed do generally like to assist a woman they care for with a problem they can solve. You further affirm that Bill's anger is the issue here.

What testimony could you, as a leading expert in the difference between 'malethink' and 'femalethink', give to prove that Bill's anger was justifiable? Or was it? As you tell, under oath, a little-known difference between men and women, you could hear a pin drop in the courtroom. The jury is transfixed.

They are dismissed to decide the case. When they return, the foreman says, 'Guilty, your honour. In fact, you should lock up Leil and throw away the key.'

What testimony could you have given about men and women to bring in this unanimous decision? You told them that Leil overlooked a crucial element in the male psyche. As expert witness, you testify that, given his gender conditioning, he had every right to get hot under the collar for being asked to help on a problem *that the woman could obviously solve herself*.

Those are the key words – 'that the woman could obviously solve herself'. A man does not tend to be angry when his aid is sought on a genuinely tough problem, or one that involves a quality that he obviously excelled in, such as physical strength. *The Journal of Personality* reports that men, unlike women, neither expect – nor give – support to anyone who has made an *avoidable* mistake. (Of course, they don't want you to mention it when *they're* the ones who have committed the blooper. But they don't expect sympathy either.)

As expert witness, you explain to the jury. 'Nobody told Bill *he* was cute when he was a little boy crying because he skinned his knee. From aged 4 up, nobody kissed *his* boobie and put a plaster on it. He had to take it like a man. Little girls, on the other hand, are coddled and cuddled. Mummy dries her little tears and kisses them away.'

Sisters, that does not mean you will never again seek a male's assistance with a problem. If the crisis is a *bona fide* one, he will be pleased and honoured you put your trust in him. Mine eyes have seen the coming of countless concealed male smiles when asked to unscrew the cap from a bottle of old nail polish, or when their help is sought on showing me the way to get somewhere from a map. Why? Because they know they are superior in physical strength or map-reading.

*But*, take him a problem you could have solved yourself and you have a very different ending. Women, suppose you misplaced the car keys; you forgot to lock the garage door, or you wore pretty little shoes on your tootsies to go out, and now you don't want to walk from the restaurant to the movie because your feet hurt – BIG DEAL! (I've done them all.) But, unfortunately, he *does* make a big deal out of it.

'How could you have lost the keys; they were right here?'

'You forgot to lock the garage door? Do you know how much my new racing bike in there cost?'

'I've told you a hundred times – wear sensible shoes!'

> Sisters, it may not be conscious, but he probably expects you to take your punishment like a man, too. Don't be upset. Just let him lecture and take it calmly. Affirm that you will change your ways, and then don't hang on to it. Let it slip out of your grasp like a bar of soap. If you don't, he just might let you slip through his fingers.

**CLAUSE 42 ♀**

## Let Him Lecture

I will not be upset when a male chides me for some meaning-less little blooper. It's not his fault. He can't help it. It comes from his gender conditioning as a kid.[63] I'll really listen and then I'll say something like, 'You're right. I'll be more careful in the future.' Then we'll both forget about it.

For women only

Sometimes, instead of lecturing, men will just stand there sto-ically while you scramble frantically for your keys. ('Why isn't he helping me find them?' you're grumbling under your breath. You're assuming he's thinking, 'This brainless twit, she loses everything.' Not true. More likely his mind is many miles away on yesterday's football game.)

Or he'll let you go out in the middle of the night in your bathrobe to lock the garage door you left unlocked. Or he'll let you walk in your bare stockings five blocks from the restaurant to get the car with him because you wore uncomfortable shoes.

You're thinking, 'What a brute! Couldn't he, just for once, go and lock the garage door even though it's my fault? Couldn't he, for once, be gallant and give my poor sore tootsies a rest by getting the car himself and then coming to pick me up?'

Unfortunately, males sincerely believe it's better for you to 'learn your lesson' like he was forced to do as a kid. I hope I don't sound like I'm betraying my sex when I say, 'Go ahead. Take your punishment "like a man".' You are learning a lesson, but not in leaving garage doors unlocked or wearing comfort-able shoes. *You're learning a lesson on how to get along with the man in your life and make him love you all the more!*

# Chapter Forty Four

# How would you handle this, dear?

Now, gentlemen, when it comes to asking advice, you too must do your bit to bring harmony and love to the land of male–female relationships. Some of the recent literature on the subject has been too 'black and white'. While it is true that men want to feel needed and women want to be cared for, there is a crossover. A part of the male cries out, 'I want to be cared for', and a part of the female yearns to be needed.

Without prejudice, the world now accepts as fact that women are more sensitive than men when it comes to recognizing the subtleties in relationships. Don't be embarrassed, fellas. They've got a few more years of it under their belts than you. Look at any nursery-school class. The boys are spread out all over the room with Lego bricks, alphabet blocks, beanie bags and toy trucks. The little girls are clustered in groups drawing with crayons *together*, moulding clay *together*, playing with dolls *together*, plaiting *each other's* hair and drying *each other's* tears. If a disagreement arises, they prefer to find a compromise than battle it out.

A study reported in the journal, *Sex Roles*, said that 'Boys engage in more aggressive and rough and tumble play as well as more functional, solitary dramatic and exploratory play ... whereas girls produce more parallel and constructive play as well as more peer conversations.'[64]

So, putting these two facts together – women wanting to feel needed too, and being proven 'better' at some relationship issues, what does that suggest to you gentlemen?

If you guessed 'ask her advice on certain relationship issues', you are right.

## ❋ It's not just for schmoozing her

Asking a woman's counsel is not just a charade to please her. You can receive some valuable advice and come across as a compassionate leader at the same time. Let's say you are an upper-middle-management man at a large company and you must fire someone who reports to you. Not a pleasant task. However, I guarantee that one of your female colleagues will have insights that can make the situation less distasteful for you and the poor chap (or chapess) you have to let go.

At the women's leadership conference I mentioned earlier (*see page 50*), there was one seminar on hiring and firing. Practically every participant had, in fact, been faced with the 'heartbreaking' task of having to let someone go.

Twenty people attended – 15 women, the moderator and 4 men. We went around the room, each narrating how we had handled firing an employee.

Each of the women in the group had a sensitive suggestion, such as taking the employee to lunch, letting the employee use the office for another couple of weeks as a job-hunting base, and even offering to make calls on the employee's behalf for another position. One woman, who had to let a good employee go due to drastic budget cuts, gave a small party for her and let her save face by telling everyone she was resigning for a better opportunity.

The four men? To a man, each did it with a sharp, clean cut on a Friday afternoon. Surprise announcement: 'Charlie, old buddy, I hate to do this to you but I have to fire you because [the reason]. And it's best you have your things out of here before Monday morning.' I could tell from icy expressions on the women's faces that they were feeling not terribly warm towards the men that day.

Gentlemen, you win a woman's respect or love when you handle a situation effectively, but with heart. If these men had consulted with just one of their female colleagues before firing Charlie, they could have picked up a few ideas on how to discharge him without blasting him.

In social relationships as well, women constantly have their antennae turned to pick up keys to your character, your beliefs, your values, your ways of looking at the world. Right from the start, a woman is like an intrepid Sherlock Holmes, instinctively examining everything you say under a microscope. If she starts to consider you as a possible partner, she pulls out her microscope, dons her lab coat and takes an even more thorough look.

If you're ever puzzling over how to handle a touchy situation that involves people's feelings or egos, 'handling it like a man' could come across as 'handling it like a crude brute'.

> The best way to avoid her 'Crude Dude' designation, and win her heart at the same time? Go to her for advice with the full recognition that, when the good Lord assembled women, they were given a few extra sensitivity bits.

CLAUSE 43 ♂

## Seek Her Social Assistance

Whenever I face a 'people problem', I will seek the assistance of the brightest woman in my office, or my life. Not only will it help my relationship with her, but I may even get a good workable idea!

For men only

# Chapter Forty Five

# I just want you to be happy!

Women, before leaving the lab, we should take yet another peek through the microscope at the neurons circulating in the male brain.

It is a well-known fact, yet it has failed to make its way into the vortex of the female brain – men, God bless them, really do feel responsible for our happiness.

If we complain about something, a man feels responsible. No matter how much we protest and say, 'Oh that's silly', or 'Love, it's not your fault', he feels he is to blame. When you complain that the restaurant wasn't up to scratch, he feels like the chef, the waiter and waiter's assistant all wrapped up in the body of one big failure – him. You didn't like the movie? Suddenly he feels like he's the director, the actors, the lighting engineer, the sound engineer and costume designer all rolled into one big failure – him.

I once went to a terrible movie with a wonderful man. We hit it off immediately, or so I thought. I actually had a fleeting fantasy of sitting by the fireplace with him decades hence with dogs at our feet and children playfully pulling at my knitting and punching at his newspaper.

As we drove to the restaurant for dinner after the show, I shared my cinematic insights with him – worthy, I thought, of a member of the Academy. The film was set in Elizabethan times and my keen eye had actually picked out a wristwatch peeking out from the folds of a footman's sleeve. (He would then realize my attention to detail.) I commented on the gaudiness of the castle. (He would, of course, then recognize my design talent for our future home together.)

When we arrived at the restaurant, I was thrilled to discover he was a fellow wine lover. As I peeked over his shoulder at the wine list, I let him know that I knew it was second-rate, lest he think I was not a connoisseur of Bacchus' choice beverage. As we sipped our red wine from the flute-shaped glasses, I urbanely bemoaned the absence of round goblets. (He would, of course, then realize what a superb hostess I would be.)

Our dinner was mediocre, the service worse. In an effort to let him know how discriminating I was, I let him know. 'But who cares?' I exclaimed, batting my mascara-laden lashes. 'The company is sublime.'

It may have been a no-star film and a one-star restaurant, but it definitely was, in my opinion, a five-star date. We arrived on my doorstep and I tarried momentarily lest he want to take me in his arms and declare his everlasting love. He let the moment pass, and I, smiling at his desire to impress me with his gentlemanly nature, squeezed his hand in understanding, and whispered, 'Goodnight'.

As I drifted off into happy dreamland, I half expected the phone to ring. It would be him, telling me what a marvellous time he'd had and asking when he could see me again. And again. And again.

The phone didn't ring that night, nor the next, nor the next. He never called me again. *How was I to know he'd feel like the \*@!&^$ director of the movie, the chef of the restaurant AND the wine waiter?* We didn't have all the studies and popular books on gender differences in those days. And I wasn't smart enough to figure out by myself that, even if a male agrees with your critiques, he'll take your disappointment personally.

---

**CLAUSE 44 ♀**

## 'You Make Me Sooo Happy'

I will remember that *whatever* emotion I express, men will feel responsible – and if he can't fix it, he feels like a failure. Therefore, I will think twice, no thrice, before ever, ever, ever complaining around a man. I'll save that for my girlfriends, who will understand we're just hanging out a little disapproval to let it dry.

For women only

---

Gentlemen, what should you do in the case of a rotten movie and a rancid meal at the location of your choice? Well, first of all, try to rid yourself of those decades of gender conditioning that make you feel responsible. Realize that, nine times out of ten, contrary to everything you've ever been taught, she does NOT blame you. Same, nine times out of ten she accepted the date because she wanted to be with *you*, not because she wanted to see one of the worst ten movies of the year followed by a trailer for a snuff film. Then try the octopus tartare at the new restaurant with the lousy wine list. Additionally, if she's savvy about gender stereotypes, she'll be worried that you may feel

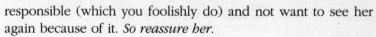

responsible (which you foolishly do) and not want to see her again because of it. *So reassure her.*

Of course she'd be happier if the flick had been a block-buster and the restaurant not so lacklustre, but that's minor.

> *You* are what matters most. Laugh off the movie and the dinner that made you gag. Tell her you'll let her pick the next movie and restaurant the two of you go to. (The subtext of that one is 'There WILL be a next time.' And that, gentlemen, is something a woman who likes you *always* wonders about.)

Then – now, here's the important part – dig down deep into your soul, and try to come up with a creative compliment ... and the more poetic, the better. Women *love* words.

**CLAUSE 45** ♂

## SHE'S the Ball Game, Not the Ball Game

I will remember that, for a woman, our relating to each other is the main event – not the movie or the meal. No matter how rotten the activity was, *I will give HER rave reviews.* For example, after a bad movie, I'll say something like, 'I'm sorry the movie was such a bummer, but being with you made it beautiful.' (Yes, women love a poetic soul!)

For men only

## Chapter Forty Six

# Hyperbole as aphrodisiac

Gentlemen, the exaggerated and poetic compliment is not just for the joy of the receiver. Men who have mastered the artform are irresistible to women. Why is it you think that Italian men are considered so sexy? Is it their tall, dark and handsome looks? First of all, on average, Italian men are shorter than English men. Dark? Most are, but dark is not the preferred colouring. Handsome? No more or less handsome than English men.

Is it because they are better in bed? Not according to one of my female friends, who has enjoyed both foreign and domestic hanky-panky.

Then why is it that women swoon over Italian men?

I found out in an unfortunate way. All of the waiters on the ship where I was cruise director were Italian. My dinner table was a large one near the centre of the dining room, and I always made a point of inviting single people, travelling alone, to join me for meals.

Each week on the first night of the cruise, the waiter would pretend almost to drop his tray because he was so struck by the beauty of one of the single women at my table.

'Ohh, Signorina. And for you? What may I bring you this evening? I am honoured to serve such a beautiful woman.' Usually that's all it took. My female passenger would be a goner. In the entire season, only one woman saw through it: 'Oh, gimme a break,' she moaned. So, the next night, the waiter moved on to another of my passengers. The waiter always followed up his discovery act with a question for me. 'Signora Leil, where did find such a *bellissima donna* on this ship?' (I was tempted to say, 'Cut the crap. You know you choose one every cruise.') He would make it quite clear by his allusion to her that if she didn't understand that '*bellissima donna*' meant 'beautiful woman' by the beginning of the meal, she sure would by the end. Everything she ordered, he'd say '*Benissimo*', which means 'excellent choice'. Often the waiter and his assistant would fall into a mock scuffle on who was going to refill *bellissima donna*'s water glass. If she happened to drop a napkin or a fork, the waiter would race to pick it up and stay on his knees beside her to talk.

All in all, it was pretty disgusting ... but boy, did it work! I shudder to think how many *bellissima donnas* disembarked at the end of the cruise with torn nighties in their suitcases and sated smiles on their faces. They'd be dreaming of their future life in Italy with Giancarlo, Franco, Roberto, Marco or Umberto.

The only problem was that Giancarlo, Franco, Roberto, Marco or Umberto never called them again because they'd be pursuing another *bellissima donna* at my table the following week. And have you ever tried to ask for a Giancarlo, Franco, Roberto, Marco or Umberto on the phone in a ship that had several hundred waiters all named Giancarlo, Franco, Roberto, Marco or Umberto?

More than once, when disembarking, I saw two *bellissima donnas* (who had been my passengers on different cruises) waiting on the dock for the same lover ... and a Giancarlo, Franco, Roberto, Marco or Umberto hastily ducking through the crowd to avoid them.

Sad, but true. But how can we take this sad tale, gentlemen, and make it a happy one? Very simple. Learn how to compliment your lady love. Chances are you are better-looking than most of the dining-room Lotharios. You are probably brighter and better educated. And you're sure to be more ethical when it comes to women. But, as a nationality, you have not learned an important lesson. A little poetry in your words of love goes a long way. Rent the Italian movie *Il Postino*. Read a women's romance novel. Read the English poets ...

'How do I love thee? Let me count the ways ...'

'My love is like a red red rose ...'

'Come live with me and be my love, and we will all the pleasures prove ...'

You get the idea. Whether you are telling your new girl-friend she is beautiful, or your wife of fifty years that you love her, choose words that could be said in a poem or set to music. Express your feelings in a lyrical way. No matter how clumsy the result, she will love you for your attempt.

**CLAUSE 46** ♂

## My Lyrical Love

I will tell my girlfriend or wife of her beauty, or my love for her – in a lyrical way – at least once a day.
For men only

# Chapter Forty Seven

# Understanding my clam

After watching the Channel 2 news the other evening, there was a programme I wanted to see on cable 41. Being in no rush, I decided on a leisurely surf all the way up, channel by channel. (A great excuse to get a quick peek at all those candy for the brain shows that nobody ever admits to watching, like *Baywatch* reruns.) When I reached Channel 27, I spotted Robert Mitchum, happily snuggled into an armchair reading a magazine, much to the chagrin of a pouting Jane Russell. Being a fan of both late greats, I stopped surfing just long enough to get the gist of the show. Jane was suffering yesteryear's ADD (Attention Deficit Disorder). Her character was not getting enough of it from husband Robert. The 1951 movie was called *His Kind of Woman*, and it was, indeed, some kind of awful.

Continuing my leisurely finger voyage, I stopped briefly on a *All in the Family* rerun. Edith Bunker was employing *her* version of feminine wiles to get husband Archie's attention as he sat silently transfixed by the 'goggle box'. Finally, Edith Bunker blurted out accusatorily, much to Archie's surprise, 'You never talk to me any more.' That brought a full can of laughter and applause from the audience. (Such reactions result when we recognize the hilarious truths in our own lives.)

Next in my channel surf, came an *I Love Lucy* rerun. Lucille Ball was whining to on-and-off screen husband Desi Arnaz that they didn't communicate. She accused him of talking to everyone except her.

'But Loosi. I tell you everything that's on my mind.' Laughter and applause. (*Refrain*: Such reactions result when we recognize the hilarious truths in our own lives.) As the episode continued, it became evident that he did tell her everything that he considered important. It's just that, like most males, he didn't consider his every passing thought important enough to impart. Whereas Lucy, like most women, would have been quite content drifting along on her man's stream of consciousness – regardless of whether the stream ended up any place he thought important.

I began to pick up a recurring theme and I remembered the countless times I've been in the company of a male – whether he was a date at dinner, a PMR at a party or a male colleague just walking down the street. I always felt we had to make conversation, because if he and I weren't talking I felt something was wrong. Unless we were sharing ideas, I felt we weren't being compatible.

The Jane Russell character felt the same, Archie Bunker's wife felt the same and Lucy Arnaz felt the same. I am sure we are not the only four women in the world who want more communication from the men in our life.

The next day, that was proven to me in a small upstate town where I went for a manicure with Cindy (*see page 168*), the best nail technician in the country, who doubles up as the town gossip journalist. To her credit, she doesn't reveal names, but Cindy is an entire broadcasting station with a new audience of one every hour on the hour. (She likes it when I tell her that I get my international news from the *New York Times*, my national news from the TV and my local news from her.)

As I sat down and submitted 10 chewed and chipped nails for her scrutiny, I opened with my usual original and precisely worded refrain – 'So Cindy, what's new?'

She responded with her traditional two-word overture (which signals the coming of the latest and juiciest town gossip): 'Nothing much.'

Now Cindy does not exactly need a need a clam opener to pry out the latest pearls of local gossip. All it takes is a sentence or two of encouragement. 'Oh, come on Cindy. I've been on the road for almost a month. What's everybody talking about?' 'Everybody', of course, in Cindy's world of nails and hair, meant 'women'.

'Oh, it's the same old stuff', she replied. Then she launched into her half-hour programme of news and pogrom against the husbands. 'They're complaining about the weather and that their husbands are work-obsessed and don't talk to them. Especially the younger ones. They're really upset because they say their honeys talked a lot when they were dating. Now they've all turned into clams ...'

There, I had it – the evidence I needed! From 1950 right on up into the new millennium, women were (and still are) complaining about men's obvious lack of loquaciousness. Cindy and I joked about silver-tongued princes turning into grunting frogs, rather than vice versa.

'No, not frogs,' she said. 'Nowadays brides wake up to their handsome prince and he's turned into, not a frog, but a clam!'

The hooting and yelling of all the nail techs and customers within earshot confirmed the verity of her observation. (*Refrain*: Such reactions result when we recognize the hilarious truths in our own lives.)

##  Who talks more – men or women?

Suppose you are on a quiz show. The studio audience holds its breath while the host asks you, 'For one million dollars, can you tell us, please ...

do men talk more than women? _____
do women talk more than men? _____
or is it about 50/50? _____'

Don't peek!

Is that tick your final answer? If you guessed that men talk more, you are now a millionaire. There have been countless studies on verbosity, and not one was able to prove that women spoke more.[65]

So why do women have the erroneous reputation of being terminally chatty? Some speculate that the stereotype evolved from men's historical belief that women (like children) should be seen and not heard, so whenever they do speak some male listeners think it's more than proper.[66] Others attribute it to the fact that women talk more about people, feelings and relationships.[67] Because the home is more appropriate for these softer topics, it often seems like they talk more – because they do it at home. But the men more than made up for it at work. In both 'words per day' and amount of time spent talking, men came in first. [68]

Men, on the other hand, prefer topics such as business, money and sport. Money and business are relevant to their jobs, so they really gab it up there. And sport? Well, sport is an important way of male bonding.

Also, talking means something different to men. For them, it is a way to call attention to themselves and their ideas – a competing and conquering of sorts. When a man is at work, he's competing for position. When he's with his buddies, he's competing for who's up and who's down. When he's on a date, he's competing to win you. But, at home, happily married or snugly seated with his significant other, he feels no need to compete. The result is contented *silence*.

## ✹ Clams à la grecque

I have a friend, Nicole, a very beautiful young woman whom men swarm around like bees swarm around honey. She is the daughter of one of my clients, and when we met she unofficially adopted me as 'Big Sis'. Even though men find Nicole irresistible, she is able to resist most of them. In fact Nicole is quite discriminating and seldom is intimate with any of her suitors. However, Dimitri was a different story.

When she met Dimitri, she knew he was the one. He was very tall, very dark and very, very suave. Dimitri was born in the States but his father was a Greek shipping magnate and he had travelled all over the world. Additionally, he was an avid reader so he was very well versed in just about any subject that interested Nicole.

But the best thing about Dimitri, Nicole told me, was that he really knew how to treat a woman. She had been dating him for six months and he had taken her to two plays, one opera, six movies, one ballet and countless fine restaurants. Every time he came to pick up her up for a date, he brought her a beautiful fresh flower. 'This guy really knows how to court!' she told me. I felt for sure they were on a beautiful winding path that would eventually wind up at the altar.

Whether she was playing hard to get, or whether her principles were stronger than her passion, I'll never know, and I didn't probe. But six months into the relationship, still she had not been intimate with Dimitri

Then, one Sunday afternoon, Nicole called me in tears. Between sobs she blurted it all out. 'I'm afraid it's all over with Dimitri. He's no longer interested in me. I don't think he'll ever call me again.'

'Oh, Nicole, I'm so sorry. What happened?'

'Well,' she confided, 'last night I invited him to stay over at my house.' She paused dramatically, and then added 'All night.' I was expected to know what she meant, which, of course, was as easy as peeling a banana.

'Oh no, he was terrific,' she sobbed. 'And I thought I was too,' she added, I suppose thinking Big Sis would doubt her allure.

'So this morning, I asked him if he'd like some breakfast. He said, "That would be great." But – but – but, while I was fixing him an omelette, he picks up the newspaper from my doorstep, goes into the living room, and starts reading!

'If that wasn't enough,' she sniffled, 'when I serve the eggs and sit down for us to eat together, he's still reading! I couldn't believe it.

'I asked him if the eggs were OK, and he smiled and said, "Yes, they're great." And then he goes back reading. Leil, I couldn't believe it. There I am staring at ... not at a lover, but *the back side of a newspaper*? He hates me because of last night. Does he think I'm cheap? Is it because he's Greek?' she asked in desperation. 'Is it because, when a man gets what he wants, he's no longer interested?'

It sounded as though Dimitri had passed his physical exam with flying colours, but left a bit to be desired in the oral department. Of course, he should have understood women better and talked with her warmly over breakfast. But, since he didn't, Big Sis had to explain the facts of life to her. No, not the birds and the bees – she had that part down to a T – but about clams.

---

I tried to explain to her that, to many men, talking is to win something – an argument, the respect of a boss or his colleagues, a woman.[69] And, when he is feeling completely comfortable, there is no need to talk. To many men, life is a talk show – and everything he says must be right. But that's work! And when he's with the woman who loves him, he can happily relax, and be quiet.

---

'Nicole,' I said, 'Dimitri reading the newspaper at the breakfast table was most probably an indication that he feels completely at ease and relaxed with you.' I told her the story of Wordsworth and Coleridge ...

Perchance you haven't heard the story which, although it is about two dead, white poets (a genre I was told never to quote), holds an eternal truth. Wordsworth went to visit

Coleridge at his cottage. He walks in, sits down and does not utter a word for three hours. Neither does Coleridge. Wordsworth then rises and, as he leaves, thanks his friend for a perfect evening. And means it!

As I talked, it sounded as though the telephone was in less danger of being short-circuited due to Nicole's tears. I think she began to understand.

Incidentally, her story has a very happy ending. Nicole's name is now Nicole Stephanopolis.

### CLAUSE 47 ♀

## My Silent Partner

I will NOT think that, just because my man isn't talking to me, it means he is upset. Unless there are other indicators, I'll assume his silence just means that he's feeling peaceful and non-competitive. I'll let him savour the silence and go happily about my business.

For women only

'Hey, that sounds pretty good,' I can hear you gentlemen say. 'Great, no more of her asking, "How was your day?", when all I want to do is read the paper. No more of her asking, "Is something bothering you, honey?", when all I was doing was scratching my head. No more of her saying, "You never talk to me!", when all I was doing was figuring out a problem from work. And, best of all, no more of her offering "Penny for your thoughts!" Hooray! Hooray!'

Not so fast, brothers. Yes, all of the rewards above can be yours. But you have to do your part, too. What if I told you that, for a scant 15 minutes per calendar day, you can make her feel like you rival Romeo. You can make her very happy indeed – both romantically and sexually. (Which, of course, makes you happy sexually.)

Do you agree that the first impression you make on someone new is important? I'm almost sure you do. But the old
phrase, 'You never have a second chance to make a great first
impression', is only half true. Even though you don't have a second chance at the *very* first impression, you have thousands of
second chances at the little first impressions she gets every time
you see her. What happens first when you or she walks into a
room is what stays in her heart for a long time.

Here is the technique to give her the impression that you are
not the clam, but a loving and interested friend, significant
other, husband. I call it the 'Minute-an-Hour Treatment'. *Quite
simply, give 100 per cent of your attention to your woman for
the number of minutes that correlates with the number of hours,
up to 24, since you last saw her.*

Here are the rules.

## The eight-minute treatment

If you and she have been apart for more than eight hours, such
as at work or on a business trip, devote the FIRST eight minutes of your time 100 per cent to her. Put down your briefcase,
your luggage, your newspaper and tell her about your day. Ask
her about hers. Be sure to work a kiss or an 'I love you' into
your repertoire.

## The five-minute treatment

If you've been apart for a half-day or up to five hours, devote the
first five minutes of your time 100 per cent to her. Make small
talk. Work a little compliment somewhere into the dialogue.

## The two-minute treatment

When you've been apart for just a couple of hours, make sure
she has 100 per cent of your attention for at least two minutes.

## The one-minute treatment

And, if you've only been apart for up to an hour, give her at least 60 seconds when you first meet up again.

Your wife/girlfriend/significant other is not as high-maintenance as you think. Start using the Ten/Five Clause tonight and you'll see the difference in her happiness. All of those mini first impressions you make each day add up to an overall impression of a man who cares about the minutiae in her life. And that, dear gentlemen, is contentment to a woman. We are not such complicated creatures after all.

**CLAUSE 48 ♂**

### The Minute-an-Hour Treatment

I will give the woman in my life one minute of undivided and devoted attention for every hour we have been apart. Additionally, every time she walks in the room if we haven't really been apart, I'll give her a smile, a wink, a blown kiss or just a loving gaze. (For extra guidance, see Appendix E.)
For men only

# Part IV

# Networking

*Recruiting Knights for
my personal Round Table*

# Chapter Forty Eight

# The world's best contact sport

*(Once you learn how to play it)*

I sincerely hope you never need to suffer (as I did) in order to be to convinced of the need for faithful friends and true love in your life. But if ever something untoward happens, you want to make sure that you're surrounded by a strong team, who will support you until you get back on your feet.

If you are blessed with a close family, you've probably already got a pretty good support system. But sometimes even their love is not enough. Let's say, heaven forbid, a drunk driver hits your car. Due to your severe injury, you must undergo a rare type of surgery. Of course your family will do everything they can to care for you but, unless they are *insiders* in the medical community, they may not be able to find just the right specialist to make you better than new (or the right lawyer who can win a just settlement to pay for the operation!).

In any industry, there are the second-rate practitioners, the standard ones, the stars and the superstars. The superstars are those who are most knowledgeable. They address their conventions and write articles for their industry publications. The top lawyers and surgeons are on the cutting edge (no pun intended) of their fields, renowned within their professional 'communes', but relatively unknown outside of it. And only the insiders know who's who.

You might be tempted to say, 'Why? If I need a specialist, my doctor knows who to refer me to.' Or, 'If I need a lawyer who specializes in personal injury, my lawyer can refer me.' That's not good enough! Their patients or clients (i.e. you) are important to them. But, more important to them by far are their family and *personal friends*.

If you want one of the top boys or girls on your case, you have to know someone who is not just going to give you 'the party line', 'I am not permitted to make recommendations' or 'They're all good.' You want an insider friend, so you can get the real score on these national or international experts.

Local superstars are significant Knights, too. In your home town, or nearby, there are bound to be superstar dentists, accountants, bankers, travel agents, vets, insurance experts, fire-fighters, politicians, headhunters, journalists, motor mechanics and sales folk – all of whom welcome your business. There are also very approachable superstar police officers, politicians, postal workers, journalists and radio/TV media celebrities. These are great Knights to have sitting at your Round Table.

'Success' comes before 'Work' only in the dictionary. In real life, 'Work' comes before 'Success' – and 'Networking' comes before both of them.

# Chapter Forty Nine

# 'Networking?' Did I hear you say 'networking'?

Many people abhor the whole idea of networking. I've heard all the excuses:

'Networking is when you become an insincere, grovelling sycophant boot-licker to anybody who might be able to help you.'
'Networking is pretending you like someone so you can get something out of them.'
'I tried networking last Thursday and it didn't work.'
'Networking makes my nose too brown.'

People suffer two big misconceptions about networking. One, they think it's selfish; and two, they feel uncomfortable mingling and meeting strangers. We're going to cure both these conditions.

Because networking has achieved a bad name with some people, I'm going to give it a new name. 'What's in a word?' you ask. 'Will just changing its name make it any more palatable?'

Ask 'pro-choice' people about the word 'abortion'. Ask people living alternative lifestyles about the word 'perversion'. Ask people who support freedom of expression about the word 'pornography'. (Please note that I am *not* making judgements about the terms used above. I merely present them as my case for 'What's in a name?')

I'm changing the name 'Networking' to 'Sharing Your Gifts', or 'Sharing' for short. That's really what networking is all about. It's Sharing your talents and gifts with new people you like, and letting them share theirs with you.

Sharing is as much *giving* as getting. Often it's more. Is it work? Yes. It's like exercising by doing sit-ups, lifting weights or running, to take care of your body and strengthen your muscles. Some people enjoy it. Others don't enjoy the actual workout, but they're thrilled with the results.

It's the same with Sharing. Some people love the mingling, the talking, the exchanging of telephone numbers, email addresses, numbers or business cards. For those who don't enjoy the minute-to-minute mingling, think of Sharing as a pleasant workout. It strengthens you to be ready to take care of yourself and your loved ones now, and for whatever surprises are round the corner.

For example, say you have an ageing parent who can no longer live at home. You definitely don't want to put Mum or Dad in an old-age home you know nothing about. But if you have Shared with someone knowledgeable – perhaps a geriatric nurse – he or she can suggest who to turn to for home care, or can recommend an institution that will offer a caring and loving environment for your parent.

Some of your old friends are moving into your area and have asked you to help them find a home. But you know nothing about rents and prices of houses. You and your friends are in luck if you've already Shared your Gifts with an estate agent. Due to his or her connection with you (a friend), your estate agent will give them better service.

Let's say that you've done very little travel in your life and now you're taking your first big trip, right across Europe. You'll have a much more fun, and less expensive, trip if you've previously Shared your talents with a travel agent. Because he or she is your friend, you'll get personalized service.

> You may still say, 'I hate Networking.' But I'm sure you can't say (and mean) 'I hate Sharing my Gifts with people I really like.' Don't think of 'networking' in the old sense of brown-nosing people who can help you. See it as actively seeking people you genuinely like. Then the two of you share your God-given abilities and learned talents with each other so that you are better able to take care of yourself and your loved ones.

**CLAUSE 49** ♂ ♀

## Sharing My Gifts

I will force myself to go to events and find people I can 'Share' my talents with for an aspect of my life that is even more important than my work – my personal life and the well-being of those I love.

# Chapter Fifty

# Plan ahead!

One of the most valued Knights sitting at my Round Table is a fellow speaker named Jeff, who, selflessly, has done dozens of favours for me. He's recommended me to his clients for speeches and he's *the* man to call whenever I need to get the lowdown on a speaker's bureau or anything else in the 'speaker world'.

Some time ago, he called and said his beloved brother and his wife, and their two kids, were coming to New York and they were dying to see *The Lion King*. At that time *The Lion King* was the hottest ticket in town and you had to wait almost a year even to get tickets for a Wednesday matinee. And they wanted tickets on Friday night!

Jeff (like practically everyone else in the United States outside of New York City) figured that, just because I lived in the Rotten Apple, I had connections and could render the impossible. Sure, Jeff.

Well, foolishly, that's precisely what I said. 'Sure, Jeff.' As I hung up I wondered how on earth I was going to go about getting Jeff's brother, Jeff's wife and little Amanda and Mitchell tickets to *The Lion King*. I didn't know any big-deal ticket agents. I didn't know any hot-shot PR people who can always wangle seats for their clients. I didn't even know any unscrupulous slimy ticket scalpers who illegally sold tickets for scandalous prices. I felt terrible, because Jeff had Shared his Gifts with me so much. Finally, I was being offered the opportunity to Share back, and I was going to have to let him and his family down.

The only person I knew who was remotely connected with theatre was Kam, an actress. But she, like most performers, is between engagements 95 per cent of the time. And, when she was performing, it was mostly in off-off-off-off-Broadway shows. The closest she ever got to Broadway was my office on lower Broadway, where she did part-time secretarial work. 'Well,' I said to myself. 'It's worth a shot.' But I knew it was a *long* long shot.

With no expectations whatsoever, I called Kam and explained the situation. She said she'd get back to me. I had hardly put down the phone when she called back and told me she was 99 per cent sure that she could get them seats on that Friday if they didn't mind not all sitting together.

After I extracted my jaw from the phone mouthpiece, I managed to mumble, 'Hmmma, hmmma, hmmma, Kam, how did you manage to do that?'

It turns out she was dating an actor whose day job was selling tickets in the theatre where *The Lion King* was playing. He told her that they always have a dozen or so people turning in tickets because their trip was cancelled or whatever. And, instead of selling them to anyone of the countless numbers crowding outside the theatre – who offered him bribes of everything from money to their firstborn male – he would save the first four tickets that came in for Jeff's kin from Columbus, Ohio.

Thank heavens for Kam. I lucked out on that one. But I won't always have a friend who is dating someone who works in the ticket office of a hot show. And, even if I did, he wouldn't always be the type of guy who can sneak the family of a friend of a friend of his girlfriend to the top of the list. I resolved at that moment to research who gets tickets how, and put that person on my list of 'People I'd like to Share My Gifts with'. (You may notice I'm not telling whether I succeeded or not, lest other out-of-town friends crawl out of the woodwork wanting me to get *them* tickets.)

Think about what needs might crop up in your life during the next year. Then imagine who can be a solution to those potential problems. You don't want a case of last-minute panic like mine.

# Chapter Fifty One

# The guide to sharing your gifts

Many Networking guides will tell you how to sidle up to the people you want, get their attention, get them to like you, and go for what you want. Instead, let's reverse that. This 'Handbook of Sharing' starts with what YOU bring to the table. 'It is more blessed to give than to receive', and all that. (It's also a smarter way to go about the whole thing.)

Think about what qualities, talents, gifts or knowledge you have that would benefit anyone who knew you. Many of your gifts will be outside the job arena. For example, my PMR Phil, a freelance business writer, is not rich. He's not famous. And he's not well connected. But Phil has a multitude of other qualities that make him an excellent Knight to have sitting at anyone's Round Table.

Phil is an obsessive computer genius and will not rest easy until he's solved a friend's software problem. In fact, whenever a friend has any kind of computer quandary, he takes it on as his own and tirelessly pursues the answer.

Recently one of his friends needed some expensive dental work. He did a thorough raking of the Web for her. Two days later, he finally dug up the solution on one of the 1036 sites he had scoured for information. He found some highly acclaimed dental researchers who would do the work for free, as long as she would agree to a few time-consuming but harmless tests. Sometimes I picture Phil like a restless golden retriever in a rocket. Shoot him out into cyberspace, and he lands safely back on terra firma with his tale wagging and the information you wanted secured safely between his teeth.

He also has an excellent legal mind and will inspect every angle of a contract with the care of a guard making the midnight rounds with a torch. Then he'll pick out any potentially bothersome clause, like a monkey picking fleas out of its fur, and explain it to you.

The list goes on. He never has a bad word to say about anyone, and his loyalty to his friends is unwavering. Qualities like these are priceless today, because they're the type money can't buy.

Maybe you are a Phil to your friends. You may not have precisely these qualities, but undoubtedly you have many others that make having you as a friend an invaluable gift. One thing is certain: you are a resource for everything you know; and the more you know and learn, the better Knight you are.

For some people, networking is easier if they think of it as giving rather than receiving. Imagine yourself sitting as one of the 150 proud Knights siting around Arthur's great table. When the time comes for you to be knighted as one of King Arthur's legion, you are going to give five reasons why someone would want to be your friend.

There are probably 50 reasons so it's going to be hard to narrow it down to just five. In this list, you can put anything – from a special quality you have, to a particular knowledge you possess.

For instance, perhaps you are unfalteringly honest, so anyone who has the pleasure of knowing you can have faith that he or she will always get a candid answer to anything asked. Perhaps you know more about current rock groups than anyone else, so people can benefit from your recommendations about which concert to buy tickets to. Perhaps you know all about gardening, so you can suggest to your friends what will grow best in their soil.

If you don't come up with five, ask your family or friends what they think your valuable and sharable qualities are. Often you have no idea that your natural talents could have such value to your friends.

 ## Networking, it's kids' stuff too

Christine, a single mum who also works as a dental assistant, was giving a small tea party for a friend of mine who just had a book published. During the tea, Christine's two daughters were scurrying around getting everything ready for their exciting afternoon. Their mum had just bought a microwave and the girls were thrilled that it could actually make popcorn – and you didn't have to put any oil in the pan. They had popped a huge batch and decided to sell it with lemonade out front. They made a sign – 'Lemonade 25 cents, Popcorn 15 cents' – and raced out to the front lawn to open up shop.

After an hour or so, Sarah (the older daughter) came in stuttering, tears dripping into her mouth. 'Mummy, we sold a few lemonades, but nobody's b-b-b-buying our popcorn. And we have t-t-t-tons of it left.'

While we were trying to console her, explaining that it wasn't her fault, people just don't eat popcorn on a warm day, the phone rang. Christine answered it and I heard her in the kitchen sharing the popcorn story with the caller. Then she was silent for a minute or so. The next thing I heard was, 'What a great idea. We'll try it.'

Christine returned with a big smile on her face. 'Sarah, go get the crayons and some paper. It's going to help you sell your popcorn.' Drying her tears with her fists, she scurried off to get the tools. I asked Christine what was up. She said that the call was from a new friend she had met at a National Association of Women in Business networking event. She was an advertising copywriter who was interested in finding a good root-canal specialist, so she was calling Christine for a recommendation. 'When I told her about the popcorn fiasco, she suggested a different wording on the sign.'

Sarah returned holding her crayons and paper out to her mother, with a look of total trust that mummy was going to perform miracles with the multicoloured magic wands. And so she did. She took the crayons to the big paper and wrote a few words in big kid-like letters. She told Sarah and Ashley to go and post it on the stand. Sarah asked what it said, and Christine just responded, 'It's magic words that will make people want to buy popcorn.'

She was right! An hour later, both girls returned, looking exhausted but happy ... and carrying a big, empty bin of popcorn.

What had the top Madison Avenue copywriter, who had worked on campaigns for companies such as Cadillac, suggested as the popcorn slogan?

'Today only. FREE POPCORN when you buy one lemonade, 50 cents. Popcorn has no butter. No salt. No calories. No taste.'

Everyone walking by who saw the sign stopped, laughed and, of course had to taste the tasteless popcorn. Even people who were driving by pointed it out and many stopped to buy a lemonade and nibble on the popcorn.

Just like this advertising copywriter probably would not have guessed that her talents could have helped a dental assistant with two kids, you may not see how your particular talents can help someone else. But I'm sure they can. A Knight doesn't always have to fulfil a big need in someone's life. Knights can plug small holes, too. For Christine, a single mum, her daughters' happiness was no small hole.

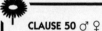

**CLAUSE 50** ♂ ♀

## Knight Time-Sharing

Seated as one of the 150 proud Knights at King Arthur's Round Table, I submit these as my five top gifts:

1_____

2_____

3_____

4_____

5_____

I will Share selflessly my gifts above as my friends' needs arise, and accept graciously when they offer me theirs.

## Chapter Fifty Two

# Do you carry enough friend insurance?

Hopefully, you are comfortable with what you can *give*. It is now time to get comfortable knowing what you can *get* from letting others Share with you. Recently I saw an advert for online banking, which showed a pile of little plastic bath ducks strewn all over the floor as though they had been thrown down in a huff. The caption under the chaotic topsy-turvy mess was 'My life'. The next photo showed a nice neat line of ducks, swimming in procession one after the other, not wavering one millimetre from the formation. The caption for this photo was 'My finances'.

I could have had a similar ad for me several years ago. One photo would be me all trussed up to give a speech. I'd be dressed up in a stylish suit, carefully pressed blouse, freshly shined shoes, carefully coiffed hair and freshly painted fingernails perfectly matching my lipstick. The caption under that one would be 'My career'. The caption under the second photo would be 'My car'. Here would be my 10-year-old banged-up bucket of bolts which, much to my chagrin, spent half its life at the car mechanic's.

Why didn't I chuck it and buy a new car? It wasn't that I couldn't afford it. It wasn't that I didn't want a new car. It was just that I didn't know anything about cars and I didn't know anyone who did! So, year after year, I kept putting the painful process of buying one off, all the while making sure that my motorists' card with the extra towing insurance was in the glove compartment.

Then something happened – what people call a wake-up call. I was driving to a speech at a recreation centre, and as I drove to the back of the building to park, I noticed two work-men walking towards the building. I parked and, not knowing where the main entrance was, ran to catch up with them. I overheard one say to the other, 'Did ya see that little piece of s♂'* that the speaker drove up in?'

That was it! I resolved to get a new car immediately. I know I paid far too much and didn't get the best car I could for the money. But that was the price I paid for not having friend insur-ance in the car department.

I'll never make that mistake again. I also resolved to never be without a knowledgeable contact for every conceivable predicament I might find myself in. I needed to fill my Round Table with Car Salespeople Knights, Accountant Knights, Doctor Knights, Lawyer Knights, Car Mechanic Knights, Plumber Knights, – the list goes on for me. And it does for you, too.

Why is it that a man and a woman are more apt to go out when they meet at a singles' function than if they meet in, say, a museum? Because the mindset at a singles function is love. They are more open to the idea of love walking in the door. Everyone of the opposite sex they meet is judged as a poten-tial date.

When we get serious about Sharing our Gifts, we will begin to look at everyone we meet as a potential Knight. The next time your sister mentions she's going out with a cruise ship cap-tain, squelch your jokes, 'Boy, if he ever takes you and all your luggage on a cruise, he'll have to get a bigger ship. Har har.' Instead, ask to meet him. Your brother is going out with an accountant? Don't ask if she has the usual credentials. You know: 'Is she appallingly dull, unimaginative, timid, spineless, no sense of humour, tedious company and irrepressibly drab?' Har-de-har har. Instead, ask to meet her.

In your lifetime, you will in all probability buy six cars, have four houses painted, make five moves, buy twelve insurance policies, four trips abroad and purchase innumerable major appliances. You'll call a plumber 36 times and an electrician 16. In addition, you will dine at thousands of restaurants, engage half a dozen lawyers and buy food and telephone services every day.

To get the best deal in these, you should definitely have a car salesperson, a painter, a plumber, an electrician, a removal firm, an insurance broker and a travel agent on your Sharing Gifts list. So you can get the advantage when it comes to products and food, you should also seek someone who works at a major appliance store, a grocery store and the telephone company. These folks can let you know about the best deals beforehand  and, if they're close friends, they might even put the purchase through them so you can take advantage of their employee discount.

**CLAUSE 51** ♂ ♀

## Knight Recruiting Clause

I will be on the constant lookout for people I like who are the best in their particular field. I will Share my Gifts with them, and go out of my way to become their friend. I will aim to fill in every blank in the list below (see page 256).

When you've filled in every line below with the name of at least one person whom you consider more than a purely professional contact, you'll have a pretty impressive friend insurance policy.

## One man's Knight is another man's nobody

Below the last name, you will find a few blank spaces for you to fill in 'specialist' Knights who might be important to you in your particular life. For instance, a skydiving champion or head of the school board might make great Knights for *you*, but since I'm not jumping out of aeroplanes or have no kids at school they are worthless to me. I'd rather have Jeff and all of his speakers' bureau knowledge, which would bore you to tears. These last few lines are for your 'Just for Me' Knights.

But, just like your policy expires if you don't pay the premiums, your friends will expire into acquaintances if you don't keep paying the premium. The cost? Very little, considering the benefits. It's an occasional card, an email, a phone call. It's sending them a clipping of something they are interested in. It's sending birthday and Christmas cards. Think of each of the above as logs to throw on the fire in order to keep the friendship warm.

Friendship is caring about the friendship just as much as it is deep communication. When I lived in France, Alain and his wife Charlotte owned the little gymnasium I used to go to. We never communicated any deep feelings or philosophies (mainly because I wouldn't have been capable of it in French – and his English was worse than my French, if that's possible!), but the relationship was quite pleasant. Every year since, we've exchanged Christmas cards and Alain occasionally sits down and writes a letter. Yes, the old-fashioned way – with pen, paper, envelope, stamp.

There were many people I was closer to when I worked in France, but, because Alain and Charlotte kept up the contact, I still consider them friends. I've invited them to come and visit me, and I know there's always a place for me to stay in their tiny coastal town.

As you look at the following list, you may think, 'But why would I need a vet? I don't even have a pet.' *You* may not have one, but remember: as a Knight, it's all for one and one for all.

There's a pretty big chance you've got some dog-owning Knights sitting at the table, and one of their dogs is going to get sick as a dog someday and he or she will need a vet.

 ## The Knights at my Round Table

| Job | Name of person I know |
| --- | --- |
| Accountant | _____ |
| Artist | _____ |
| Banker | _____ |
| Car mechanic | _____ |
| Community leader | _____ |
| Elected official | _____ |
| Firefighter | _____ |
| Headhunter | _____ |
| High-ranking police officer | _____ |
| House painter | _____ |
| Insurance expert | _____ |
| Lawyer | _____ |
| Local celebrity | _____ |
| Media personality | _____ |
| Mortgage broker | _____ |
| Religious leader | _____ |
| Travel agent | _____ |
| Tree surgeon | _____ |
| Vet | _____ |

| Other Knights | Name |
| --- | --- |
| _____ | _____ |
| _____ | _____ |
| _____ | _____ |
| _____ | _____ |
| _____ | _____ |
| _____ | _____ |

## Need more? Don't stop here. Get more paper!

Many years ago, I visited Africa. The hotel where I stayed had a cocktail lounge, where visitors could sit in safety and look out for wildlife. There was an animal check list on each of the cocktail napkins – each time you saw a giraffe or an elephant go by, you could check it off.

At the risk of sounding cynical, make the above your mental cocktail napkin and, at all cocktail parties and other events, look for the various human animals you have a need for in your life.

There are a few folks who are potentially more necessary to you than any of the above. The ones I'm talking about have the ability to help you in more important ways than the best lawyers, the highest-ranking politician or the biggest celebrity in your town. Can you guess who they are? (Hint: no, it's not your family.)

Before I tell you the answer, let me hop up on my soapbox. While I'm preaching away, maybe you can guess the answer.

Most of the Western world is blessed with freedom – to move, to go into any line of work we want, to have any type of friends we wish, to follow any religion, and to bring up our children pretty much as we see fit. Our lifestyles are in a constant state of flux. We are driving less and teleworking more (i.e. using home computers, telephone, email to maintain contact with our colleagues). Nowadays, nearly two-thirds (60 per cent) of all women work (this figure increases to 75 per cent for women aged 25–34).

Diversity exists not only in the workplace. Our neighbourhoods are also becoming more diverse – it is not unusual to find representatives of a variety of different cultures, religions within a very small radius of one's home. It is quite common to find working mums and dads living next door to stay-at-home non-working mums and dads, who are living next door to telecommuting mums and dads, who are living next door to home-business mums and dads. When it comes to working together, corporations spend millions of pounds promoting understanding and better communication between the genders and races. And, as communication increases, wonderful cross-cultural friendships have developed in the workplace.

The only thing that remains constant is change.

Have you guessed where I'm going with this? Right. What we need is more communication and friendship in our neighbourhoods. These days, it is rare for us to know more than 20 of our neighbours. (In New York, where I live, it's unusual if anyone knows *anyone* who lives nearby – including one's next-door neighbours!)

Several years ago I was on a business trip when an embarrassingly complimentary article about my speaking engagements came out in a magazine. They had even published my phone number so, naturally, I fantasized how my phone would be ringing constantly, with numerous calls from dozens of big-deal prospective clients.

The day after the magazine was on the news-stands, I couldn't wait to beep in for messages. I had my pen and pad all poised to write down their numbers. My phone rang once, twice and then a curt computer-generated voice from my answering machine informed its owner, saying, 'Sorry, this machine is not taking messages. Goodbye.'

'Goodbye'? Thanks a lot. That's what all my big-deal prospective clients were going to hear, and that's what it was going to be – all right, goodbye client.

I worked out what happened. When re-recording, I must have hit the wrong button and left it on the computer-generated 'outgoing only' message setting. My machine wasn't exactly state-of-the-art and there was no way I could correct the problem by remote. But, with a simple push of a button by a live human being, my machine could have been instantly purring away again with my brilliant message designed to dazzle prospective clients.

But who was I going to call? My roommate was away and no one else in the building had the key. And, even if they had, I wouldn't have felt comfortable asking them that favour. That is a sad commentary on the loneliness of life in a big city.

I have told this story in my seminars since and was surprised to hear that many participants who live in smaller communities, in much more civil parts of the country, would have had exactly the same problem. When there is a problem – who ya gonna call?

## Chapter Fifty Three

# Who ya gonna call?

Think about it. Suppose you are at a business dinner at a restaurant an hour away from home. The maître d' comes to your table to tell you you have an urgent phone call. You discover it's your babysitter, who sounds hysterical. She tells you that your 3-year-old has locked herself in the bathroom and is crying uncontrollably. *Who ya gonna call?*

Now, let's say you're sound asleep one night. You get a panicky call from your brother-in-law. He thinks your pregnant sister is about to go into labour and his car won't start. 'Stay calm,' you tell him. 'I'll be right over.' As you jump into your jeans, you remember, 'Oh no, MY car's in the shop being fixed!' *Who ya gonna call?*

Or, how about this one – has it ever happened to you? Because it has to me. You're happily driving along the motorway in your car, humming to the music. Then the news comes on. Usual stuff – waging war and rioting in far-away places. Disastrous hurricanes, tornadoes or downpours in faraway places. Political news from faraway Washington. Then comes the local news. Top story – a fire raging in 'Ohmygod, that's MY neighbourhood!' Your foot presses the accelerator almost to the floor. You risk getting a ticket, but you need to know whether your house is still a house or a charred pulp. You zap into the next service station and race to the phone booth, but .... *Who ya gonna call?*

Dozens of problems arise throughout the year where calling a good neighbour is the solution.

# Chapter Fifty Four

# Making deposits in the good neighbour account

Just like you need to put money into a bank account before you can draw any out, you need to put some emotional investment into your neighbours before you can draw any favours out.

How do you put value in the good neighbour account? In a whole host of ways. Take the time to stop and chat when you meet on the street. Give a small party and invite the neighbours. Those who don't know everyone in the neighbourhood will be especially grateful. It gives them the opportunity to meet the other neighbours when they might be too shy to take the initiative on their own.

Invite some neighbours to dinner or brunch. If there is a television show 'event' you know you are both going to watch, invite them over to see it with you. If you know they like a particular actor or director and you have the video, invite them to come view it with you. Folks living alone will really value this. People with families often don't realize, when the shadows start to fall, the loneliness of the long evening ahead for many who live alone.

Remember your neighbours when you're travelling, and buy them a small present. Or, better still, buy their kids a tiny gift. You can also send them a card remembering their 'Special Day'.

Do you live in a neighbourhood where most of the folks are married, and there are only one or two single or divorced people? You meet someone you think they'd hit it off with? Give them a surprise. Fix the two up on a blind date. Now that's a great present!

Call after a big snowstorm or other weather-related incident to see if your neighbours suffered any damage. That's treating them like family and letting them know you are there for them. It's wonderful, especially for older folks, to know that one of their neighbours cares.

If new people move into your neighbourhood, invite them to tea. (Hey, this is nothing new. In 1922, Emily Post practically laid down the law. You *must* invite new neighbours over for tea.)

Someday your neighbours may be the most important family members you have, and all due to their proximity.

**CLAUSE 52 ♂ ♀**

## Good Neighbour Clause

I will make one of the following deposits in my good neighbour account, at least once a month:

1. Give a party.
2. Call a new neighbour.
3. Invite them to dinner or weekend brunch.
4. Invite them to watch the game, the Academy Awards, etc.
5. Give a little gift to them or their kids.
6. Plan a nice surprise – a blind date for singles?
7. Make two friendly phone calls, especially to lonely neighbours.

# Part V

# Marketing me!

*Just like Hollywood celebrity makers
promote a star*

# Chapter Fifty Five

# How's my packaging?

Some years ago, when I was just getting interested in public speaking, I was invited to join the committee to choose a speaker for an upcoming association convention. My colleague, Charlotte, the chairperson, asked several members to come and watch demo tapes of speakers giving a real speech in front of a real audience.

On the way to the meeting, I mentally calculated how long the choosing process was going to take. Charlotte had been sent 25 press packets and tapes. I multiplied 10 minutes (the average demo tape length) by 25. 'Let's see', I thought. 'That's 250 minutes – four hours minimum. Then we discuss each one, that's another five minutes. Five times 25 is 125. Then ... Oh, the heck with it,' I figured, 'we'll be there well into the evening.'

I arrived at noon and the five of us sat around with coffee and sandwiches, catching up on the latest association buzz. I looked at my watch and gently suggested that maybe we should get started viewing the tapes. So, Fran, the chairperson's assistant, cleared the table and laid out a multicoloured slew of folders, placing the speaker's photo on top of each.

Charlotte started at the left of the long table. She picked up one photo, dropped it in the wastebasket and said, 'No, not this one.' Instant extinction. Fran scurried over, scooped up the folder and demo tape and filed them in the same rubbish bin.

Charlotte then picked up the second, 'Nope, not this one.' It met the same fast fate. I was flabbergasted. Like dealing a deck of cards, she worked her way down the line of all 25 photos and, spending less than two seconds on each, trashed most, and put a few in the 'Let's look at their tape' pile. Never once did she read any of the material in the packets.

From 25 speakers, she had it narrowed down to seven whose looks she liked. She handed Fran the first tape to put in the VCR and it started to roll. The speaker came on screen. After two or three sentences into her speech, Charlotte shook her head. The others nodded in agreement. 'Eject! Bin!'

The group was a tiny bit more merciful to the next speaker. Her tape lasted about 25 seconds before Fran pressed the eject button.

I nearly suggested that we watch more of each tape but, by the time I could open my mouth, the next tape was on. This time it was a brilliant sales trainer and speaker whom I had just met. He's a little barrel of dynamite who keeps audiences rolling in the aisles. I'd heard him tell the sensational story he was performing on the tape and I knew, once he got to the punchline in about 15 seconds, that he'd have the gig. But seconds into the tape, two of the women said in unison, 'Too short.' My poor friend Jeff was rejected and ejected before he'd got the group to the first guffaw.

Their sudden-death decisions reminded me of many years ago, when I would stand with other young star-struck hopefuls in the wings of a big theatre. When called to the stage to audition, we'd be blinded by the bright lights, knowing that somewhere out there, in the shadows of the darkened theatre, an unseen producer was poised, preparing to pounce and pronounce our fate. One by one, we'd start to do our thing. After delivering just a few lines, the fat, sweaty, cigar-smoking (or so we assumed) producer roared, 'NEXT!' Hopes vanished. Dreams dashed (until the next audition).

Back to the present ... Another six or seven speakers met the same dismal destiny. Each time Charlotte said 'No', what came to mind was the gruesome image of a guillotine and the speaker's head rolling down the long table, *plunk*, into the wastebasket.

Finally a speaker came on screen who captured their attention in the first few seconds. She was a tall, regal-looking woman with frosted blonde hair, a slight English accent, a twinkle in her eye, and was wearing a blindingly bright-blue suit. Beautifully packaged person, beautifully produced tape. They watched it all – all eight minutes of it. And Patricia was chosen as the convention speaker.

I had heard Patricia give a seminar at the National Speakers' Association, which I had recently joined. Since I was one of her fans (like everyone else who'd ever heard her speak), Charlotte gave me the assignment of calling Patricia and giving her the good news. Our meeting adjourned at 2 p.m.

Driving home, I thought, 'How unfair! Everybody made snap judgements. What if the speaker, like many people, gained force gradually? What if, two minutes into the tape, the speaker suddenly took on the power of Franklin Delano Roosevelt or the pathos of Mother Teresa? Or maybe the wit of Lucille Ball or the intelligence of Einstein?'

No good. Too late! It's all up front, or nothing. What you see is what you get. And what you get is what you saw... all 10 seconds of it. You blinked? Sorry, you missed it. NEXT!

When I phoned Patricia the next morning, I complimented her on her demo video and we discussed her upcoming speech. While chatting, I got around to telling her about the choosing process which I thought was so unusual. I assumed she'd share my surprise at how little they watched of the speakers' tapes.

'Oh sure, everybody makes choices like that nowadays,' she said. 'People don't have time any more – time to go through your information folder with a fine-toothed comb. All they want is your photo, your topic and how you come across to an audience – your charisma.'

Patricia, who teaches seminars on how to be a successful speaker, should know. She continued, 'What they're buying is how you look, how you sound, how you dress and your personality. It's assumed you'll have the message. In other words, they are buying YOU for the hour, the half-day or the full day you are in front of their group. You *must* get their attention in the first few seconds.'

# Chapter Fifty Six

# What they see is what they think they get

Now, with a few more years of speaking under my belt, I look back and appreciate the wisdom of Patricia's words. Whether it's fair or not, whether we like it or not, it's an irrefutable fact that, whenever you enter a room, 'IT' has already happened. Everyone who has glanced your way has come to a quick verdict. They've passed judgement on your clothing, your expression, your grooming and how you carry yourself. They've judged your hairstyle, and could probably tell you when you washed it last. Even your fingernails and shoes don't escape their scrutiny!

Some people have already categorized you as a 'Potential Friend', 'Potential Love' or 'Potential Contact'. Others have written you off – just on the way you look. The first few seconds you are reflected in their eyeballs are critical, consequential, conclusive, crucial, major, meaningful, momentous, heavy duty, not-to-be-sneezed-at. (Can I say it any stronger?)

If you still don't believe it, let's go to the videotape. There was a study published in the *Journal of Personality and Social Psychology* called 'Half a Minute: Predicting Teacher Evaluations from Thin Slices of Nonverbal Behavior and Physical

Attractiveness'. One by one, college professors, high-school principals, teachers and students saw 30-second clips of individuals. From just that half-minute glimpse on film, they were asked to predict how that person would perform, and how they would feel about that person by the end of the semester (term). At the end of the semester, the teachers, administrators and students were again polled on how they felt about the person, now that they had known them for several months.[71]

People had guessed so accurately, from having only seen 30 seconds of the person at the beginning of the semester, that the researchers conducted a second study, reducing the glimpse to just 15 seconds. Still – amazing accuracy. Finally they did a third study and showed the people only a six-second glimpse. Many were *still* able to predict how they would feel about someone months later. *Who says looks, clothes, hairstyle and body language don't count?*

Incidentally, these first impressions carry more weight in love than in friendship. People leave you 'on stage' a little longer when you're 'auditioning' for the role of friend than they do for the role of loved one. But not much!

# Chapter Fifty Seven

# You're the brand manager

*(And the product is YOU)*

Theatrical performers, professional speakers and all others whose livelihood depends heavily on their appearance, have coined a term for this crucial aspect of their lives. They call it 'Personal Marketing'. They think of presenting themselves like marketing a product. They are the brand managers who have the final say on every minute detail, and each choice is vitally important.

Big companies spend millions of pounds on supposedly arbitrary choices. Managing directors, artists and marketing executives lie awake at night worrying about issues like the colour of the package, the size of the type, the glossiness or matt of the paper used for the wrapping. Nothing is left to chance. Every conceivable aspect is considered, and its impact thoroughly studied.

In fact, company employees don't even trust their own judgement when it comes to deciding what the fickle public really wants. A few years ago, I wrote a corporate history for a leading market research firm called National Family Opinion (NFO). The company determines the public's preferences in products and packaging for important clients such as Procter and Gamble, Eastman Kodak and Kraft Foods.

Many companies now hire NFO and other research firms to discover, for example, whether when taking a shower people prefer to lather up with a big bar, a little bar, an oblong bar, a round bar, a square bar or a rectangular bar ... or whether they like their suds in pink, in blue, in green or in white ... or whether they like to have writing on the bar or not.

(Incidentally, with regard to the issue of 'writing or no writing', the answer turned out to be a definite NO. Ageing baby-boomers – who usually take showers without their glasses on – might pick up the bar of soap while being doused with water and, seeing some writing on the soap, fear that it may be some sort of warning. What a drag to have to grab for a towel, then trail water all over the house to find your glasses, put them on your wet face, secure the slippery bar in your hands, just to read that it's only the name of the soap.)

Then there's the packaging. Does the public like their soap in a paper package or in a box? What colour do they prefer the packaging to be? Should it have big lettering or little lettering? And on it goes.

Supposedly arbitrary attributes can make or break a product. A supermarket shopper has about a five-second window (yes, research firms have timed this, too) in which to decide whether to grab the soap in the red wrapping, the blue wrapping or the environmentally correct, all-ingredients-listed, no-animals-used-for-testing, politically correct, light-brown-earth-coloured, recycled-paper-with-green-letters-and-no-dye wrapping.

Where is all this leading? To YOU, of course! People make exactly the same five-second (or less) decision when they look at *your* 'packaging'. They decide if they want to buy your act or not, and, just like carefully calculated variables determine the success or failure of a product, your variables (that is, *your packaging*) can determine whether you succeed or fail in the land of love, business or friendship.

A big part of it starts right where we began in *How to Make Anyone Like You* – with confidence in the product called 'you'.

# Chapter Fifty Eight

# Beauty is as beauty feels

Nowadays, the insult 'She's so thin, she has to wear snow-shoes when she takes a shower' is a compliment. Many women would smile smugly if they overheard someone say this about them. You can never be too rich or too thin, they say. Thin is in, slender is splendour.

It seems that, no matter how good-looking someone is, everyone has a gripe about his or her own appearance. This is *not* the way to become a people magnet, as you'll see. And the biggest gripe – surprise, surprise – revolves around weight.

Once, trying on some clothes in a department store, I overheard two young women in the next cubicle complaining. Apparently unhappy with her image in the mirror, one griped, 'What a jelly belly I am! Why can't I get rid of this paunch? Ohmigosh, do you think I'm pregnant?'

The other woman, equally displeased with the image staring back at her, said, 'Stop complaining. Ol' Thunder Thighs here can't even get these jeans on!'

I must admit my warped curiosity got the better of me and I lurked around the jeans department so I could get a gander at Jelly Belly and Ol' Thunder Thighs when they left. No one came out of the dressing rooms for about five minutes except two very attractive and slender young girls, who dejectedly put some size 12 jeans back on the rack. As they left, I heard them commiserating on their failure to cram their 'chunky trunks' into the tiny jeans. If I hadn't recognized their whining voices, I would never have dreamed that those two willowy creatures were the complainers of a few moments ago.

Well, if nothing else, the desire to be slender is testimony to a country's affluence because, in impoverished societies, 'jelly bellies' and 'thunder thighs' are coveted measurements.[72] Women's rights activists should also be delighted at the girls' attitude, because history shows a direct correlation between skinny-mania and women's control of economic resources.[73]

However, neither of these facts will console Jelly Belly and Ol' Thunder Thighs when they sit in front of their TV tonight, watching reruns of *Beverly Hills 90210* or *Melrose Place* and bemoaning how much skinnier than themselves Donna and Amanda are.

Why mention these two actresses instead of a myriad of other attractive (but emaciated) media women? Because a study, conducted in the years when the show was at its most popular, proved a direct correlation between *Beverly Hills 90210* watchers and women's eating disorders such as anorexia nervosa and bulimia nervosa – bingeing, then purging through laxatives or the old unhealthy (not to mention disgusting) finger-down-the-throat, weight-control home remedy.[74]

According to the same study, women who watched other popular shows, like *Seinfeld* and *Northern Exposure* (who starred normal-weight women, Elaine and Maggie), suffered fewer eating disorders. And watchers of *Designing Women* and *Roseanne*, which starred a couple of heavyweights (Suzanne and Roseanne), had fewer eating disorders still.

Does that mean that the shows were the cause of the disorders? I don't think so, but in a similar study researchers asked women which of three models they liked best: Kate Moss (thin), Cindy Crawford (average) or Anna-Nicole Smith (heavy.) This time there was an inverse relation between the number of women suffering severe eating disorders and the number of pounds these models tipped the scales at. I'm not entirely convinced by their findings, but the researchers decided that they proved that thin media personalities were causing women to have eating disorders. Which brings us neatly to the weighty subject of this chapter ...

Medical professionals have proven, beyond all reasonable doubt, that today's exaggerated standards of thinness are not healthy. And, between Kate Moss, Cindy Crawford and Anna-Nicole Smith, which body shape do you think most males most go for? Cindy Crawford's, of course. This and other observations convinces me that men like a well-shaped woman, not the sort of female who is so thin she doesn't even have a shadow.

Think of the great sex symbols of yesteryear – Betty Grable, Marilyn Monroe, Lana Turner, Hedy Lamarr, Dorothy Lamour, Rosalind Russell, Carmen Miranda – Talk about Jelly Bellies! And, if Dorothy Lamour ever got one of today's wrestlers in a headlock with her thighs, he'd never get up again. (Not that he'd want to, necessarily ...).

Yes, men do like thin. In fact, in an analysis of personals ads, 'thin' topped the list of 28 qualities men sought in a potential date[75] (whereas 'financially secure' topped the women's wish list). However, at the time of writing, men still prefer their women to be a little heavier than most extremely fashion-conscious females want to be. (Have you ever seen protruding collarbones and ribcages in a pin-up calendar?) But, if we're not careful, the male interpretation of a thin woman will get dangerously close to a woman's exaggerated, almost unattainable standard of thinness.

Furthermore, if men are beginning to appreciate a much thinner woman, then it's women's darn fault. To substantiate high fashion's influence on taste, Nigel Barber wangled a foundation grant to study curvaceousness in women (another example of a 'Nice work if you can get it' assignment). Barber contrasted the vital statistics of Miss America contestants and Playboy bunnies (a male's fantasy of ideal women) with those of *Vogue* models (more a female's view of ideal women).[76] He tracked their curves from about 1921 until 1986 when, due to political pressure, the measurements of Miss America contestants became a secret as carefully guarded as the formula for Coca-Cola.

His findings? Generally, a female's vision of the 'Ideal Woman' is getting thinner, and thinner, and thinner – and has far fewer curves than the male's erotic example of feminine pulchritude. Thanks to female fashion editors – and, perhaps, some designers in the industry, who are quite pleased that their own curvaceousness is now rivalling the more boyish measurements of the top models – that is changing. The male concept of the ideal woman is, happily, still behind theirs. But, as the calendar flips from year to year, the girls on it are becoming thinner, too. Researchers speculate that this is a response to the beauty images women are putting forth.

Incidentally, women, don't believe everything you see in a magazine regarding weight. I was once picking up some photos at a retoucher. John, the retoucher, was hovering over a photo. He said to his assistant, 'If I airbrush any more, there's going to be nothing left of her.' I peeked over his shoulder and saw a beautiful bikini-clad blonde with hardly any waist. I could tell from the opaque pigment around her belly that a good 10 per cent of it had already been blown away and his airbrush was still spraying strong.

## 🌼 Thunder Thighs wins Olympic gold medal for love

As is so often the case, it's not the actual product, but how it is *advertised* that makes or breaks it. And it's the same with people. Promote yourself as beautiful, and you seem all the more so.

I was visiting my good friend Bonnie several months ago. She is no lightweight (mentally or physically); in fact, she's pretty weighty in both departments.

Anyway, we were sitting on the couch, talking after dinner. The subject turned to her happy marriage and I was joking that, if they gave an Olympic gold medal for 'How much your husband loved you', she would have no contenders.

Our conversation was interrupted by her husband, who had just come back from a business trip. As if on cue to confirm my recent statement, the first thing he did was race over to the couch, scoop her up in his arms and say, 'Hi, gorgeous.' Now, if you knew Bonnie's measurements, scooping her up is no mean feat. A few sarcastic unfeeling souls might even say that *he* should get the gold medal – for weightlifting. He gave Bonnie a big effusive loving kiss, paid his respects to me, and then excused himself to unpack.

I said, 'Bonnie, how do you do it? How do you keep Tom so enraptured by you?' I hope that I did not, by the tone of my voice, insinuate 'in spite of the fact that you're so overweight'. However, Bonnie must have understood that most people would have thought of the question in that light because she just laughed and, fluffing her hair in a mock gesture of 'Aren't I beautiful?' said, 'Well, Tom just accepts my own opinion of myself and I guess I'm pretty narcissistic.' As if to highlight that, she turned around several times, as gracefully as a model on the catwalk.

When we sat down again, we fell into a fascinating discussion. She told me she never makes any disparaging remarks about her own body. She has never asked Tom, 'Honey do you think I'm too fat?' She always wears sexy underwear, sleeps in see-through teddies and, she told me, she even does sexy dances around the bedroom for Tom.

'You don't let him see your cellulite?' I asked in mock horror, grabbing the backs of my thighs to show her I was no stranger to that orange-peel-like puckering all women get on their legs.

Bonnie said, 'Cellulite? You've got to be kidding. I once referred to those as my "dimples", and now Tom likes to nibble my "cute little dimples"!'

Bonnie is, of course dieting and exercising. She is working at weight loss as much as any overweight woman. The important thing is that, even before she sheds the pounds, she has pride in her own appearance. She loves her own body, and therefore so does Tom.

Do I hear you asking, 'Does that mean I should be narcissistic?' And the answer is, 'Yes, a little.' If you're sceptical, please check out a study in the *Journal of Sex Research* on precisely this topic. It states that 'Women's relationship status is directly related to their own subjective view of themselves and their sexual self esteem, NOT to their actual body size or the objective researchers' rating of their physical attractiveness.' In other words, if you feel beautiful and act like you are beautiful, it definitely magnifies your man's view of your beauty.[77]

Even more important (perhaps) than the echo-effect adoration you receive from him is the effect that feeling beautiful has on your health. In an address to the medical community called 'Psychosomatics of Beauty and Ugliness', researchers gave evidence supported by doctors of medicine, psychiatry, psychoanalysis and family therapy that if you feel beautiful you will be healthier and less apt to be ill.[78]

CLAUSE 53 ♀

### I Am Beautiful

For the sake of my health and my relationships, I will NEVER again make negative remarks about my appearance, most especially my weight. Nor will I ever hide parts of my body from my man. If I think I'm beautiful, he will too.

For women only

 ## Gentlemen, lest you feel left out of the beauty game ...

Don't! Because the same goes for you. The reason I write this clause for women is that as a species you're not quite so hard on yourselves. Oh, sure, you occasionally check to make sure nobody is looking. Then you turn sideways in the mirror to check to see if your contour is a bit more convex. Or you furtively hold a mirror up to the back of your head for a weekly inspection to see how many hairs you've had to say 'Happy landing' to. But generally you pass muster when it comes to not complaining to your buddies or your woman about your looks.

However, if you'd like to get a few more women whispering, 'He's so-o-o handsome' when you pass, then – are you ready for this – you need to become a 'good mover'.

A good what? I'm sure you've seen the really cool dudes in the magazines advertising Calvin Klein undies or Armani jackets. They've got that intense 'I can see right through your dress' look in their eyes and just enough five o'clock shadow to certify their manliness. The really cool part is the way they're standing, weight on one foot, jacket held by one finger and casually thrown over their right shoulder, head cocked at just the right angle. In the modelling business they're called 'good movers'. And you can do it, too.

You don't need to go around posing all over the place, or you'll end up looking like just that, a poser. But do start paying attention to how you move. Strong masculine movements are in – have a good stride. Courteous movements are in – stand up when she returns from the ladies' room to the restaurant table. Protective movements are in – offer the lady your arm when you cross the street. Loving movements are in – straighten her collar or adjust her hair after putting her coat on.

**CLAUSE 54♂**

## I'm a 'Good Mover'

I will become aware of the way I move and cultivate manly and mannerly movements.
For men only

# Chapter Fifty Nine

# What can I change?

## *And what am I stuck with?*

Everyone has what in personal marketing are called 'elective traits', 'partly elective traits' and 'non-elective traits'; in other words, the things we can change, the qualities we may be able to change and those we can't change. (Well, we can try, but few of us have the time, the inclination or the money to have our noses fixed, our eyelids clipped, our chin(s) lifted, our legs liposuctioned and our buttocks tucked. That means that we're pretty well stuck with the bodies we've got.)

## Non-elective traits

These include qualities like your height, your complexion, your cheekbones, your eyes and your lashes, although some people are not convinced that these latter are entirely non-elective. When I was in high school, for example, one of my girlfriends came upon an article in a women's beauty magazine. It said that gently tugging on your eyelashes made them grow. That night, at our Potluck pillow party, seven other girls and I sat around tugging at our own and each other's lashes. The next morning, looking into each other's bleary, bloodshot, semi-lashless eyes, and the pile of little lost hairs all over our pillows, we got our first painful lesson in 'Don't believe everything you read.'

## Partly elective traits

You also have partly elective qualities. If you have no metabolism problem and always avoid chocolate, ice cream, doughnuts and anything else 'naughty' and nice to eat, then your weight is a partly elective trait. Skin moisture is another such trait: if you drink lots of water, avoid the sun and religiously use moisturizer, then your skin will be more supple.

## Elective traits

Finally we arrive at the obvious and extremely elective traits. These are, of course, from top to bottom, your hats, hairstyle, jewellery, clothing and shoes. There is enough material on this subject to tangle the Web, but let's just take one example – glasses. Sooner or later, everyone (yes, *everyone* by the time they reach the age of 40) has to think about the prospect of needing ocular assistance.

##  To see or not to see

Let's say you are single and your job has just transferred you to a new city. They've given you a place to live, moving expenses and a pay rise. The company doctor has given you your 80,000-kilometre checkup and you're in super shape. Great. But unfortunately he or she hasn't introduced you to any new friends – especially ones of the opposite sex. You're feeling a tad blue about this.

So, you figure, now is the time for a 'whole new me'. You say to yourself, 'I'll go out and buy a new wardrobe with the extra money and get new glasses. Or, hmmm, should I get contact lenses? Glasses? Contact lenses? Glasses ... Contact lenses ...'

A study entitled 'The Effects of Eyeglasses on Perceptions of Interpersonal Attraction' (or, in plain English, how good-looking people think you are with and without glasses) came up with two different answers – one for each sex.[79]

The researcher (probably a bespectacled chap himself) showed photographs of people to a group of men and women gathered in a laboratory. Sometimes the subjects in the photos were wearing glasses, and sometimes not. He then asked the folks in the laboratory to rate how good-looking they thought the subjects were.

The results concerning the women were not a surprise. (Remember the old retro chant, 'No one makes passes at lasses who wear glasses'?) Sadly, the glasses brought the woman down a notch or two in the looks department. However, the consensus was that the men were better-looking with their specs on.

Their critique? 'Makes him look more intelligent'; 'He is more intellectual that way'; 'Looks more important.' Now, this isn't to say that glasses don't have the same effect on the perception of a woman's *personality*. Still, it's a sad commentary on our society that 'She looks more intellectual' doesn't necessarily go hand in hand with 'She's more attractive.'

But, rather than bemoaning human nature (predominantly male nature in this case), let's see how we can take this lemon and turn it into lemonade.

Women, since eyeglasses do make you look more intelligent or intellectual-looking, let your contact lenses have a beach holiday in their saline solution while you're out applying for a job or attending a brainstorming session. Bring out your glasses and give them a little spit and polish – it's brains rather than beauty that will win the day.

## ✺ The best case of self-packaging I ever witnessed

Let me tell you about the best marketer I ever met. She is a gorgeous Miss Georgia runner-up who is an editor at a major women's magazine. The magazine business is ruthlessly competitive: heads roll daily like bowling balls, and starting salaries are low, but for those who scramble to the top of the heap there are many financial and lifestyle rewards.

Women dominate the women's magazine industry and my new acquaintance knows that – if she is to stay at the head of the pack of the fierce female rat race – the rodents with long claws ahead of her must have no green in their eyes when they look her way. The top dogs (and we all know what female dogs are called) had to like her. Consequently, Marianne wears no make-up to work, dons drab-coloured, very conservative suits that cover her 38–26–36 figure making her look almost like a 38–38–38, and balances out-of-fashion glasses on her nose. Is she doing the right thing? Is Miss Georgia going to be just a runner-up in real life, too? Or is she going to win this time?

I had the opportunity to sample, first hand, some of almost-Miss Georgia's tactics. I had made her acquaintance at an after-work networking party for our chamber of commerce. That afternoon, she was wearing a very straight, mahogany-coloured suit, which made her look like the side of a bookshelf. Her hair was tightly twisted into a chignon, which was covered by a net, and she wore large round glasses.

As we talked, Marianne mentioned that she had an idea for a book she wanted to write – anonymously, of course because, it would dish a lot of inside dirt on the magazine publishing business. I told her about the man who was my book agent at the time, and how he might take to her idea. This, mixed with my budding feelings of friendship for almost-Miss Georgia, prompted me to suggest that we three get together sometime.

A week or two passed and I didn't give it much thought. So, imagine my surprise when my agent, whom I'll call Justin (not his real name), called me with the friskiness of a teenager (which, for an 80-plus-year-old man is pretty good). He said, sounding like his liver was all a quiver, 'Leil, your friend Mimi stopped in this morning, and she said you'd like us all three to have dinner.' I hadn't heard Justin that excited about anything since he told me the time when he signed up a million-dollar author. Mimi was no million-dollar author. 'Wait a minute!' I said to myself. 'Who is Mimi?'

'Uh, Justin,' I hesitantly said, 'it must be one of your other authors. I don't know any Mimi.'

'Oh yes, you do,' he assured me. His voice had the effervescent, squished sound that syllables make when squeezed out through ear-to-ear grins. 'You met her at the last chamber of commerce meeting.' When he told me what magazine she worked for, it all came back. He meant Marianne. Sure, I'd be happy to join them for dinner.

As I put the phone back in on the hook, I wondered how 'Let's do lunch' had got upgraded to 'Let's do dinner.' Marianne must have put together some terrific book proposal.

Cut to Friday night. Justin and I arrived at the restaurant about the same time. The maître d' seated us with Justin facing the entrance, so he could keep an eye out for Mimi. During our chat, Justin kept looking towards the door. 'Keeping his eyes out' was an understatement. He looked like he couldn't keep them *in*.

Suddenly, as though someone had kicked him under the table, his head jerked up and his eyes seemed to start spinning like tops. I turned around to see what was making them gyrate out of control.

I was stunned. But she was stunning. Practically half the restaurant (the male half) became unabashed rubberneckers as the beastly beautiful woman with shiny brown hair down to her waist (and her cleavage almost as far) slunk over to our table. Justin jumped up, immune to his toppling water glass, as he clasped Mimi's hand.

After a spate of pleasant small talk, the waiter handed us our menus, which were handwritten in tiny cursive script. As I pulled out my granny glasses to read the menu, I noticed that Mimi's gorgeous hazel eyes were focusing, no problem, on the tiny letters.

After we had ordered, I told Mimi I was considering getting contact lenses too, and asked where she bought hers.

'Oh, I don't have contacts,' she replied.

'But, Marianne, when we met, weren't you wearing glasses?'

'Oh those,' she laughed gleefully. 'Those are just an office prop.'

Got it!

I was torn between admiration – not for her God-given good looks (I was as green-eyed as any other woman in the restaurant), but for her flexibility. She hid her talents under the proverbial barrel at the office, when she knew that would get her further up the corporate ladder. But, brother, did she flaunt them when she knew that was the best strategy.

At one point, Justin went happily floating (as well as a plump 80-year-old man with a cane *can* float) off to the men's toilet. Marianne and I then indulged in a little girl talk.

She told me that she always engaged the help of an image consultant with her wardrobe. It was her image consultant who suggested the little 'brown mouse and big glasses' style for the office and for networking events, where there were primarily women present. (I must admit, had she looked like she did at the restaurant at the chamber of commerce gathering, I probably would not have been as comfortable 'offering' her my agent.) And, for 'seducing' a literary agent (not sexually, but in the sense of getting him interested in her book), her image consultant had picked out the dress she was almost wearing.

Since the money I was making at the time came nowhere near to Marianne's salary, I knew I could never afford an image consultant, but I told her that someday I hoped I could.

Marianne said, 'Expensive? You've got to be kidding. In the first place, you save oodles of money, because an image consultant puts your old clothes together with her talented eyes so you don't have to buy any new ones. Besides,' she said picking up the bottle of wine that Julian had ordered, 'my image consultant's hourly fee costs a lot less than this.' She gave me the phone number of Julia, who works at a trendy New York art gallery by day and moonlights as an image consultant.

## ✿ Just add a scarf here, pin that there and don't get caught *dead* in that!

I thought for about a month and finally plucked up the courage to call Julia. Somehow the idea of having an image consultant was just too 'la di da' for me. But, it turns out to have been one of the smartest calls I've ever made.

Julia came over one evening and did a complete (what she calls) 'closet analysis'. Throughout the evening it was her cacophony of:

'Keep this.'

'Trash that.'

'Keep this.'

'Oh, God. Never wear that!'

'Ooh, this is terrific.'

'And this is *you*.'

'Don't be caught dead in that.'

'This goes with that.'

'That is great with this.'

'Now, this will work beautifully if you just add this scarf.'

'Put some kind of a brooch there.'

An hour and a half later, and exhausted from jumping in and out of skirts, blouses and dresses – and holding up black tights, beige tights and every scarf and piece of jewellery I'd collected over the past 20 years, I had gained all kinds of esoteric self-knowledge I never had before. How could I have gone through life not knowing pale beige was me and white was death on me. How did I know that red was dynamite on me – but, if there were any blue in it, I looked like a corpse. I must have learned how to tie a scarf 50 different ways.

When it was all over, I contentedly collapsed on the couch piled high with clothes and calculated how much money I had saved. On the double-digit fee I paid Julia, I realized I'd probably never have to buy any clothes again. I was a very happy woman – and so, I am sure, was the Salvation Army the next day, when they came to pick up three bags of clothes that, Julia commanded me, 'Don't get caught *dead* in that!'

We could go on ad infinitum. But I'll spare you and simply say this. Make sure your packaging – from their first sight of you right on down to your smell – is carefully calibrated to attract the kind of friends and loves you want. And, unless you're an expert in not only fashion, but human nature, but what others find appropriate and attractive, let a pro do the job for you.

Yes, gentlemen, you too. Or, perhaps I should say, *especially* you.

**CLAUSE 55** ♂♀

## Who, ME? Hire an Image Consultant?

I will keep an open mind and realize image consultants are not just for superstars and the residents of Easy Street. I'll start asking around and, if I can find a good one, I will hire him or her – at least once – to conduct a complete 'closet analysis' for me.

## Chapter Sixty

# The making of a star – me!

Have you got time for a story? It's a short one and it's true. Maureen's story can help make you be loved by everyone who hears your tale.

Earlier in this book, I mentioned my PMR (Platonic Male Roommate) Phil (see pages 9 and 98). Maureen is his girlfriend – and she is an admitted 'secondhand rose'. She told me how she got her nickname.

Maureen had a sister two years older and, when she was growing up, always got hand-me-downs. This bothered Maureen – a lot. She *hated* hand-me-downs. She even *hated* the phrase ... until a tragic turn of events changed her feelings about them.

Maureen's sister, while studying at New York University, met a bright chap who was studying filmmaking. They fell in love, got married and Darlene moved to California with her new husband. Within six years, her brother-in-law had become one of Hollywood's top film producers and, naturally, her sister attended practically every Hollywood opening. And, heaven forbid, she couldn't wear the same dress to two openings!

Knowing how Maureen had grown up hating hand-me-downs, Darlene didn't dare offer them to Maureen. Instead, she donated some to charity and let the rest pile up in the spare-room closet.

Once about 10 years ago, when Maureen was visiting Darlene for Thanksgiving, she opened the spare-room closet to find something and was, as she puts it, practically blinded by the array of beautiful glittering dresses. One by one, she took them out of the closet and started trying them on.

Enter Darlene. 'Collie, do you like those gowns?'

'Like them? They're beautiful!'

'They're yours!' They both had a big laugh, and from then on Maureen was hooked on Darlene's hand-me-downs. Every month, a box would arrive with a Hollywood postcode, filled with a beautiful skirt, a jacket, a sequined sweater or a glittering gown.

Time passed and Maureen's started filling up. So she started giving the clothes to her friends, who *loved* them. In fact, Maureen told me, she has a few friends who actually have the nerve to phone and ask her, 'What's in this month's care package?' so they could get a first crack at the designer goodies.

Then several years ago, Darlene became very ill with breast cancer. After a mercifully short time, because she was in great pain, she passed away. Maureen, who hates sympathy, decided to wait before telling her friends. She was grief-stricken enough, without having to talk about it repeatedly with her many friends.

But some of them still continued to call asking about the care package. What could Maureen do? All up and down Second Avenue, where she had been walking for years to get to work, she had passed thrift shops. Often she would see gowns or other beautiful designer clothes in the window with ridiculous prices like $15 or $25 (£10 or £15). Aha! That was the solution. She bought several things and, as usual, distributed them to her friends.

Maureen's eyes welled up with tears when she told me, 'You know, Leil, it was like I was doing something that Darlene would have wanted me to do. I felt like I was paying her homage by getting these beautiful clothes and giving them to my friends.'

Eventually, she told her friends what had happened. But she had come to enjoy her weekly trips through the thrift shops so much that the tradition continued.

One day, Maureen (who was visiting Phil that day) reached for a bag she had brought over to the loft. She said, 'I hope you won't take this as an insult, but when I saw it I thought it was so "you".'

She handed me a plain brown paper sack and I reached in and felt a fabric as soft as a rose petal. Jokingly I said, 'Oh, a sack of mice ears – just what I always wanted!' But then I pulled out a beautiful, black Yves Saint Laurent dress, which would make any woman look terrific. It was the perfect little black dress that I had been seeking for years. It scrunches into the size of a sparrow, and folds out without a wrinkle. My mouse-ear dress has followed me on every trip I've made since. (In fact, I'm wearing it in the photo on this book.)

Why have I told you this rather long story? Because it leads us to something you can do in your life that will make you beloved in the sense that many celebrities are. Until very recently, I grew up thinking that success comes only to the ones who deserve it or, occasionally, to the very lucky. With very few exceptions, like those who are born into a celebrity family, I assumed that the actors, singers, dancers and musicians who make it are the most talented ones.

I also assumed that celebrities in the more 'serious' sectors – medicine, business, academia, fashion and even food were the best and the brightest in their world, and that's why they became celebrities.

But how wrong I was! I discovered, quite by accident, that behind most celebrities is a highly sophisticated marketing technique that separates the visible from the invisible, the powerful from the powerless, and the star from the satellite.

How did I come upon this discovery? Some years ago, when I had a radio show, PR people would call asking me to interview some relatively unknown person such as, for example, 'the dentist who invented implants'. Big deal. Unless someone were in the market for implants, the subject was a snore, a sure dial-turner. I managed to say no as gracefully as possible to the dentist's insistent PR person and was just about to hang up, when 'Wait!' he said. Then came the story.

Dr Molar (name changed, of course) and his brother Joshua were brought up in a poor family in Brooklyn. David had always wanted to be a dentist and worked hard to put himself through dental school.

Their father had dentures, and both boys had vivid memories of seeing teeth in a water glass with bits and pieces of the evening's meal floating around them – not the most pleasant sweet-dreams send-off. Inspired by this aversion, David had been toying with the idea of implanting some tiny nail-like rods in the jaw to hold teeth rather than hook them on to existing teeth. But he was still years away from actually getting anyone to agree to this (then) unheard-of procedure.

However, about a year into his research, his younger brother Joshua smashed his Harley Davidson into a tree and lost six of his front teeth. David had got his first guinea-pig patient – perhaps sooner than he may have wanted. In order to have the materials made quickly when there was no prototype, he had to borrow money against his home. But it paid off because, today, 10 years later, Josh still has his implants – and 'now lives in Georgia, where corn-on-the-cob is one of the local specialities', the PR person told me. And now Dr David Molar is the world's leading implantologist.

'Hmm, that does sound interesting,' I said. And Dr Molar came on my show. The response to his story was tremendous.

Lets analyse it. David's story had it all:

- Being brought up in a poor family automatically gets the public's sympathy.
- David had a dream which he had to follow – a dream inspired by a childhood experience.
- He worked hard and brought himself up by the bootstraps, putting himself through dental school.

- He appeals to the younger, more hip audience because his brother had a Harley Davidson.
- Family tragedy always makes for good publicity.
- David risked all because he believed in his ideas.
- He finds solution and makes family member happy.
- He's now at the top of his profession – a winner in spite of the odds.

Was the story true? Who knows. ('And who cares?' ask the PR people.)

Since then, I've made friends with a few people involved in promotion, who tell me they do, in fact, take liberty with the truth. In fact three men who have studied the celebrity-making process say there are 22 major celebrity storylines.[80] A few of the most popular are:

*The accidental meeting* Diana Ross and the Jackson Five
*The big break* Whoopi Goldberg in *The Color Purple*
*Success–adversity–success* Judy Garland
*The fatal flaw* Richard Nixon – paranoia
*Mum or Dad's footsteps* Liza Minnelli
*Young, dramatic death* James Dean
*Revenge* Lee Iacocca
*Need to prove something* Maria Shriver
*Outrageous behaviour* publisher Larry Flynt
*Unexpected type makes good* Woody Allen

Maureen's story was true. But it also makes her more beloved by her friends. If someone were a PR person trying to get her some media interviews, her story would have many elements, including:

*Glamour* a millionaire movie mogul brother-in-law
*Humour* turnaround on hand-me-downs
*Tragedy* a sister who meets an early death

*Pride and nobility* not wanting sympathy from friends, so not telling anyone about her sister's death

*Sacrifice* spending time scrounging through the dusty racks of second-hand shops for her friends.

In fact, Maureen's story is becoming family history to the children of her other brothers and sisters. They know that Aunt Maureen buys beautiful clothes for her friends in tribute to Aunt Darlene.

# Chapter Sixty One

# What's *your* story?

Think about your life for a minute. Is there anything that is, of course, true that is the stuff of which legends are made? Look at the themes in the previous chapter. Are you the first in your family, say, to go to college? Did you have to overcome some great adversity? Are you doing a wonderful job of following in Mum or Dad's footsteps? Did you get a big break? Have you made a great sacrifice? Have you risked something to achieve your goals?

Stories are powerful. As a professional speaker, I know how significant stories are to the learning process. Stories are what make the material memorable. And a story about your life makes *you* memorable.

Telling your personal story to a potential friend helps move the relationship along because, chances are that it's personal, and an early sharing of a little vulnerability, or a heart-rending 'the laugh's on me' story, brings people closer.

There are dozens more themes that people love to hear. Pretend you are a celebrity-maker sitting in a big PR company's office on Madison Avenue, New York City. You are brainstorming with several colleagues on how you can become a celebrity in your family or your life.

Don't think of it as self-serving or selfish. People love to love a celebrity; otherwise, we wouldn't be such a celebrity-driven society. I love Maureen and her story, and that love makes me happy. And people will love you too, when you take the true facts of your life and weave them into a true story. Rehearse it for the pleasure of everyone you are going to become friends with in your life.

**CLAUSE 56** ♂ ♀

## My Star Story

I pledge to think of all the true stories in my life. I will choose one or two, and share them with potential friends or loved ones.

## Chapter Sixty Two

# Getting to know me, getting to feel free'n'easy

During my seminars over the past few years, I've distributed coloured cards – quite conventionally, pink for women and blue for men. I invite participants to write down any question they might be hesitant to air in front of the others. I read these during the break and open the questions to discuss later in the seminar.

One of the most popular questions is, 'What one quality immediately attracts you to someone of the opposite sex?'

Overwhelmingly the women answer that they like a man who is sure of himself, a man who is confident in his life, his choices and his opinions. Many men answer the same way. They say they want a woman who knows who she is, where she's going and what she wants out of her life. What this boils down to is a *sense of self*.

About a year ago, there was a man named Marty in one of my relationship seminars. Marty was tall. He had strong, striking features, penetrating brown eyes, wavy dark hair and an infectious quicksilver smile. In short, Marty was a hunk. During the seminar, he had asked a wide variety of interesting questions and it was obvious that some of the women in the group found him very attractive.

That 'What one quality ...?' question had come up during the session and everyone agreed that being centred or having confidence or a strong sense of self was crucial.

Marty raised his hand and asked, 'How, precisely would you define a sense of self?' His one little question was like the kid who took his finger out of the dyke: answers gushed forth from dozens of participants because they could sense that this question was coming right from Marty's heart.

The answers were varied, but they had an underlying theme:

- 'It's knowing you are in life and what your purpose is.'
- 'It's knowing how you feel about God.'
- 'It's knowing the choices you have and making the ones that are best for you.'
- 'It's knowing how you feel about the important things in life.'

The answers kept coming, and they all had one thing in common. Every one started with the words, 'It's knowing....'

After the seminar, Marty graciously came up and thanked me for having spent so much time on his question.

'Marty,' I said, 'there is no need to thank me. I didn't consciously spend time on it. Your question was so good, everyone wanted to answer it.' We continued chatting for a while and he asked me if I would like to join him for a late supper.

I was flattered and joked that it would break the hearts of half the women in the room if he were to walk out with me. Deadpan serious, Marty looked at me and said, 'That's my problem. Women. They always like me at first. But they lose interest real fast. I hardly ever get a second date. I thought maybe you could give me some hints.'

Now I was genuinely curious. I couldn't imagine what it could possibly be. He was one of the best-looking men of more than 50 in the room. He was well spoken, very articulate, obviously intelligent – everything a woman could want, to all outward appearances.

As we were driving to the restaurant, I made small talk by asking if he had seen a currently very popular movie. He said yes he had. I asked him what he thought about it.

'Well, I don't know really ...' he answered. Continuing on the same theme, I asked him if there were any other films he'd seen recently. He said he loved movies and had seen practically all of the good ones. I asked him what his favourite film of all time was.

'Oh, it's hard to choose,' he said.

Certainly nobody could accuse Marty of being opinionated on movies. I noticed that Marty had a rack of CDs in his car, so I changed the subject to music, asking him what kind was his favourite.

'Oh, all kinds'.

'Any favourite artists?'

'Not really, I like listening to all of them.'

I was beginning to pick up a trend here. We discussed a few other subjects in which Marty was well versed but had no real opinions.

Since I speak on networking and conversation, for over a year I'd been collecting a list of topics people talk about. Every time I heard an interesting discussion, I'd make a note of it in a notebook I carry with me at all times.

After we placed our order in the restaurant, I told Marty what I'd been doing and asked if he minded if I asked his opinion on a few things.

'Of course, Leil. I'd be happy to.' He said, 'I think it's great what you're doing and I'd like to help in any way I can.' (Little did Marty know that the point of this exercise was to help him.)

'Ok, Marty, here goes. What's your favourite season?'

'Oh, they're all great.'

'If you could travel anywhere in the world, where would you want to go?'

'Oh, gosh. That's a tough choice. I never really had to think about it.'

'What do you think motivates people?'

'Lots of different things – money, freedom.'

'What motivates you, Marty?'

'I never really pinned that down.'

'What is your favourite food?'

'I love eating all kinds of different cuisines.'

'Any favourites?'

'No, they're all good.'

'Do you like art?'

'Yes, I love art. I go to the galleries whenever I can.'

Bingo! I thought I'd struck lucky with this one. Marty seemed even more enthusiastic with his last answer, so I decided to stay with it.

'How do you think computers have affected art?'

'I don't know really.' I tried another tactic.

'What is your favourite style of art?'

'Oh, Leil, there's so many.'

'I mean, in general. Impressionists? Expressionists? Modernists? Surrealists?'

'I like them all.'

At this point, I wasn't sure whether Marty really knew much about art or was bluffing. Since I knew just a tad about the Impressionists, I asked him what he liked about Impressionism.

'Oh, lots. The dabs and strokes of primary colours I guess.'

We were getting somewhere, I thought. 'Which Impressionists do you like best?'

'Oh, all of them.'

'Marty, which ones?'

'Well, I guess Monet, Manet, Degas, Utrillo, Van Gogh, Gauguin ...'

The guy knew his stuff, all right. *What Marty didn't know was Marty*. And that was his problem. His wonderfully curious and inquiring mind knew about a lot of things. But he hadn't come to any solid conclusions on most of them. He didn't really know himself. This left a big hole in his personality.

Before we can bring others into our life, either as friends or as lovers, *we must know who we are and how we feel about the important things in life*. Marty knew more than most people about a wide variety of subjects. He just hadn't organized it all in his mind. It's like having hundreds of good books in your home, but never organizing them on a bookshelf. They're piled haphazardly in the middle of the floor, so, no matter how marvellous the books, your living room looks like a mess.

It was obvious that Marty had never sat down and had conversations with himself. He never asked himself questions like these:

- What do I believe about God?
- What influence did my parents have on me?
- What are the most important qualities I would want to pass on to my children?

These are questions that some people don't have to verbalize and answer for themselves. They naturally have a strong sense of self and they just know the answer. These people appear more centred. They look more confident because they know who they are, where they come from and where they're going. I've heard them referred to respectively as 'old souls' rather than 'confused young souls'.

Have you ever seen a baby in his cot? One day he discovers his big toe: 'Ooh, what's that?' He plays with it, pats it around a little, grabs it. He's getting to know his body. Or perhaps a little tot, who suddenly discovers she has a belly button. 'Mummy, mummy, what's this?' She doesn't need to think about her belly button any more when she's grown up because she has the quiet confidence to know where it is and that it's always going to be there. We need to have the quiet confidence that our beliefs, values and principles are always there.

The other day on television, I saw a young black boy, about six years old, sitting at a baby grand piano. His little feet didn't even reach the pedals but, like Mozart as a child, he could listen to any tune and then play it back beautifully. The rest of us would have to practise for years to attain any musical expertise.

It's the same with our principles and beliefs. Some people just automatically *know* themselves. Others of us must ask ourselves a series of questions to attain that self-knowledge. No matter how much we practise on the piano, we might never become musical virtuosos, but we can all become the world's leading expert on ourselves. The way to do this is to have a series of interviews with ourselves.

You will find a list of self-discovery questions in Appendix B. To help solidify your sense of self, answer one each day. There is one for each workday of the year. Anchor your interview to something you do on a daily basis – for example, while shaving or putting on your make-up, while commuting to or from work. It will only take about five minutes. With each passing day, you will feel yourself becoming more and more centred. You will see patterns emerging, and soon you will know yourself much better.

Another way to do the exercise is with a friend or loved one. Discussing these subjects helps spark your thinking even more. But only partner with someone with whom you can be completely candid. *Don't skimp on this one – it's too important.*

**CLAUSE 57** ♂ ♀

## Gaining Self-Knowledge

Each day, I will set aside some time to get to know myself. I will ask myself one of the questions in Appendix B. Just like I am being interviewed, I will think the answer through thoroughly .

Incidentally, from what I've told you about Marty, how old do you think he was? Reading this, I would have guessed he was around 22, 28, perhaps? Maybe 30 would be pushing it. No, Marty was 45 years old! Developing a sense of self is not a matter of age; it's a matter of mentality. We're never too old to start putting all the pieces of our belief system together.

# Chapter Sixty Three

# Give yourself a priceless gift

'Maybe it all began at Camp Mohawk. Hmm, or was it that double date in my dad's old Ford? No, no – it must have been when we sat next to each other in, ugh, Latin. Whenever it started, we swore we'd be friends for life. Where is she now?' I wonder.

'He was the first boy who ever slipped his hand under my sweater and whispered "I love you" in my ear. The stars were like fireworks when we both looked up at their flickering and promised to be together for ever. Where is he now?' I wonder.

For some strange reason, memories like these flash on my windscreen whenever I'm driving in a new city. Maybe it's because I don't know where they live now, and every once in a while someone passes me on the motorway who looks like a long-lost friend or love. I put my foot down on the accelerator – sharpish.

But then I have to remind myself that whoever passed looked like my friends did *then*, not now.

They say that if you stand on the corner of 42nd Street and Broadway in New York City, sooner or later you'll see everyone you ever knew. I spend a lot of time on that corner in the half-price theatre tickets queue. Sometimes I mutter to myself, 'Old hippie' when a long-haired beggar asks for a handout. Or I whisper to a girlfriend how a passing mink-clad socialite has obviously had a face-lift.

Could the old hippie be the boy who gave me my first kiss under the stars? Could the obviously pruned matron be the pal I swore eternal friendship with?

So many people I once called 'my best friend' have passed me by or pulled off on the hard shoulder and disappeared in my rear mirror. People I once trusted with my deepest, darkest secrets are now strangers to me.

A little over a year ago, I was surfing the Web after an especially pensive drive from Los Angeles to San Diego in a blinding rainstorm. As though my fingers were on a Ouija board, I started typing in the names of old friends whose faces had flashed before me with each swipe of the windscreen wipers. A dozen or so came up with no matches, but I had three good hits.

I found Irene, my best friend in college. She wanted to be a Fado singer. Her name came up as a fundraiser to bring musical troupes from Lisbon to America. And there was Ricky, my first boyfriend, with his very own Web page. Ricky was going to raise polo horses professionally. His page didn't mention polo horses, but it did tell about his Ford dealership in our home town. And Jayne, a real Anglophile. She was going to be ambassador to England. Her name came on screen in a list of people who had spoken at The English Speaking Union.

What if their fingers had clicked on *my* page? Would they all smile, remembering my exaggerated dreams, only to find the reality just as so different?

I debated long and hard before calling them. Each lived in a different city, so I decided to leave it to destiny. If my work ever took me to within several hundred kilometres of them, it would be fate's hand pushing us together.

I have seen all three now, and wouldn't trade the experience for the world. Ricky and I remembered the days when our mere touch was a wonder and our whispers sounded like thunder.

Jayne and I laughed and we cried. Irene and I even rolled on the floor in hysterics. The intensity of emotion was something we all forgot we were even capable of.

Would I want to see them again? Would they want to see me again? Probably not. But the one meeting with each was so special that I beseech you to do the same. Whatever new friends or lovers you find through using the clauses in *How to Make Anyone Like You!*, please enrich your life with the old faces as well.

**CLAUSE 59** ♂ ♀

## Find an Old Friend or Old Love

I will look up at least one old friend and (if I'm not hurting my current love) one old love. I will spend a few hours with them – no expectations other than maybe savouring the special sentiments we once shared. (And probably realizing *why* I left him or her in my rear mirror.) Whatever happens, or doesn't happen, I know we will both receive a priceless gift. We will each come away with a fresh and profound new sense of self.

# Appendix A

# How to say it to the opposite sex

These are examples of the do's and don'ts in the Dis-Guys and De-Gurrl My Dialogue clauses. ♀ is the symbol for how a woman can best communicate to a man, ♂ marks the most effective man mode.

1. ♀ *Say what you want:* I'd like to go to lunch at the new restaurant.
   ♂ *State an observation first which leads to what you want:* I've heard the food at the new restaurant is good. *Or ask a question which leads to it:* What do you think about trying the new restaurant today?
2. ♀ *Say what you mean:* John, I want this report on my desk by this afternoon.
   ♂ *Soften it:* Jane, I'd prefer it if you could get the report to me by this afternoon. Is that possible?
3. ♀ *When interrupting:* John, I see you are busy. However, this has to be read and signed before noon.
   ♂ *When interrupting:* Jane, I apologize for interrupting you when you're so busy, but this has to be read and signed by this afternoon.

4. ♀ *Speak more facts than feeling*: John, you got the promotion? You deserved it. You were definitely the best candidate.

   ♂ *Add feeling words to the dialogue:* Jane, you got the raise? I'm so happy for you. We all felt you were definitely the best candidate.

5. ♀ *Drop tag lines:* John, I think it's time we wrapped this meeting up.

   ♂ *Add tag lines:* Jane, I think it's time we wrapped this meeting up, don't you?

6. ♀ *Show appreciation and trust:* John, I appreciate how you were able to win over that tough client this morning. But I knew you could do it all along.

   ♂ *Show caring and respect:* Jane, I really respect the way you handled that tough client this morning. If there is anything I can do to make dealing with him any easier for you, please let me know. I'm here for you.

7. ♀ *Apologizing:* Unless you really mean you are sorry, say nothing. This is difficult for women because we are so accustomed to filling holes in the conversation.

   ♂ *Apologizing:* This is easy for women, tough for men. Just two words – 'I'm sorry.'

# Appendix B

# The e-mail sent to me by Dr Stan on 'smart women'

Ever noticed how the real witch in the carpool always has the guy who knows how to cook a soufflé, who sends flowers, who is frequently heard to say, 'You're so right, darling'? What's wrong with this picture? She's not even nice. Exactly. She's smart.

Smart women get the nice guys because they don't lower their standards for men – or anyone else for that matter. Smart women take the attitude that if this is the best you can do, they'll just go to the dance without an escort, the movie without a date, and the rest of their lives without the true companion constantly celebrated on FM radio. A smart woman has figured out that her biological clock is not really ticking that loud, that her grandmother was still fertile well into her fifties, and, anyway, if she had wanted a rug rat, she would have had one by now.

Smart women have also worked out that all the media hype about not finding a husband when you're growing older is promulgated by male-owned media machines to make women desperate and compliant. To make sure that men will always have their pick of scared women to choose from and that they won't have to work any harder at being decent.

Smart women have learned that the important question is not

'Will I ever get married?' but 'Do I want to get married?' (Or 'Why on earth would I want to get married?')

Smart women know that you can ALWAYS settle for less than what you really want. You can always get serious with a guy you're not really in love with or one who doesn't treat you exactly right. So there's no point in making any compromises today or tomorrow either for that matter. There's always going to be time to do the wrong thing. Smart women aren't lonely enough. They've noticed you get a lot done when you're on your own. Smart women have often drawn the conclusion that sugar daddies aren't worth it. If you allow someone to buy you, he's going to think he owns you. (Imagine that.)

Smart women know it's a heck of a lot easier to figure out what you're good at and make your own money than it is to entertain some tyrant. This frees you up to see a nice guy, whether he has money or not. Smart women have also freed themselves from the psychological need to be dominated by their men. Smart women like to feel powerful themselves, and appreciate men who can handle that. Smart women have adopted a firm line with men that can best be summarized as 'treat me right or take a picture of me'.

I have an architect friend who has an even better line. Whether it's a design not worth building or a relationship not worth any more investment, she growls, 'NEXT!'

Smart women are over men who fear commitment, who can't control their hormonal urges, who grunt instead of making conversation, who aren't reasonably punctual, who won't spring for an occasional evening out on the town, who don't listen, who don't know how to be supportive of their smart women's dreams.

Smart women know that being a jerk doesn't make a guy exciting. Smart women are excited by men who call every day without being pushy, who do what they say, who know how to say 'I love you' and, more importantly, how to act out that love in 100 ways that prove it. In other words, smart women are no longer attracted to the bad boys. I've been out with all the bad boys. Yawn. Been there, etc. Now they cultivate the bad boy in the nice boys they go out with, which is something COMPLETELY different.

Take it from a grateful, recovering nice woman: smart is better.

# Appendix C

# What love equity theorists would say about your compatibility

On the 'Bo Derek' scale of one to ten, (ten being tops, one being zip) rate yourself and the partner of your choice. Then add up all of partner's (or desired partner's) scores. Put his or her total at the bottom. Then add all of your scores and put the total on the bottom.

|  | Partner | Me |
|---|---|---|
| 1) Physical appearance | _____ | _____ |
| 2) Possessions or money | _____ | _____ |
| 3) Status or prestige | _____ | _____ |
| 4) Information or knowledge | _____ | _____ |
| 5) Social graces or personality | _____ | _____ |
| 6) Inner nature | _____ | _____ |
| **Partner's total** _____ | | **My total** _____ |

Now, subtract the smaller number from the larger. What is the difference?

**Difference in the two numbers:** _____

If it is five or above, the theorists say the relationship probably wouldn't work. (The higher-scoring partner would get bored or take advantage of the relationship. The lower number would always feel he or she didn't measure up.) Four is borderline. Three is OK. Two and one are great. Zero? That's a marriage made in heaven!

# Appendix D

# Reading her subconscious 'sex signals'

Be careful with the following. As in learning any foreign language, you will make a few mistakes at first and think she is saying one thing, when she is really saying another. Also, just as words make up sentences, these individual body movements make up what is called 'gesture clusters'. With practice, you will be able to read 'gesture clusters', not just individual movements, to have a more accurate reading of her interest in you. The numbers following the movement are for relative importance only.

**When you approach her, her body...**
Turns away (–5)
Straightens up (+3)
She pulls in her tummy or tightens her buns (+1)
Doesn't show any physical reaction (0)
Turns full body toward you (+4)
She starts swaying to the music (+4)

**While talking with her, her body is...**
Leaning back (–4)
Sitting or standing straight up (0)

Leaning toward you (+3)
Directly facing yours (+4)
At an angle less than 90 degrees away (+1)
More than 90 degrees away (–5)

**Her arms are...**
Crossed in front of chest (–2)
Rubbing or grooming herself (+3)
Touching you occasionally (+5)
Relaxed on lap or hanging down (0)

**And her legs...**
Are crossed toward you (+2)
Are crossed away from you (–2)
Are uncrossed knees facing you (+3)
Are uncrossed and open facing you (+6)

**Add bonus points if also...**
She uncrosses legs DURING the conversation (+2)
She plays with her hair (+2)
She runs her fingers around a glass (+3)
She puts one hand on her hip (+2)
She caresses her upper arm (+2)
She caresses her thigh (+4)
She puts on lipstick or powder (+4)

# Appendix E

# The minute-an-hour treatment

Gentlemen, for those of you who welcome a little extra guidance in Clause 48: the Minute-an-Hour Treatment, here are some examples.

You come home from work. She's already there. You've been away nine hours so that deserves…

**The nine-minute-treatment.** Don't make a nosedive for the newspaper or the television dial. Give her a kiss and say, 'How was your day, honey?' She'll tell you and then you, *without her asking*, give her a short version of yours in a nutshell.

Then give her another hug or a kiss and tell her you'd like to read the paper now, or see the news, or go wash the car, whatever. You have now done your bit to make her as happy as a butterfly in a garden of sunshine and flowers. (Hopefully she'll fly around and do her thing and let you do yours.)

'Wait a minute,' I hear you saying. 'If I encourage her like that, she'll never stop talking.' Not true. Why? Because you sharing your thoughts about your day *without her asking* is not about the details of your workday. It's about her *feeling* close, and receiving affirmation of your love. That's what any previous 'nagging' was really about anyway.

**This time you've only been apart a few hours.** She comes back from the night course she's taking, from the meeting she's attended, from the laundrette, from picking the kids up – from anything that's only kept you apart a few hours. Check your clause, brothers. This only requires the five-minute massage. Ask her about the meeting, the class, the laundrette, the school – listen and follow it up with a compliment like:

'I really admire you're working all day and then having the energy to attend a class.' 'Sounds like some pretty important work you are all doing. Was everyone at the meeting?' 'Was the laundrette empty? I worry about you going there after 6 p.m. if it is.' 'Did you have to wait for the kids? Were a lot of Mums there or did most of the kids take the bus?' (And say it like you care!)

Listen to her and ask a few more questions for a few minutes and you've given her complete gratification that you care about the details of her life.

**Now we come to the short form ten/five**. This is ten seconds and five seconds. When she's been away only an hour or so, say working on her computer upstairs, and she comes down. If you're reading the paper, put it down when she walks in. Smile at her. Throw a quick question if you have time for it. 'Computer working OK?' 'Were you on-line?' 'Get much e-mail?' Listen. Give affirmation you've heard and then you can go back to your paper.

**The thirty seconds and under treatment.** Whenever she walks into the room, put your newspaper down, sometimes even click the mute button on the TV, be sure to let your eyes follow her lovingly. Smile. If you're in the mood, blow a kiss. Sometimes it only takes three seconds. In fact, there is something you can do that is quick as a wink. It's, well, a wink! She'll find it very sexy and loving. She'll think about it all day long, and she'll respond to your kisses more warmly at night.

# Appendix F

# On developing a deeper sense of self

Choose the same time each day so you anchor it to another activity – while eating breakfast, commuting, showering, etc. Take as much time as you need to find the answer for your self.

How do I feel about what's happening in the environment now?
What motivates people?
What is my favourite season?
How do I feel about pornography?
What are my feelings on sexual harassment?
Am I a slob or a neat freak and do I defend either?
How do I feel about joke-telling sessions?
What do I think the future of the computer is? The web?
What's really important to me?
What's my idea of a perfect first date?
What is my favourite holiday?
What is my favourite meal?
Would I die for something I believed in?
What does art mean to me?
What influence did my parents (grandparents) have on me?
What are my favourite books?
What is an ideal relationship to me?
What would retirement mean to me?
Do I believe in extraterrestrial life?

If I had only a few months to live, how would I spend it?

What do I think happens after death?

Is there a God?

Who is my favourite fashion designer?

What do I think the best investment is?

If I won a ticket to travel anywhere in the world, where would I go?

How do I feel about the mayor of my city?

What really gets me angry? Why?

How to I feel about extreme 'political correctness'?

If I could be famous, what would I want to be famous for?

If I could afford to collect anything, what would I collect?

What is 'honour' to me?

What do I think is the cause of most relationships failing?

What is my favourite song? Why?

What does loyalty mean to me?

What do I think is our country's influence around the world?

What do I think about most when I'm just waiting in line?

How do I feel about organ donation?

How do I feel about aging?

Who do I think is the world's greatest artist, in any discipline?

What are the most comfortable clothes to me?

Who is my favourite author?

How do I feel about industrial air pollution versus progress?

What is one thing I learned this week?

Who was my first best friend?

What is my favourite time of day?

What do I like to watch on television?

What do I think about the relationship between government and religion?

How much of a perfectionist am I?

How do I define 'spirituality'?

Do I think there will ever be a universal language?

What are my top-ten favourite web pages?

How do I feel about wrestling as a professional sport?

How was the universe created?

How do I feel about hunting?

What's the best thing about being the age I am? The worst?

How are kids born now and growing up with the Internet going to be different?

What's my favourite rainy weekend activity?

What's the worst date I ever had?

What is my opinion of the local newspaper?

What new personal rituals would I like to create?

What makes a leader?

How do I feel about animal testing if used to create a product to help humans?

Did I have a happy childhood?

Do I think most people lie a little? A lot?

What was the happiest day of my life to date?

What is my purpose in life?

What is my worst fear?

How do I feel about body piercing?

Do I want big commercial chains like McDonald's or Starbucks in my town?

Can I tell if somebody is lying? How?

Do I procrastinate much? If so, on what and why?

How do I feel about meditation?

How do I feel about religion?

How do I feel about the town I was born in? How has it changed?

If I could change just one thing in my life, what would it be?

What is my favourite cartoon, and why?

How do I feel about the importance of eating breakfast?

What importance do the ancient philosophers have on today's way of life?

What does democracy mean to me?

How do I feel about school reunions?

Do I have any limiting patterns? If so, what could I do to change them?

What role does music play in my life?

How do I feel about television advertising?

Am I a 'dog person', 'a cat person', or do I prefer any other animal as a pet?

How do I feel about the institution of marriage, in general?

How do I feel about marriage for me? Will it/has it been good?

Am I superstitious? If so, about what – and why?

What was my first job, and what did it mean to me?

Do I tend to suffer more from claustrophobia or vertigo – or neither?

Do I think we should limit world population in some way?

Do I believe in unconditional love?

If I had to live life in confinement, how would I re-adjust?

Do I think people are basically good or bad?

Should infomercials be banned?

Do I prefer watching the Oscars, the Emmys or the Grammys, and why?

What is my opinion of Madonna?

How much do I believe of what I read in the magazines?

Will we be a totally web-based culture ten years from now? Is that a good thing or bad?

What is my favourite dish?

Whose cooking do I most prefer ? (Mine? Mum's? Other's?)

Do I believe in the 'big bang' theory of the universe?

Do I think we should have legislation limiting buying foreign products versus domestic?

How do I feel about eating meat versus being vegetarian?

If asked, 'Who are you?' what would I answer?

Are political elections fair? Why?

Do I believe any of the popular diets work?

What world leader do I feel has had the most positive impact on humanity?

If I could speak a second language, what would it be? Why?

Do 'nice guys' finish last?

How do I feel about artificial insemination?

Should people know their family tree? Why?

Who is my favourite singer?

Do I think volunteering can really get things done?

What is my favourite subject to talk about?

If I were reincarnated as an animal, what would I be? Why?

How would I feel if I were asked to give a speech?

I must give a speech on anything I like. What is it about and to whom do I give it?

How do I feel about soap operas?

How do I feel about 'finding love on-line'?

How do I really feel about each of my family members?

Am I happy? Why?

If I could change just one thing in my life, what would it be?

How will or how does my life differ from my parents' lives?

What are some of the illnesses members of my family tree have had?

Were/are my parents happy?

What would/do I wish for my children?

What would/does having children mean to me?

Do I have a satisfying sexual life? Why?

At what age should someone retire? How about me?

Am I happy with the wardrobe I have?

Do I prefer travelling by train, plane, bus or car? Why?

Do I think people can be motivated and change through listening to motivational speakers and audiotapes?

If I owned my own company, how would I reward my employees?

What do I think cars of the future will be like?

If I could live in any era, what would it be?

How do I feel about my life right now?

# Notes

1. Potts, Marilyn K. (1997) 'Social Support and Depression among Older Adults Living Alone: The Importance of Friends Within and Outside of a Retirement Community', *Social Work* 42(4): 348 (15).
2. Rotundo, E.A. (1993) 'American Manhood: Transformations in Masculinity', in *The Revolution to the Modern Era*, New York: Basic Books.
3. Snyder, M., Berscheid, E. and Glick, P. (1985) 'Focusing on the Exterior and the Interior: Two Investigations of the Initiation of Personal Relationships', *Journal of Personality and Social Psychology* 48: 1427–39.
4. Aleman, Anna M. Martiez (1997) 'Understanding and Investigating Female Friendship's Educative Value'. *Journal of Higher Education* 68(2): 119(21).
5. Sternberg, R.J. and Grajek, S. (1998) 'The Nature of Love', *Journal of Personality and Social Psychology* 47(3):12–29.
6. Wright, Paul H. (1982). Men's Friendships, Women's Friendships and the Alleged Inferiority of the Latter. Sex Roles: A Journal of Research 8 n1 p1-20.
7. Roberto, Karen A. 'Qualities of older women's friendships: stable or volatile?' International Journal of Aging & Human Development, Jan-Feb 1997 v44 n1 p1(14).
8. Wartik, Nancy (1997-) The Surprising Link to Longer Life. McCall's v124 n9 p104(5).
9. Malloy, T.E., Yarlas, A., Montvilo, R.K. and Sugarman, D.B. (1995) 'Agreement and Accuracy in Children's Interpersonal Perceptions: A Social Relations Analysis', *Journal of Personality and Social Psychology* 67: 692–702.

10. O'Brien, S.F. and Bierman, K.L. (1988) 'Conceptions and Perceived Influence of Peer Groups: Interviews with Pre-Adolescents and Adolescents', *Child Development* 59: 1360–65.
11. Merten, D.E. (1997) 'The Meaning of Meanness: Popularity, Competition, and Conflict among Junior High School Girls', *Sociology of Education* 70: 175–91.
12. Sprecher, Susan (1998) 'Insiders' Perspectives on Reasons for Attraction to a Close Other', *Social Psychology Quarterly* 61(4): 287(1).
13. Burgoon, J.K. (1993) 'Interpersonal Expectations, Expectancy Violations, and Emotional Communication', *Social Psychology Quarterly* 61(4): 287(1).
14. 'The Possible Woman', annual women's leadership conference organized by Linda Wind of Kennesaw State University; *possiblewoman@mind-spring.com*
15. James, Deborah and Clarke, Sandra (1993) 'Women, Men, and Interruptions: A Critical Review', in Deborah Tannen (ed.) *Gender and Conversational Interaction*, New York: Oxford University Press, pp. 231–80.
16. Clancy, Patricia (1986) 'The Acquisition of Communicative Style in Japanese', in Bambi B. Schiefflin and Elinor Ochs (eds) *Language Acquisition and Socialization Across Cultures*, Cambridge: Cambridge University Press, pp. 213–50.
17. Ueda, Kieko (1974) 'Sixteen Ways to Avoid Saying "No" in Japan', in J.C. Condon and M. Saito (eds) *Intercultural Encounters with Japan: Communication - Contact and Conflict*, Tokyo: Simul, pp. 184–92.
18. Graham, Dee, *et al.* (1995) 'A Scale for Identifying Stockholm Syndrome Reactions in Young Dating Women', *Violence and Victims* 10(1): 3–22.
19. The National Speakers' Association annual conference.
20. Morman, Mark. T. and Floyd, Kory (1998) 'The Overt Expression of Affection in Male–Male Interaction', *Journal of Research* 38 (9/10): 871(11).
21. Arkowitz, H., *et al.* (1975) 'The Behavioral Assessment of Social Competence in Males', *Behavioral Therapy* 6: 3–13.
22. Henderson, Lynn (1997) 'Mean MMPI Profile of Referrals to a Shyness Clinic', *Psychological Reports* 80(2): 695(8).
23. Pilkonis, P.A., Heape, C. and Klein, R.H. (1980) 'Treating Shyness and Other Psychiatric Difficulties in Psychiatric Outpatients', *Communication Education* 29: 250–55.
24. Izard, C.E. and Hyson, M.C. (1986) 'Shyness as a Discrete Emotion', in W.H. Jones, J.M. Cheek and S.R. Briggs (eds) *Shyness: Perspectives on Research and Treatment*, New York: Plenum, pp. 147–60. Hamer, R.J. and Bruch, M.A. (1997) 'Personality Factors and Inhibited Career Development: Testing the Unique Contribution of Shyness', *Journal of Vocational Behavior* 50: 382–400.
25. Sanderson, W.C., DiNardo, P.A., Rapee, R.M. and Barlow, D.H. (1990)

'Syndrome Co-morbidity in Patients Diagnosed with a Dsm-iii-revised Anxiety Disorder', *Journal of Abnormal Psychology* 99: 308–12.

26. Capsi, A., Elder, G.H. and Bern, D.J. (1988) 'Moving Away from the World: Life-Course Patterns of Shy Children', *Developmental Psychology* 24: 824–31.

27. Garcia, S., Stinson, L., Ickes, W., Bissonnette, V. and Briggs, S. (1991) 'Shyness and Physical Attractiveness in Mixed-Sex Dyads', *Journal of Personality and Social Psychology* 61: 35–49.

28. Bruch, M.A., Gorsky, J.M., Collins, T.M. and Berger, P.A. (1989) 'Shyness and Sociability Reexamined: A Multicomponent Analysis', *Journal of Personality and Social Psychology* 57: 904–15.

29. Cheek, J.M. and Buss, A.H. (1981) 'Shyness and Sociability', *Journal of Personality and Social Psychology* 41: 330–39S.

30. Bruch, M.A., Giordano, S. and Pearl, L. (1986) 'Differences Between Fearful and Self-Conscious Shy Subtypes in Background and Current Adjustment', *Journal of Research in Personality* 20: 172–86.

31. Alfano, M.S., Joiner, T.E. and Perry, M. (1994) 'Attributional Style: A Mediator of the Shyness–Depression Relationship?', *Journal of Research in Personality* 28: 287–300.

32. Goode, Erica (1998) 'Social Anxiety, Old as Society Itself', *New York Times*, 20 October.

33. Noriyuki, Duane (1996) 'Breaking Down the Walls', *Los Angeles Times*, 5 February.

34. Lowndes, Leil (1996) *How to Make Anyone Fall in Love With You*, New York: Contemporary Books.

35. Walster, E., Walster, W.G. and Berscheid, E. (1978) *Equity: Theory and Research*. Boston: Allyn and Bacon.

36. Morman, Mark. T. and Floyd, K. (1998) Source: Sex Roles: 'Overt Expression of Affection in Male-male Interaction', *Journal of Research* 38(9/10): 871(11); Ekman, E. and Friesen, W.V. (1969) 'The Repertoire of Nonverbal Behavior: Categories, Origins, Usage, and Coding', *Semiotica* 1: 49–98.

37. Rabinowitz, F.E. (1991) 'The Male-to-Male Embrace: Breaking the Touch Taboo in a Men's Therapy Group', *Journal of Counseling and Development* 69: 574–76.

38. Shotland, R. *et al.* (1988) 'Can Men and Women Differentiate Between Friendly and Sexually Interested Behavior?', *Social Psychology Quarterly* 51(1): 66–73.

39. LaFontana, Kathryn M. and Cillessen, Antonius H.N. (1999) 'Children's Interpersonal Perceptions as a Function of Sociometric and Peer-Perceived Popularity', *Journal of Genetic Psychology* 160(2) June: 225(1).

40. Adler, P.A., Kless, S.J. and Adler, P. (1992) 'Socialization to Gender Roles: Popularity among Elementary School Boys and Girls', *Sociology of Education* 65: 169–87.

41. *New York Times*, 24 April 1999, p. 14.

42. See note 27 above.
43. Mitchell, W. (1988) *It's Not What Happens to You, It's What You Do About It*, New York: Phoenix Press.
44. See note 43.
45. The title of one of W. Mitchell's inspirational speeches.
46. Murstein, Bernard I. (1980) 'Love at First Sight: A Myth', *Medical Aspects of Human Sexuality* 14(9).
47. Margaret Mead (1935) *Sex and Temperament in Three Primitive Societies*, New York: William Morrow.
48. Liebowitz, M.R. (1983) *The Chemistry of Love*, Boston: Little, Brown.
49. Murray, Sandra L. and Holmes, John G. (19XX) 'Seeing Virtues in Faults: Negativity and the Transformation of Interpersonal Narratives in Close Relationships', *Journal of Personality and Social Psychology* 65(4): 707(16).
50. Helen Fisher (1989) 'The Four-Year Itch', *Natural History* (October): 22–3.
51. Liebowitz, *Chemistry of Love*.
52. Liebowitz, *Chemistry of Love*.
53. Dutton, D.G. and Aron, A.P. (1974) 'Some Evidence for Heightened Sexual Attraction under Conditions of High Anxiety', *Journal of Personality and Social Psychology* 30: 510–17.
54. Byrne, Donn (1971) *The Attraction Paradigm*, New York: Academic Press.
55. Byrne, Donn, *et al.* (1970) 'Continuity Between the Experimental Study of Attraction and Real-Life Computer Dating', *Journal of Personality and Social Psychology* 1:157–65.
56. Perper, Timothy (1985) *Sex Signals: The Biology of Love*, Philadelphia: ISI Press.
57. Perper, *Sex Signals*.
58. Oguchi, Takashi, *et al.* (1997) 'Voice and Interpersonal Attraction', *Japanese Psychological Research* 39(1) (March): 56–61.
59. Bruder-Mattson, S.F. and Hovanitz, C.A. (1990) 'Coping and Attributional Styles as Predictors of Depression', *Journal of Clinical Psychology* 46: 557–65.
60. Shumaker, S.A. and Hill, D.R. (1991) 'Gender Differences in Social Support and Physical Health', *Health Psychology* 10: 102–11.
61. Barbee, Anita P., *et al.* (1993) 'Effects of Gender Role Expectations on the Social Support Process', *Journal of Social Issues* 49(3): 175(16).
62. Smythe, M. and Huddleston, B. 'Competition and Collaboration: Male and Female Communication Patterns During Dyadic Interactions. Constructing and Reconstructing Gender', Albany: State University of New York Press.
63. Moller, Lora C., *et al.* (1992) 'Sex Typing in Play and Popularity in Middle Childhood', *Sex Roles: A Journal of Research* 26(7/8): 331(23).
64. See note 63.
65. James, Deborah, and Drakich, Janice (1989) 'Understanding Gender Differences in Amount of Talk' Ms., Linguistics Department, University of Toronto.

66. James and Drakich, 'Understanding Gender Differences'.
67. Lakoff, Robin (1975) *Language and Woman's Place,* New York: Harper and Row.
68. Lakoff, (1975) *Language and Woman's Place.*
69. Spender, D. (1985) *Man Made Language,* London: Routledge & Kegan Paul
70. Dupont, Kay (1997) *Handling Diversity in the Workplace,* American Media Publishing.
71. Nalini, Ambady and Rosenthal, Robert. (1993) 'Half a Minute: Predicting Teacher Evaluations from Thin Slices of Nonverbal Behavior and Physical Attractiveness', *Journal of Personality and Social Psychology* 64(3): 431(11).
72. Sobal, J. and Stunkard, A.J. (1989) 'Socioeconomic status and obesity: A Review of the Literature', *Psychological Bulletin* 105: 260–75.
73. Anderson, J.L., Crawford, C.B., Nadeau, J. and Lindberg, T. (1992) 'Was the Duchess of Windsor Right: A Cross-cultural Review of the Socioecology of Ideals of Female Body Shape', *Ethology and Sociobiology* 13: 197–227.
74. Harrison, Kristen (1997) 'Does Interpersonal Attraction to Thin Media Personalities Promote Eating Disorders?', *Journal of Broadcasting & Electronic Media* 41(4): 478(23).
75. Smith, Jane E. *et al.* (1990) ' Single White Male Looking for Thin, Very Attractive ...', *Sex Roles* 23: 675–85.
76. Barber, Nigel (1998) 'Secular Changes in Standards of Bodily Attractiveness in American Women: Different Masculine and Feminine Ideals', *Journal of Psychology* 132(1): 87(8).
77. Wiederman, Michael W. and Hurst, Shannon R. (1998) 'Body Size, Physical Attractiveness, and Body Image among Young Adult Women: Relationships to Sexual Experience and Sexual Esteem', *Journal of Sex Research* 35(3): 272(10).
78. Czechowicz, H. and Diaz de Chumaceiro, C.L. (1988) 'Psychosomatics of Beauty and Ugliness: Theoretical Implications of the Systems Approach', *Clinical Dermatology* 6(3): 9–14.
79. Hasart, Julie K. and Hutchinson, Kevin L. (1997) 'The Effects of Eyeglasses on Perceptions of Interpersonal Attraction', *Journal of Social Behavior and Personality* 8(3): 521–8.
80. Rein, Irving J., Kotler, Philip, Stoller, Martin R. (1997) *High Visibility.* NCT Publishing Group.

## About the Author

Leil Lowndes is an internationally acclaimed communications expert who coaches top executives of Fortune 500 companies as well as frontline employees to become more effective communicators. She has spoken in practically every major U.S. city and conducts communications seminars for the U.S. Peace Corps, foreign governments and major corporations. In addition to engrossing audiences on hundreds of TV and radio shows, her work has been acclaimed by the *New York Times*, the *Chicago Tribune* and *Time* magazine. Her articles have appeared in professional journals and popular publications such as *Redbook*, *New Woman*, *Psychology Today*, *Penthouse* and *Cosmopolitan*. Based in New York City, she is the author of four books including the top-selling *How to Talk to Anybody About Anything* and *How to Make Anyone Fall in Love with You*.

If you come across any little tricks of Big Winners in your life, share them with Leil – so she can share them with others, credited in her next book, of course, to you.

Leil's mailing address is Applause, Inc., 127 Grand Street, New York, NY 10013.

Or e-mail her at leil@lowndes.com

Leil's website address is http://www.lowndes.com